Ex Líbris

Randy Manning

© APCo

Voices of the Civil War

Voices of the Civil War · Second Manassas

By the Editors of Time-Life Books, Alexandria, Virginia

Contents

THE FIELD AT SECOND MANASSAS

*The Battle of Second Manassas raged across the fields and woods
west of Bull Run. An artist's rendering depicts the ground where
the principal actions took place.*

Groveton-Sudley Road

Stony Ridge

The Dump

Unfinished Railroad

Deep Cut

Brawner House

Groveton

Warrenton Turnpike

Young's Branch

Chinn Ridg

Lewis Lane

Chinn House

Chinn Branch

Sudley Ford

Sudley Church

Bull Run

Matthews Hill

Dogan Ridge

Dogan House

Stone House

Stone Bridge

Henry House (ruins)

Henry Hill

Lewis Ford

Bull Run

Manassas-Sudley Road

The Road to Manassas

Shuffling into line for dress parade on the Fourth of July, 1862, their colorful Zouave uniforms ragged and soiled, the soldiers of the 5th New York Volunteer Infantry saw little cause to celebrate the 86th anniversary of the founding of the republic. For more than a year the nation had been torn asunder by the Civil War, and the mightiest and best-trained military force ever assembled on the continent—Major General George B. McClellan's Army of the Potomac—had failed, at great cost in suffering and blood, to put an end to the rebellion of the Southern states.

Three months after joining McClellan's army on the Virginia Peninsula for an ambitious campaign to capture Richmond, the New York Zouaves had seen the Federal legions outmaneuvered, outfought, and compelled to retreat to a defensive perimeter on the banks of the James River. They had been stopped short seven miles from the Confederate capital. In a week of unprecedented carnage, known as the Seven Days' Battles, the Army of the Potomac had lost nearly 16,000 men. The 5th New York, more than 900 strong when they began the campaign, now mustered only 350 men, many of them racked with malaria, typhoid, and dysentery.

Standing at parade rest that July 4, the New Yorkers listened as their adjutant read a characteristically flamboyant address from the army commander, dubbed Little Mac by his admiring troops: "Soldiers of the Army of the Potomac," McClellan's proclamation stated, "Your achievements of the last ten days have illustrated the valor and endurance of the American soldier. Attacked by vastly superior forces, and without hope of re-enforcements, you have succeeded in changing your base of operations. . . . Your conduct ranks you among the celebrated armies of history."

"It was eloquent and true," noted Zouave Alfred Davenport. "But eloquence and eulogy were swallowed up in the stern realities of the dead and dying, the wounded on the road, the sick and wounded left behind to be made prisoners, the unknown and unremembered graves, and the individual suffering of every survivor. Each man had an experience of his own, and the battle of a life-time is epito-

In spring 1862 Federal cavalry and a group of children face off across Bull Run at Sudley Ford. It was a critical crossing point during First Manassas, but the Federals ignored its potential in the second battle.

mized in a short ten days of such experience."

McClellan's inspirational oratory could not mask his singular lack of success. "This has been a defeat," Zouave George Leavitt concluded. "General McClellan has failed to accomplish what this army could have accomplished." Leavitt's comrade, 16-year-old Charles Brandegee, agreed: "The Army of the Potomac if properly managed ought, could, would & should have entered Richmond."

That the Federal army did not enter Richmond had much to do with McClellan's innate caution, his tendency to inflate enemy numbers, and his personal disdain for President Abraham Lincoln and the Republican administration in Washington. But above all it was the military skill of Little Mac's Confederate counterpart, General Robert E. Lee, that had so dramatically reversed the fortunes of war on the Virginia Peninsula.

A man of aristocratic lineage with a distinguished record in the prewar Regular Army, Lee was the most highly regarded officer to cast his lot with the Confederacy. His dignity, reserve, and quiet determination elicited an almost instinctive respect from his subordinates. "The fear of incurring his displeasure at all times enforced implicit obedience," wrote Alabama colonel William C. Oates.

But there was more to Lee than his dignified image and management skills. He was a consummate campaigner, a skilled tactician, and a daring strategist. Knowing the odds the Confederacy faced, he was ever willing to risk defeat to attain victory. As Captain Joseph Ives put it, "Lee is audacity personified."

Though Richmond had been saved, the Seven Days' fighting had cost Lee's Army of Northern Virginia more than 20,000 men, nearly a quarter of his force. Moreover, Confederate success could not disguise the fact

that a lack of coordination and initiative on the part of subordinate commanders had, on several occasions, prevented Lee's forces from achieving a decisive victory—what might have been the destruction of McClellan's army. Even Major General Thomas J. "Stonewall" Jackson, the eccentric military genius whose brilliant spring campaign in the Shenandoah Valley tied down thousands of Federal troops and kept them from joining McClellan, had failed to live up to his reputation during the Seven Days' Battles.

With McClellan bottled up at Harrison's Landing on the James, Lee bolstered his army with reinforcements, overhauled his subordinate command structure, and pondered the lessons of the recent campaign.

But Lee would have little time for rest or reflection. A new Federal threat was looming to the north, in the person of Major General John Pope and his Union Army of Virginia.

Born in Kentucky and reared in Lincoln's home state of Illinois, the 40-year-old Pope had rough edges to his personality. The tall, burly midwesterner was in many ways the diametrical opposite of the dapper, meticulous McClellan. Pope exuded bravado and energy; "He spoke much and rapidly," an English correspondent noted, "chiefly of himself." Most importantly for the Lincoln administration, Pope was a staunch Republican with a string of minor but conspicuous victories in the war's western theater, and therefore an appealing alternative to the cautious, conservative Democrat McClellan.

Pope's Army of Virginia comprised some 50,000 troops, organized in three corps commanded by Major Generals Franz Sigel, Nathaniel P. Banks, and Irvin McDowell. The force was scattered over a wide area from the foothills of the Blue Ridge east to the city

of Fredericksburg on the Rappahannock River. Initially intended to cooperate in McClellan's advance on Richmond, these troops had shifted to the defensive with the failure of the Peninsula campaign and now served to block Lee's way to Washington.

Fired with ambition and eager to excel in his new assignment, Pope urged Lincoln and General in Chief Henry Halleck to abandon the Peninsula and transport the Army of the Potomac to northern Virginia, whereupon the united force would launch a drive to Richmond. McClellan, who suspected such a move to be the precursor to his removal from command, strongly objected to Pope's strategy. But McClellan's views held little stock with Lincoln and Halleck, and on August 4 the Army of the Potomac was ordered to join Pope's forces along the Rappahannock.

Soon after taking charge of the Army of Virginia, Pope issued an address intended to boost the morale of his soldiers. The address had quite the opposite effect, and its repercussions would haunt the general throughout his controversial tenure in command. "I have come to you from the West, where we have always seen the backs of our enemies," Pope proclaimed; "Let us look before us, and not behind." Rejecting the ideas of "lines of retreat" and "bases of supplies," Pope embraced a concept of total war that left little distinction between enemy soldiers and civilians. His troops would forage off the countryside, hold citizens responsible for guerrilla attacks, and require them either to take the oath of allegiance to the United States or be forcibly deported from within Federal lines.

This thinly veiled slap at McClellan's conservative strategy and concern for private-property rights served to alienate many of Little Mac's Army of the Potomac before they ever arrived in Pope's sector. When he got wind of the orders, Major General Fitz-John Porter, the Fifth Corps commander and McClellan's closest adviser, characterized Pope as "a fool" and "an ass." Some of Pope's own subordinates likewise disparaged the proclamation as bombastic and self-serving rhetoric. Brigadier General Marsena R. Patrick branded Pope a "demagogue," and Brigadier General Robert H. Milroy called him a "miserable humbug-bag of gas."

Beyond the moral question of Pope's ruthless approach to warfare, many believed his orders would lead to breaches of discipline on the part of his soldiers. "The resulting effects of these orders were to license the brutality of our soldiers towards their victims," wrote one of General Sigel's staff officers; "pillage and arson ceased to be crimes." Captain Charles H. Walcott of the 21st Massachusetts thought "Those few days of legalized rapine did more to demoralize and weaken the army than an average unsuccessful campaign."

If Pope's style of war caused grumbling among the Federals, it kindled the outright hatred of his Southern foes. The *Richmond Examiner* branded the Yankee general "an enemy of humanity." Lee informed Confederate president Jefferson Davis that Pope "ought to be suppressed if possible."

Lee's desire to "suppress" Pope was complicated by the fact that the Army of Northern Virginia, and Richmond itself, still lay between two powerful Federal armies. Uncertain of McClellan's intentions, on July 13 Lee ordered Jackson to shift his two divisions by rail to Gordonsville, 60 miles northwest of Richmond. By July 19 Jackson's 18,000 troops were in position, securing the crucial rail junction. Eight days later, with McClellan showing no sign of emerging from Harrison's

Landing, Lee reinforced Jackson with Major General Ambrose Powell Hill's 4,000-man division. Advising Jackson to beware of "an unexpected blow" from Pope, Lee gave his trusted subordinate free rein "to drive if not destroy the miscreant."

Deploying Brigadier General Beverly H. Robertson's cavalry as outposts along the Rapidan River to his north, on July 29 Jackson led his infantry south into Louisa County, a region yet untouched by war where his men could rest and the horses fatten on lush forage. After a week's hiatus, Jackson's tough "foot cavalry" marched back to Gordonsville and continued north along the Orange & Alexandria Railroad toward Orange Court House and the Rapidan. After several weeks conferring with the administration in Washington, Pope had taken the field in person, and the Confederate troops were eager to confront their reviled opponent. "Just wait till Old Jack gets a chance at him," John Casler of the 33d Virginia heard a soldier remark; "he'll take some of the starch out of him."

Meanwhile, Pope had determined to unite his scattered forces at Culpeper Court House, about eight miles north of the Rapidan. Linked with the defenses of Washington by the Orange & Alexandria line, Pope saw Culpeper as a good base of operations from which to launch a strike south across the Rapidan, past Jackson's left flank, and on to sever the Virginia Central Railroad between Gordonsville and Charlottesville. Pope had been told of the imminent arrival of Major General Ambrose E. Burnside's Ninth Corps at Fredericksburg, 14,000 strong, fresh from a successful campaign in the Carolinas. Once McClellan's forces made their appearance, his numerical superiority would enable Pope to launch a full-fledged advance on Richmond.

In fact McClellan, loath to yield up his beloved Army of the Potomac, was dragging his feet on the Peninsula. Despite Halleck's orders to evacuate Harrison's Landing, on August 7 McClellan shifted a number of troops north to Malvern Hill, the scene of bloody fighting on July 1. The move briefly alarmed Lee as precursor to an advance of McClellan's force; but it soon became apparent that it was only a feint, Little Mac's last hurrah before grudgingly complying with his superiors' instructions. Nonetheless another week went by before the Army of the Potomac began marching toward their point of embarkation at Newport News.

Lee, meanwhile, was eager for Jackson to exploit his opportunity before Pope was further reinforced. "I would rather you should have easy fighting and heavy victories," Lee declared. "I must now leave the matter to your reflection and good judgment." The presence of a foe that was powerful but still geographically dispersed was reminiscent of the challenge Jackson had faced in the Valley campaign. When his scouts informed him that only the 11,000 troops of Banks' corps had arrived at Culpeper, that half of McDowell's corps was still at Fredericksburg, and that Sigel's troops were strung out along the roads from the Blue Ridge, Jackson decided to strike the first blow.

Jackson planned to unite his forces at Orange Court House, cross the Rapidan on August 8, and with a two-to-one advantage in numbers, attack and destroy Banks before the rest of Pope's troops arrived at Culpeper. Success would hinge upon rapid marching and good strategic coordination, the very traits that Jackson had manifested in his Valley campaign. But unfortunately for Southern hopes, Jackson's soldiers, subordinate commanders, and particularly Jackson himself proved unable to execute the maneuver according to plan.

In temperatures reaching as high as 96 degrees, scores of Confederates collapsed by the roadside with heatstroke and exhaustion. The army covered little ground on August 7, and the next day matters were further complicated by Jackson's characteristic disinclination to explain his plans to his subordinates.

While A. P. Hill's division waited at Orange Court House for Major General Richard S. Ewell's troops to take the lead as Jackson had initially ordered, Jackson had meanwhile changed his mind and instructed Ewell to cross the Rapidan at Liberty Mills, some six miles to the west. Although Hill was apparently never informed of the change, Jackson was enraged when he arrived at Orange with Brigadier General Charles S. Winder's division and found Hill still waiting for Ewell's troops. Winder's division pushed on, its ailing commander following in an ambulance, and crossed the Rapidan at Barnett's Ford to link up with Ewell's force. But Hill's troops got caught up in a massive traffic jam of wagons and artillery, the day wore on, and a frustrated Jackson was forced to postpone his attack and go into camp for the night. The fight, if it came, would have to take place the following day.

On August 9, eager to make up for lost time, Jackson urged his 24,000 men through the torrid heat toward Culpeper. Ewell was in the lead, Winder following, and Hill pushing to close the gap that had opened during the misunderstandings and confusion of the previous day. Shortly after noon, the Confederate vanguard reported a large Federal force drawn up to meet them south of Culpeper, near the gentle slopes of Cedar Mountain.

The leader of that force, Major General Nathaniel P. Banks, the 46-year-old commander of Pope's Second Corps, was the quintessential "political general"—a man of great influence and thus important to the Union war effort, but an officer of questionable military skill. A former Speaker of the House of Representatives and governor of Massachusetts, Banks was ambitious and brave, but he had seen his forces licked by Stonewall Jackson in the Shenandoah Valley. Despite the fact that the bulk of Pope's army had yet to reach Culpeper, the combative Pope had sent an aide to Banks with verbal instructions to deploy skirmishers to slow the enemy advance on Culpeper, "and attack him immediately as soon as he approaches." Eager to redeem his military reputation, Banks prepared to do just that—even though he would be outnumbered by more than two to one.

The ensuing engagement at Cedar Mountain would be the first clash in an epic campaign that in less than a month would shift the contending armies from the very gates of Richmond to the environs of Washington and present the Confederates with an opportunity to invade the North. Three weeks of hard marching and maneuvering would forge the unshakable resolve and confidence of the Army of Northern Virginia and confirm the greatness of its commander, Robert E. Lee. Those 21 days, known as the Second Manassas campaign, would bring humiliation to the Federals and disgrace to Pope, and would result in a second shocking disaster to a Union army on the battlefield of Bull Run.

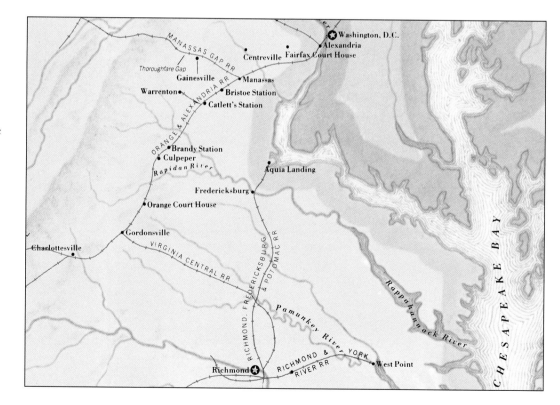

The 100-mile expanse between Washington and Richmond was the setting of the Second Manassas campaign.

ORDER OF BATTLE

ARMY OF VIRGINIA

Pope 70,000 men

From ARMY OF THE POTOMAC

I Corps Sigel

1st Division Schenck	2d Division	3d Division Schurz	Cavalry
Stahel's Brigade	Von Steinwehr	*Schimmelfennig's Brigade*	*Beardsley's Brigade*
McLean's Brigade	*Koltes' Brigade only*	*Krzyzanowski's Brigade*	
		Milroy's Brigade	

II Corps Banks

1st Division Williams	2d Division Greene	Cavalry
Crawford's Brigade	*Candy's Brigade*	*Buford's Brigade*
Gordon's Brigade	*Schlaudecker's Brigade*	
	Tait's Brigade	

III Corps McDowell

1st Division King	2d Division Ricketts	Reynolds' Division	Cavalry
Hatch's Brigade	*Duryea's Brigade*	*Meade's Brigade*	*Bayard's Brigade*
Doubleday's Brigade	*Tower's Brigade*	*Seymour's Brigade*	
Patrick's Brigade	*Stiles' Brigade*	*Hardin's Brigade*	
Gibbon's Brigade	*Thoburn's Brigade*		

Reserve Corps Sturgis

Piatt's Brigade only

III Corps Heintzelman

1st Division Kearny	2d Division Hooker
Robinson's Brigade	*Grover's Brigade*
Birney's Brigade	*Taylor's Brigade*
Poe's Brigade	*Carr's Brigade*

V Corps Porter

1st Division Morell	2d Division Sykes
Roberts' Brigade	*Buchanan's Brigade*
Griffin's Brigade	*Chapman's Brigade*
Butterfield's Brigade	*Warren's Brigade*

VI Corps

Taylor's Brigade only

IX Corps (under Reno's command)

1st Division Stevens	2d Division Reno
Christ's Brigade	*Nagle's Brigade*
Leasure's Brigade	*Ferrero's Brigade*
Farnsworth's Brigade	

ARMY OF NORTHERN VIRGINIA

Lee 55,000 men

Left Wing (I Corps) Jackson

W. B. Taliaferro's Division	A. P. Hill's Division	Ewell's Division
Baylor's Brigade	*Branch's Brigade*	*Lawton's Brigade*
Johnson's Brigade	*Archer's Brigade*	*Early's Brigade*
A. G. Taliaferro's Brigade	*Pender's Brigade*	*Trimble's Brigade*
Starke's Brigade	*Field's Brigade*	*Strong's Brigade*
	Gregg's Brigade	
	Thomas' Brigade	

Right Wing (II Corps) Longstreet

R. H. Anderson's Division	Wilcox's Division	Kemper's Division
Armistead's Brigade	*Wilcox's Brigade*	*Corse's Brigade*
Mahone's Brigade	*Pryor's Brigade*	*Jenkins' Brigade*
Wright's Brigade	*Featherston's Brigade*	*Hunton's Brigade*

D. R. Jones' Division	Hood's/Evans' Division
Benning's Brigade	*Hood's Brigade*
Drayton's Brigade	*Law's Brigade*
G. T. Anderson's Brigade	*Stevens' Brigade*

Cavalry Stuart

Hampton's Brigade
F. Lee's Brigade
Robertson's Brigade

"The towns stood like ruins in a vast desert . . . the wretched denizens had fled in cold and poverty to a doubtful hospitality in the far South."

GEORGE A. TOWNSEND

Reporter, New York Herald

In the summer of 1862, at age 21, Townsend was the war's youngest correspondent and already a veteran of the Peninsula campaign. After recuperating from a bout of typhus, he went north to report on the fledgling Army of Virginia, interviewing its new commander and traveling across the war-ravaged Virginia countryside to visit Pope's scattered troops.

I presented myself to General Pope on the 12th of July, at noon. His Washington quarters consisted of a quiet brick house, convenient to the War Office, and the only tokens of its importance were some guards at the threshold, and a number of officers' horses, saddled in the shade of some trees at the curb. The lower floor of the dwelling was appropriated to quartermasters' and inspectors' clerks, before whom a number of people were constantly presenting themselves, with applications for passes—sutlers, in great quantities, idlers, relic-hunters, and adventurers in still greater ratio, and, last of all, citizens of Virginia, solicitous to return to their farms and families. The mass of these were rebuffed, as Pope had inaugurated his campaign with a show of severity, even threatening to drive all the non-combatants out of his lines, unless they took the Federal oath of

A solitary figure leans against one of the few remaining timbers of the gutted Henry house, pounded by Union artillery during the Battle of First Manassas. When the war returned in August 1862, the hill on which it stood anchored the Federals' last line of defense.

"At last we came to Bull Run, the dark and bloody ground where the first grand armies fought and fled, and again to be consecrated by a baptism of fire."

allegiance. He gave me a pass willingly, and chatted pleasantly for a time. In person he was dark, martial, and handsome—inclined to obesity, richly garbed in civil cloth, and possessing a fiery black eye, with luxuriant beard and hair. He smoked incessantly, and talked imprudently. Had he commenced his career more modestly, his final discomfiture would not have been so galling; but his vanity was apparent to the most shallow observer, and although he was brave, clever, and educated, he inspired distrust by his much promising and general love of gossip and story-telling. He had all of Mr. Lincoln's garrulity (which I suspect to be the cause of their affinity), and none of that good old man's unassuming common sense.

The next morning, at seven o'clock, I embarked for Alexandria, and passed the better half of the forenoon in negotiating for a pony. At eleven o'clock, I took my seat in a bare, filthy car, and was soon whirled due southward, over the line of the Orange and Alexandria railroad. The country between Alexandria and Warrenton Junction, or, indeed, between Washington and Richmond, was not unlike those masterly descriptions of Gibbon, detailing regions overrun by Hyder Ali. The towns stood like ruins in a vast desert, and one might write musing epitaphs at every wind-beaten dwelling, whence the wretched denizens had fled in cold and poverty to a doubtful hospitality in the far South. Fences there were none, nor any living animals save the braying hybrids which limped across the naked plains to eke out existence upon some secluded patches of grass. These had been discharged from the army, and they added rather than detracted from the lonesomeness of the wild. Their great mournful eyes and shaggy heads glared from copses, and in places where they had lain down beside the track to expire. . . .

Some of the dwellings seemed to be occupied, but the tidiness of old times was gone. The women seemed sunburnt and hardened by toil. They looked from their thresholds upon the flying train, with their hair unbraided and their garters ungyved—not a Negro left to till the fields, nor a son or brother who had not travelled to the wars. They must be now hewers of wood, and drawers of water, and the fingers whereon diamonds used to sparkle must clench the axe and the hoe.

At last we came to Bull Run, the dark and bloody ground where the first grand armies fought and fled, and again to be consecrated by a baptism of fire. The railway crossed the gorge upon a tall trestle bridge, and for some distance the track followed the windings of the stream. A black, deep, turgid current, flowing between gaunt hills, lined with cedar and beech, crossed here and there by a ford, and vanishing, above and below, in the windings of wood and rock; while directly beyond, lie the wide plains of Manassas Junction, stretching in the far horizon, to the undulating boundary of the Blue Ridge. As the Junction remains today, the reader must imagine this splendid prospect, unbroken by fences, dwellings, or fields, as if intended primevally to be a place for the shock of columns, with redoubts to the left and right, and fragments of stockades, dry rifle pits, unfinished or fallen breastworks, and, close in the foreground, a medley of log huts for the winter quartering of troops. The woods to the north mark the course of Bull Run; a line of telegraph poles going westward points to Manassas Gap; while the Junction proper is simply a point where two single track railways unite, and a few frame "shanties" or sheds stand contiguous. These are, for example, the "New York Headquarters," kept by a person with a hooked nose, who trades in cakes, lemonade, and (probably) whiskey, of the brand called "rotgut"; or the "Union Stores," where a person in semi-military dress deals in India-rubber overcoats, underclothing, and boots. As the train halts, lads and Negroes propose to sell sandwiches to passengers, and soldiers ride up to take mail-bags and bundles for imperceptible camps. In the distance some teams are seen, and a solitary horseman, visiting vestiges of the battle; sidelings beside the track are packed with freight cars, and a small mountain of pork barrels towers near by; there are blackened remains of locomotives a little way off, but these have perhaps hauled regiments of Confederates to the Junction; and over all—men, idlers, ruins, railway, huts, entrenchments—floats the star-spangled banner from the roof of a plank depot.

After their victory at First Manassas, the Confederates, reluctant to advance on Washington, settled in around Centreville and Manassas Junction. Expecting a long stay, they threw up an extensive complex of earthworks as well as rude winter quarters, shown here shortly after they were abandoned in March 1862.

A lone sentry and three of his fellow soldiers with fishing poles hold still for the camera along the banks of Bull Run at the southern edge of the battlefield. Behind them stands a bridge of the Orange & Alexandria Railroad, the Army of Virginia's lifeline linking Pope's command with the huge depots at Manassas Junction and Alexandria.

A deserted Rebel fort looms near a pair of Union army boxcars at Manassas Junction, which by August 1862 had become a vast complex of rail sidings and supply yards. Not long after this photograph was taken, General Stonewall Jackson and his "foot cavalry" swept back into the junction, laying waste to the mountains of matériel and briefly reoccupying the forts.

MAJOR GENERAL JOHN POPE

Commander, Army of Virginia

The Union force occupying northern Virginia in the summer of 1862 found itself at odds with a hostile population who resisted in a variety of ways, including sabotage and sniping. In response, Pope issued a series of general orders that presaged the coming of total war. At about the same time, Pope composed a bombastic address to his new command that offended most of his own soldiers and took a poorly disguised swipe at his predecessor, George McClellan, for his timidity and failure to subdue the Rebels.

Generel Orders, No. 5.

Hereafter, as far as practicable, the troops of this command will subsist upon the country in which their operations are carried on. In all cases supplies for this purpose will be taken by the officers to whose department they properly belong under the orders of the commanding officer of the troops for whose use they are intended. Vouchers will be given to the owners, stating on their face that they will be payable at the conclusion of the war, upon sufficient testimony being furnished that such owners have been loyal citizens of the United States since the date of the vouchers. Whenever it is known that supplies can be furnished in any district of the country where the troops are to operate the use of trains for carrying subsistence will be dispensed with as far as possible.

General Orders, No. 7.

The people of the valley of the Shenandoah and throughout the region of operations of this army living along the lines of railroad and telegraph and along the routes of travel in rear of the United States forces are notified that they will be held responsible for any injury done to the track, line, or road, or for any attacks upon trains or straggling soldiers by bands of guerrillas in their neighborhood. No privileges and immunities of warfare apply to lawless bands of individuals not forming part of the organized forces of the enemy nor wearing the garb of soldiers, who, seeking and obtaining safety on pretext of being peaceful citizens, steal out in rear of the army, attack and murder straggling soldiers, molest trains of supplies, destroy railroads, telegraph lines, and bridges, and commit outrages disgraceful to civilized people and revolting to humanity. Evil-disposed persons in rear of our armies who do not themselves engage directly in these lawless acts encourage them by refusing to interfere or to give any information by which such acts can be prevented or the perpetrators punished.

To the Officers and Soldiers of the Army of Virginia:

By special assignment of the President of the United States I have assumed the command of this army. I have spent two weeks in learning your whereabouts, your condition, and your wants, in preparing you for active operations, and in placing you in positions from which you can act promptly and to the purpose. These labors are nearly completed, and I am about to join you in the field.

Let us understand each other. I have come to you from the West, where we have always seen the backs of our enemies; from an army whose business it has been to seek the adversary and to beat him when he was found; whose policy has been attack and not defense. In but one instance has the enemy been able to place our Western armies in defensive attitude. I presume that I have been called here to pursue the same system and to lead you against the enemy. It is my purpose to do so, and that speedily. I am sure you long for an opportunity to win the distinction you are capable of achieving. That opportunity I shall endeavor to give you. Meantime I desire you to dismiss from your minds certain phrases, which I am sorry to find so much in vogue amongst you. I hear constantly of "taking strong positions and holding them," of "lines of retreat," and of "bases of supplies." Let us discard such ideas. The strongest position a soldier should desire to occupy is one from which he can most easily advance against the enemy. Let us study the probable lines of retreat of our opponents, and leave our own to take care of themselves. Let us look before us, and not behind. Success and glory are in the advance, disaster and shame lurk in the rear. Let us act on this understanding, and it is safe to predict that your banners shall be inscribed with many a glorious deed and that your names will be dear to your countrymen forever.

Many in the North initially were impressed with Pope's bold manner. Harper's Weekly ran a favorable feature on the general (right). Ironically, because of bad timing or Harper's reluctance to acknowledge disaster, the article appeared on September 13, two weeks after Pope was defeated at Manassas and after he had been relieved of his command.

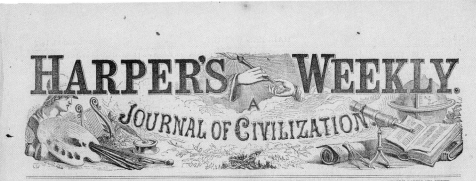

Vol. VI.—No. 298.] NEW YORK, SATURDAY, SEPTEMBER 13, 1862. [SINGLE COPIES SIX CENTS. $2.50 PER YEAR IN ADVANCE.

Entered according to Act of Congress, in the Year 1862, by Harper & Brothers, in the Clerk's Office of the District Court for the Southern District of New York.

MAJOR-GENERAL POPE.

MAJOR-GENERAL JOHN POPE, COMMANDING THE ARMY OF VIRGINIA.

"I have come to you from the West, where we have always seen the backs of our enemies. . . . Success and glory are in the advance, disaster and shame lurk in the rear."

GENERAL ROBERT E. LEE

Commander, Army of Northern Virginia

A native of northern Virginia himself, Lee was outraged by Pope's pronouncements, and crushing this new enemy became the Southern commander's first priority now that McClellan was largely contained. On July 27 Lee sent Stonewall Jackson reinforcements, along with these orders to deal with the "miscreant" Union general.

CAPTAIN HUGH A. WHITE

4th Virginia Infantry, Ronald's/Baylor's Brigade

A seminary student when war came, White agonized over taking up arms but finally resolved to "help finish it." Enlisting at Lexington in June 1861, he rose quickly to command a company in the Stonewall Brigade. Just over a year later, when he wrote this letter to his sister, his commitment had been buoyed by a string of victories.

I want Pope to be suppressed. The course indicated in his orders if the newspapers report them correctly cannot be permitted and will lead to retaliation on our part. You had better notify him the first opportunity. The order of Steinwehr must be disavowed or you must hold the first captains from his army for retaliation. They will not be exchanged. A. P. Hill you will find I think a good officer with whom you can consult and by advising with your division commanders as to your movements much trouble will be saved you in arranging details as they can act more intelligently. I wish to save you trouble from my increasing your command. Cache your troops as much as possible till you can strike your blow and be prepared to return to me when done if necessary. I will endeavor to keep Genl McClellan quiet till it is over if rapidly executed.

    Very respectfully and truly

    R. E. Lee

    Genl

But our faces are now turned towards Washington, and although we are idle now, I hope that our generals are only preparing for an advance. If invasion is feasible, we ought to try it, that the burden of the war may be laid upon the homes of our enemies, to teach them how sore a thing it is when it comes to our own doors. If we remain idle after our victories, it only requires a short time for the Yankees to recover from their defeat and panic. They are well nigh frightened to death for a while, but if we leave them in possession of all their cities and their homes, they feel secure, and soon create a new excitement in favor of the war, and push forward the poor Dutch and Irish to fill their broken ranks. If the men refuse to volunteer, they can be forced out, and we may soon expect to see another immense army gathering around us. But they have been thoroughly whipped at Richmond; their effort is seen to be foolish by their own people; and without doubt we shall ultimately be free.

In July 1862, some of the battle flags of the Army of Northern Virginia took on a new appearance, with the addition of battle honors. Here, the regimental flag of the 14th North Carolina Infantry displays the names of two battles in which the regiment fought honorably during the Peninsula campaign.

"I want Pope to be suppressed. The course indicated in his orders . . . cannot be permitted. . . . Cache your troops as much as possible till you can strike your blow."

CAPTAIN CHARLES M. BLACKFORD

2d Virginia Cavalry, Robertson's Brigade
When Blackford first encountered Stonewall Jackson, the captain was quick to note the general's spartan appearance and fervent demeanor. Later, assigned as an aide and escort to Jackson during much of the campaign, Blackford also had ample opportunity to observe his commander's eccentric behavior, including this incident 10 days before the Battle of Cedar Mountain.

Everybody in Albemarle is anticipating the arrival of the yankees but there is no danger while Jackson is in front of them. I go back to camp early this morning. Day before yesterday I was riding with Jackson and his staff investigating some roads which I expect he intends to use. We had not ridden more than five miles and it was not more than two o'clock in the day, when the General suddenly stopped, dismounted at the foot of a tree, unbuckled his sword and stood it by the tree, then laid down with his head on the root of the tree and was asleep in a second, or appeared to be so. I was amazed and glanced at the other gentlemen, who I thought were not so much surprised. The General had not said a word as he went to rest and we were equally quiet while he slept. He laid with his eyes shut for about five or six minutes, got up, buckled on his sword, mounted and rode on without any explanation or comment. He is a curious, wonderful man. No one seems to know much of him, not even those who are with him hourly. He has no social graces but infinite earnestness. He belongs to the class from which Cromwell's regiment was made except he has no religious hypocrisy about him. He is a zealot and has stern ideas of duty.

Jackson pauses to read dispatches while on a foraging expedition to Louisa County, Virginia, in late July 1862. The artist, Alexander R. Boteler, served both as a volunteer aide to Jackson and as a Confederate congressman.

AMANDA V. EDMONDS

Resident of Fauquier County, Virginia

Nicknamed "Tee," the 23-year-old Edmonds was one of the thousands of Virginians who found themselves unwilling subjects of the "Yankee Nation" when the Confederate army withdrew beyond the Rappahannock in the spring of 1862. Her diary entry for March 9 records her misgivings: "They have fallen back from Manassas. O! What will become of us." She was not long in finding out.

Last night scarcely had I gone snugly to bed and in a doze, before a tremendous barking of the dogs aroused me and then the noise of horse's feet. I jumped out of bed, raised the curtain and there were six or seven Cavalry men riding away. They had been around to the kitchen door and inquired the way to the distillery. I composed myself at last and slept soundly through the night.

But Oh! today—first we were watching five or six of infantry at work over at Aunt Margaret's. Having been all over both places, they finally had a chase after the turkeys and a grand chase it was for four or five men—believe I could have beat them *myself*. I hurriedly concealed some few of my precious treasures and put some in my pocket, among them the ambrotype of my Southern soldier friend and Syd. I was determined that if they were in my presence a Southerner should be nearer me than they; however I flattered myself in feeling better protected by having them there.

A Lt. first made his appearance. Then a gang of rough, unmanageable German and Irish. The officer said they were the worst of the division and we needed a guard. . . . he hurried off pretending he was

As in other families in the Federally occupied area, the men in Amanda Edmonds' family put on Confederate gray when the war broke out, often leaving the women as the sole defenders of home and farm. Here she poses with her first cousin, Thomas Lee Settle, who served as a surgeon with the 7th Virginia Cavalry and earlier had been the doctor who declared John Brown dead at his execution in 1859. Two of her brothers, Edward and Ben, rode with the 6th Virginia Cavalry, as did her future husband, John Chappelear.

going to send one, but none came. We fed the soldiers, who wanted eggs. Ma told them that she had sold nearly all she had yesterday, but gave them about a dozen, which was all we had. They demanded more, said she must have them. I got three with young chicks in them and put them where they could get them in the kitchen on the table. They nabbed them and off they went. I hope they will get a belly full. They searched the kitchen loft, went in the pantry and demanded the cellar and closet key. Ma took them in and told them to take a good look, but they were disappointed in not finding the *idolized tea,* which they inquired if we had. Then they wanted the meat house key and demanded four or five pieces of meat. Group after group came—infantry and cavalry all day. . . .

Sunday, but not much like it, though I have tried to make myself believe it was. Two Yankees staid with us last night acting as guard, but they slept all night. Our first visitors this morning were three on beautiful horses under the lash and spur—demanded corn and oats. Five wagons drove in and helped themselves sumptuously, the roughest of vagabond Irish and German Dutch with them. . . .

We were seated on the porch looking around on the varied scenes—here a squad, there another, some up and down the road with wagons for forage, and the three seated at their comfortable quarters (the old house); when up rode three officers. They dismounted and walked up to the porch wanting the use of the barn for a company, pretending it would be guard for the neighborhood. Ma put her veto against it, but the slick tongued out-talked her and left saying he would be back in the evening and wanted a room. He dashed away to get lodging else where for another set. This evening up they march seventy-five or [eighty] strong, headed by the slick tongued Negro stealer, every one Dutch and German with the same stripe of officers. On they go to the barn through the yard. I urged the dog on them all the time until they threatened to shoot him if he didn't stop barking. We were *dishonored* with two at the supper table—Shumaker and Memenger, whom I hope will be registered with the fallen. They are very chatty and extremely inquisitive as to the country and farming. One remarked, "Virginia was a garden spot; indeed it was a beautiful and fine country." Yes, and I hope you may all get a home on her soil not larger than six by three. . . .

This is a pretty way to subdue the Glorious South—coming and sitting down in every village for protection and trying to starve the innocent women and children out with the few men we have left behind.

LIEUTENANT ROBERT G. SHAW

Staff, Brigadier General George H. Gordon

Shaw saw his first action as part of General Banks' force that was chased out of the Valley by Jackson. In late June he became an aide to Gordon and soon complained about having "too little to do." Apparently, his fellow officers felt the same disenchantment with occupation duty and resorted to some novel ways to pass the time.

We have had a good deal of fun at some of the farmer's houses where the General has had his head-quarters. Whenever he gets hold of a Virginian, he pitches into him. First he makes them say whether they voted for Secession; then he gets them to give their reasons, and usually winds up by calling them fools and asses, and worse slaves to Jeff Davis than any black man in the country, &c., &c. At one house, some time ago, just as we were about to start, he called for the owner and told him he must sign a parole. The man said he had rather not. "Guard," bawled the General, "carry this man off." After a good deal of talk the man finally signed, but said it was pretty hard after having all his corn and provisions eaten up, and his niggers encouraged to run off, to be treated in that manner. I should have pitied him, if he hadn't been a villanous looking wretch, who, without any doubt, had often been out bushwhacking. We don't find any able-bodied men in this valley, but there are a good many who are strong enough to go out with a gun. Six were caught near here yesterday, almost in the act of firing on some of our men.

In the front lines for more than six months, once-thriving Centreville, Virginia, looks more like a ghost town in this March 1862 photograph. The Union soldiers (foreground) are part of the force that took over the town and the abandoned Rebel fort in the distance.

LIEUTENANT JAMES GILLETTE

3d Maryland (U.S.) Infantry, Schlaudecker's Brigade

Many of Pope's men were outraged by the harsh treatment of Virginians. Gillette knew the difficulties of providing for an army, but he was appalled by what happened to the family and farm of Robert Scott, a prominent politician whose moderate, pro-Union stance led Lincoln to offer him a cabinet position in January 1861.

Straggling soldiers have been known to rob the farmhouses and even small cottages, the homes of the poor, of every ounce of food or forage contained in them. Families have been left without the means of preparing a meal of victuals. . . . those removed from the scene of war's conflicts . . . know nothing of suffering on inconveniences compared with the horrors undergone by the people of Virginia. The magnificent farm of the late Hon. Robt. E. Scott of Va. has lost all the crops and means of cultivation within the past few months. Mrs. Scott told me that the negroes had absconded. That she had twenty horses, but not a kernel of corn to feed them. With her cows shot, sheep and chickens ditto, she hardly knew where she was to obtain subsistence for her large family. Mr. Scott stood with John Minor Botts in opposing secession and was at last shot by a deserter in the Union Army. His farm is now being shorn of all its worth by the renegades and straggling soldiery of the army he would have upheld were he alive. The lawless acts of many of our soldiers are worthy of worse than death. The villains urge as authority, "General Pope's order."

CAPTAIN WILLIAM T. LUSK

79th New York Infantry, Farnsworth's Brigade
Lusk, a veteran of the successful campaign along the coast of Georgia and the Carolinas, arrived in Fredericksburg on August 6 along with other troops sent north to reinforce Pope. Lusk's sentiments about the changing temper of the war were lofty, but another year of fighting would leave few in the North sympathetic with his views.

I am sick at heart in some respects, and utterly weary of the miserable cant and whining of our Northern press. It is time that we assumed a manlier tone. We have heard enough of rebel atrocities, masked batteries, guerillas, and other lying humbugs. Pope's orders are the last unabatable nuisance. Are we alone virtuous, and the enemy demons? Let us look at these highly praised orders of Pope which are to strike a death-blow at rebellion. We are henceforth to live on the enemy's country, and to this as a stern military necessity, I say "Amen!" But mother, do you know what the much applauded practice means? It means to take the little ewe-lamb—the only property of the laborer—it means to force from the widow the cow which is her only source of sustenance. It means that the poor, and the weak, and the helpless are at the mercy of the strong—and God help them! This I say is bad enough, but when papers like the ——, with devilish pertinacity, talk of ill-judged lenity to rebels and call for vigorous measures, it makes every feeling revolt. We want vigorous measures badly enough to save us in these evil times, but not the measures the —— urges. The last thing needed in our army is the relaxing of the bands of discipline. And yet our Press is urging our soldiers everywhere to help themselves to rebel property, and instead of making our army a glorious means of maintaining liberty, would dissolve it into a wretched band of marauders, murderers, and thieves. If property is to be taken, let the Government take it. That is well—but I would have the man shot who would *without authority* steal so much as a fence rail, though it were to make the fire to cook his food. I would have no Blenkers and Sigels with their thieving hordes, but a great invincible army like Cromwell's, trusting in God and marching on to victory.

Federal officers and their visiting wives mill around in the yard of a house near Manassas requisitioned for use as a field hospital. Such a peaceful scene, captured shortly before Cedar Mountain, would soon become a rarity as the campaign heated up and the casualties mounted.

Clash at Cedar Mountain

On the morning of August 9, Stonewall Jackson's troops broke camp and continued their march north toward Culpeper, destined for a clash with the forces of Nathaniel Banks at Cedar Mountain. With Brigadier General Jubal A. Early's brigade of Ewell's division in the lead, the soldiers marched along the road through choking clouds of dust. In spite of delays, confusion, and debilitating heat, Jackson was confident. "Banks is in our front and he is generally willing to fight," the general told his staff physician, Hunter McGuire, "and he generally gets whipped."

In the shadow of Cedar Mountain Jubal Early came up against Federal cavalry skirmishers—the vanguard of Banks' corps—and deployed south of the Culpeper road to engage the troopers on the rolling fields of the Crittenden farm. At about 2:00 p.m., as the other two brigades of Ewell's division wound their way up the northern slopes of Cedar Mountain, the Federal artillery opened fire, and Ewell's gunners responded.

Although the advancing Rebels held a two-to-one advantage in numbers, Banks had made skillful use of the terrain to mask the size and positions of his smaller force. Major General Christopher C. Augur's division was posted south of the road, for the most part screened from observation by a large cornfield. With soldiers dropping along the wayside with heatstroke, the two brigades of Major General Alpheus S. Williams' division hurried into the cover of thick woods north of the road. From a ridge line north of Cedar Run, the Yankee batteries rained shells upon Jackson's column as it continued to deploy astride the Culpeper road.

Eager to mount an assault, Jackson ordered Winder's division into line on Ewell's left and sent couriers to hasten the march of A. P. Hill's division, still lagging behind the rest of the Confederate force. While Jackson and Winder—who had taken the field despite being ill—were preoccupied with bringing artillery forward to counter the enemy batteries, Winder's division deployed north of the road. Neither Winder nor his brigade commanders—Colonel Thomas S. Garnett, Brigadier General William B. Taliaferro, and Colonel Charles Ronald—were aware that

On the march to Cedar Mountain, a Federal battery pauses for the camera while fording a stream on August 9, the day of the battle.

Williams' Federal division lay just across a wheat field to their east.

For two hours the Union and Confederate batteries traded salvos that caused a number of casualties on both sides. At about 4:45 p.m., as General Winder stood in the road observing the fire of his own artillery, a shell fragment tore through his arm and side, mortally wounding him. Soon after the dying general was carried to the rear, the commander of Winder's artillery, Major Richard Snowden Andrews, was also disabled with an apparently fatal wound.

The loss of the talented Winder had serious repercussions for the Confederates. General Taliaferro, who took command of Winder's division, was unable to locate Jackson. Unaware of his commander's plans, Taliaferro focused his attention south of the road where his brigade had earlier been shifted to cover Early's left. Meanwhile, Early's right had been bolstered by Brigadier General Edward L. Thomas' Georgians, the first of A. P. Hill's brigades to arrive on the field. With Hill's approach, Jackson was preparing to launch his belated advance when, at 5:30 p.m., the Federals beat him to the punch.

Following Banks' order, General Augur started forward through the cornfield south of the Culpeper road with two of his three brigades under Brigadier Generals John W. Geary and Henry Prince. Exposed to the fire of the Southern batteries on Cedar Mountain, and musketry from Taliaferro, Early, and Thomas to the front, the Union troops pressed resolutely onward. Augur was wounded and was replaced by Brigadier General George S. Greene, but the assault by his brigades had preempted an attack by Jackson's right.

Shortly before 6:00 p.m. a more dire Yan-

kee threat materialized north of the road. Breaking from the cover of the woods east of Winder's division, three of the four regiments in Brigadier General Samuel W. Crawford's brigade came surging through the wheat field that separated them from the Confederate left. Startled by the unexpected Yankee onslaught, and still confused in the wake of Winder's mortal wounding, the Rebel troops were slow to respond. Garnett's brigade managed to unleash three deadly volleys, but within minutes the cheering blue-clad soldiers had pierced the Southern line.

The left flank of Garnett's brigade caved in, and a portion of Colonel Ronald's troops—the celebrated Stonewall Brigade—was likewise thrown into disarray. Some of Crawford's Federals battled their way hand to hand through the woods north of the road, while others charged south into the left flank of Taliaferro's men.

Renewed pressure from Augur's division against the Southern right soon jeopardized the entire Confederate line. With an unexpected and unprecedented disaster in the making, Stonewall Jackson spurred his horse into the mounting chaos, cajoling and imploring his men to stand fast. So rarely had Jackson been compelled to draw his sword that he found the blade had rusted in its scabbard, and he was forced to unhook the sheathed weapon from his belt in order to flourish it over his head.

The influence of their revered commander steadied the Southern ranks, even as a lack of reserves crippled Banks' ability to exploit the Federal success. With units hopelessly intermingled and casualties mounting, Crawford's charge began to run out of steam. At that crucial moment more of A. P. Hill's troops came

storming forward at the double-quick, and the tide of battle turned.

As Brigadier General Lawrence O'Bryan Branch led his Confederate brigade against Crawford's front, Brigadier Generals James J. Archer and William Dorsey Pender swung their brigades against Crawford's right. With more than 50 percent of his troops dead, wounded, or taken prisoner, Crawford could do little more than beat a hasty retreat across the wheat field. The 10th Maine, which was held in reserve during Crawford's initial assault, along with units of Brigadier General George H. Gordon's brigade suffered severely as it tried to stem the Rebel counterattack. A squadron of the 1st Pennsylvania Cavalry charged down the Culpeper road but was hurled back.

With darkness settling over the field, Banks retreated toward Culpeper, where one of General McDowell's divisions had arrived too late to play a part in the fighting. Although Jackson's forces had carried the day, the efficient Yankee artillery was still a force to be reckoned with. When Captain William J. Pegram's Confederate battery opened up on the retreating Federals from atop an open knoll, the Union gunners caught the intrepid young Virginian in a deadly cross fire and silenced his guns.

After advancing a mile beyond the battlefield, Jackson called off his pursuit and pondered his next move. The woods and fields below Cedar Mountain were strewn with wounded and slain, the dead already decomposing in the heat. Each side had lost more than 300 men killed outright, and many more would succumb to their wounds.

The total Confederate loss of those killed, wounded, and captured was 1,418, while

Banks lost 2,403 soldiers, 617 of them taken prisoner or missing in the Rebel counterattack.

The political general from Massachusetts had shown a great deal of pluck, and the Confederate performance had been something less than brilliant. But Stonewall Jackson had saved the day, and now he was eager to move on, to carry the campaign into its next ambitious phase.

On the afternoon of August 9, with both sides itching for a fight, Jackson ran into the vanguard of Banks' corps just north of Cedar Mountain. After an interval of skirmishing and an exchange of artillery fire, the Federals attacked. First to strike were the brigades of Geary and Prince, who advanced against Jackson's center but were held off by a tenacious defense. Next, Crawford's brigade, lying undetected in thick woods, suddenly burst forth opposite the Rebel left and after a vicious struggle routed the better part of three Confederate brigades. But lacking reserves, the Federal penetration withered and was finally shattered by the counterattack of Hill's division. The Union forces withdrew in the face of a desultory pursuit, and the fighting gradually petered out with the coming of night.

"Suddenly, as if by rehearsal, all hats would go up, all bayonets toss and glisten, and huzzas would deafen the winds."

GEORGE A. TOWNSEND

Reporter, New York Herald

Armed with a pass from General Pope, Townsend conducted many interviews with officers and men of the Army of Virginia. By August 8 the young journalist was in Culpeper, where he witnessed the departure of Banks' corps as it marched south to do battle with Stonewall Jackson.

I had been passing the morning of Friday with Colonel Bowman, a modest and capable gentleman, when the serenity of our converse was disturbed by a sergeant, who rode into camp with orders for a prompt advance in light marching order. In a twinkling all the camps in the vicinity were deserted, and the roads were so blocked with soldiers on my return, that I was obliged to ride through fields.

I trotted rapidly into the village, and witnessed a scene exciting and martial beyond anything which I had remarked with the Army of Virginia. Regiments were pouring by all the roads and lanes into the main street, and the spectacle of thousands of bayonets, extending as far as the eye could reach, was enhanced by the music of a score of bands, throbbing all at the same moment with wild music. The orders of officers rang out fitfully in the din, and when the steel shifted from shoulder to shoulder, it was like looking down a long sparkling wave. Above the confusion of the time, the various nativities of volunteers roared their national ballads. "St. Patrick's Day," intermingled with the weird refrain of "Bonnie Dundee," and snatches of German sword-songs were drowned by the thrilling chorus of the "Star-Spangled Banner." Then some stentor would strike a stave of "John Brown's body lies a mouldering in the grave," and the wild, mournful music would be caught up by all—Germans, Celts, Saxons, till the little town rang with the thunder of voices, all uttering the name of the grim old Moloch, whom—more than any one save Hunter—Virginia hates. Suddenly, as if by rehearsal, all hats would go up, all bayonets toss and glisten, and huzzas would deafen the winds, while the horses reared upon their haunches and the sabres rose and fell. Then, column by column, the masses passed eastward, while the prisoners in the courthouse cupola looked down, and the citizens peeped in fear through crevices of windows. . . .

As I passed into the highway again, and riding through narrow passages, grazing officers' knees, turning vicious battery horses, winding in and out of woods, making detours through pasture fields, leaping ditches, and so making perilous progress, I passed many friends who hailed me cheerfully—here a brigadier-general who waved his hand, or a colonel who saluted, or a staff officer who rode out and exchanged inquiries or greetings, or a sergeant who winked and laughed. These were some of the men whose bodies I was to stir tomorrow with my foot, when the eyes that shone upon me now would be swollen and ghastly. . . .

A continual explosion of small arms, in the shape of epithets, jests, imitations of the cries of sheep, cows, mules, and roosters, and snatches of songs, enlivened the march. If something interposed, or a halt was ordered, the men would throw themselves in the dust, wipe their foreheads, drink from their canteens, gossip, grin, and shout confusedly, and some sought opportunities to straggle off, so that the regiments were materially decimated before they reached the field. The leading officers maintained a dignity and a reserve, and reined their horses together in places, to confer. At one time, a private soldier came out to me, presenting a scrap of paper, and asked me to scrawl him a line, which he would dictate. It was as follows:

"My dear Mary, we are going into action soon, and I send you my love. Kiss baby, and if I am not killed I will write to you after the fight."

The man asked me to mail the scrap at the first opportunity; but the same post which carried his simple billet, carried also his name among the rolls of the dead.

CAPTAIN EDWIN E. MARVIN

5th Connecticut Infantry, Crawford's Brigade
In the late morning hours of August 8, the soldiers of the 5th Connecticut, veter-
ans of General Nathaniel Banks' ill-fated spring campaign in the Shenandoah
Valley, broke camp north of Culpeper and began marching southward. Captain
Marvin, a 28-year-old Hartford native, recalled the blazing heat and the
taunts of local citizens as his column moved slowly through the town.

About 11 o'clock in the forenoon, of the 8th of August, the order came to the regiment, in its camp on the side-hill north of Culpepper, to get ready to march, on five minutes' notice, with two days' cooked rations and 150 rounds of ammunition to the man.

By noon the regiment had prepared itself and swung out into the main street of the village and joined the other regiments of the brigade. The day was excessively hot and the perspiration flowed profusely under the heat and the oppressive loads of equipments, rations, ammunition, etc., which every man was carrying. The streets were full of rumors and the "secesh," male and female, were on the alert and in high spirits, showing that they were well aware that there was to be a development of some kind. The rumor was that Jackson was advancing, and that he had already chased Bayard's cavalry back this side the Rapidan, and that meant only ten miles away. The secesh did not try to conceal their evident joy at the expected victory, and we were regaled with prophecies like this: "Old Jack will give you all you want;" "You will come back to-morrow on the double-quick if you come at all;" "You'll be whipped out o' yere right smart;" etc. None of the brigade seemed very much dispirited, however, by such talk, as they had been hearing it for a year, whenever they had chanced upon this kind of people.

There was a huge pump on the shady square, by the court house, that supplied an abundance of excellent water, and here the boys were allowed to drink their fill and replenish their canteens. For a long time there was a colonel, or officer wearing colonel's straps, not belonging to the First Brigade, and no one seemed to know who he was, who made himself servicable by working vigorously at this pump for our benefit. . . .

But the heat was excessive, more than flesh and blood could stand, and the troops had not marched a mile before men began to wilt and be overcome with it, and to fall out of the ranks in considerable numbers. The march had to be slow, consequently, with halts frequently where shade was found, to let the stragglers come up. Many were really sunstruck on that march and lay by the roadside in an almost dying condition, as far as appearances could indicate, and it was a wonder that so few of them were really seriously affected.

Confident and aggressive, Major General Nathaniel P. Banks, former railroad manager, Speaker of the House of Representatives, and governor of Massachusetts, seemed to be, in the words of a captive Confederate, a "faultless-looking soldier." In fact, Banks was ambitious and personally brave but possessed little military talent.

PRIVATE EDWARD A. MOORE

*Rockbridge (Virginia) Artillery,
W. B. Taliaferro's Division
In March 1862 Moore joined two
of his brothers in the Rockbridge
Artillery. Although sick and ex-
cused from duty since early July,
Moore took his post and fought at
Cedar Mountain. He survived
two wounds and was paroled
at Appomattox.*

We took position in the road near the corner of an open field with our two Parrott guns and one gun of Carpenter's battery, en echelon, with each gun's horses and limber off on its left among the trees. Both Capt. Joe Carpenter and his brother, John, who was his first lieutenant, were with this gun, as was their custom when any one of their guns went into action. We soon let the enemy know where we were, and they replied promptly, getting our range in a few rounds.

General Winder, commander of our brigade, dismounted, and, in his shirt-sleeves, had taken his stand a few paces to the left of my gun and with his field-glass was intently observing the progress of the battle. We had been engaged less than fifteen minutes when Captain Carpenter was struck in the head by a piece of shell, from which, after linger-

*This unexploded Federal Hotch-
kiss case shot was recovered from
the slopes of Cedar Mountain.*

ing a few weeks, he died. Between my gun and limber, where General Winder stood, was a constant stream of shells tearing through the trees and bursting close by. While the enemy's guns were changing their position he gave some directions, which we could not hear for the surrounding noise. I, being nearest, turned and, walking toward him, asked what he had said. As he put his hand to his mouth to repeat the remark, a shell passed through his side and arm, tearing them fearfully. He fell straight back at full length, and lay quivering on the ground. He had issued strict orders that morning that no one, except those detailed for the purpose, should leave his post to carry off the wounded, in obedience to which I turned to the gun and went to work. He was soon carried off, however, and died a few hours later.

The next man struck was Major Snowdon Andrews, afterward colonel of artillery. While standing near by us a shell burst as it passed him, tearing his clothes and wounding him severely. Though drawn to a stooping posture, he lived many years. Next I saw a ricocheting shell strike Captain Caskie, of Richmond, Virginia, on his seat, which knocked him eight or ten feet and his red cap some feet farther. He did not get straightened up until he had overtaken his cap on the opposite side of some bushes, through which they had both been propelled. Lieutenant Graham, of our battery, also received a painful, though not serious, wound before the day was over. This proved to be a very dangerous place for officers, but not a private soldier was touched.

By frequent firing during the campaign the vent of my gun had been burned to several times its proper size, so that at each discharge an excess of smoke gushed from it. After the captain's attention was called to it, it happened that a tree in front, but somewhat out of line, was cut off by a Federal shell just as our gun fired. Supposing the defect had caused a wild shot, we were ordered to take the gun to the rear, the other gun soon following. We got away at a fortunate time, as the Second Brigade of Jackson's division was flanked by the enemy and driven over the place a few minutes later. One company in the Twenty-first Virginia Regiment lost, in a few minutes, seventeen men killed, besides those wounded. The flankers, however, were soon attacked by fresh troops, who drove them back and took a large number of prisoners, who walked and looked, as they passed, as if they had done their best and had nothing of which to be ashamed. By nightfall the whole of Pope's army had been driven back, and we held the entire battlefield.

"Major Snowden Andrews . . . received one of those fearful wounds from which recovery is thought to be an impossibility."

The shell fragment that struck Major Richard Snowden Andrews (right) of Maryland sliced a 10-inch gash in his abdominal wall, exposing his intestines. The artillerist lowered himself from his mount and was eventually carried to the rear. Judging the wound to be likely fatal, surgeons removed debris from the cut and sewed it shut with "cotton boss and a common calico needle." To the surprise of all, he survived his terrible injury and returned to the service, only to be wounded again at Stephenson's Depot in June 1863. The major's jacket (far right) shows damage caused by the shell fragment and cuts made by the attending surgeons.

LIEUTENANT HENRY KYD DOUGLAS

Staff, Major General Thomas J. Jackson

On the afternoon of the battle, Douglas passed by the house where Snowden Andrews was being treated, and there he talked to a discouraged Dr. Hunter McGuire, Stonewall Jackson's chief surgeon. Years later, Douglas wrote a somewhat embroidered account of the artilleryman's brush with death.

*I*t was in this battle that Major Snowden Andrews of the artillery, also from Maryland, received one of those fearful wounds from which recovery is thought to be an impossibility. Struck by a piece of shell he was disemboweled and his abdominal viscera rolled in the dust where he fell: he was left without hope. Dr. McGuire, passing and seeing him, stopped to say he was grieved to see he could not be any help to him.

"Yes, that's what you fellows all say," said Andrews.

Stung a little by this, McGuire, who greatly liked him, sprang to the ground to do what he could. He washed off and restored his viscera to their proper place, stimulated him, sewed him up, gave him all the benefit of his skill and sent him to a hospital. Meeting McGuire a few minutes afterwards I said, "McGuire, is Snowden Andrews mortally wounded?"

"Well—if the good Lord will let the rest of the world take care of itself for a time and devote his attention exclusively to Andrews, he may be able to pull him through, but no one else can!"

EDWIN FORBES

Special Artist, Frank Leslie's Illustrated Newspaper
Forbes, a New Yorker, submitted hundreds of sketches from the battlefields and camps of the eastern theater to be translated into woodblock engravings for publication. His first attempts at sketching a battle, during the Shenandoah Valley campaign earlier that year, were frustrated by heavy enemy fire.

I was more fortunate on my second attempt, at Slaughter or Cedar Mountain, for I had been on the line of battle the night before, and was quite interested the following morning watching evidences of an enemy in our front. The Rebs kept well under cover, but showed several battle-flags along the edge of a distant wood, and at intervals with my glass I could see a horseman ride across the field along the line. Nothing to alarm a spectator took place until early in the afternoon. I was then watching some soldiers who were boiling green corn in a large iron boiler that they had obtained from a farmer, when I was suddenly startled by a rattle of musketry in front. I ran towards my horse, which was tied to a fence near by, and hastily mounting rode forward to the crest of the ridge on which Knapp's battery was posted, and halted near it. I soon realized that a battle had begun. The Confederates were posted on a ridge parallel to the one occupied by our forces, their position being rapidly developed by the opening fire of their guns.

Off on our right their infantry advanced, preceded by a cloud of skirmishers, who kept up an incessant fire on our men, but the compliment was returned two-fold. In their center I could see, with the aid of a glass, several batteries advancing and firing, and I knew their practice was good, as their shells burst over our heads and in rear of our position too often for comfort. The sight was magnificent, but trying to one who had no active duty to perform, so I rode over to the right, where the infantry were engaged, and saw Gen. Banks and his staff on the main road directing operations. This place soon became too hot for me, and I galloped back along the line to my original position. On my way I saw a body of Union cavalry making a charge towards the foot of Cedar Mountain, the enemy's center. It was a foolish movement, for the enemy's shells raked them badly, and this, with the ground being cut up by numberless fences, soon caused them to fall back. I watched the battle until the fire became unbearable, then, putting spurs to my horse, retreated in remarkably good order to a safe position about a mile in the rear. I here listened to the ebb and flow of the battle until, under pressure of largely superior numbers, the Union forces were compelled to fall back. I had several narrow escapes during this battle, and realized that to be a spectator was nearly as dangerous as being a participant.

Edwin Forbes made this sketch of Captain Joseph M. Knapp's Battery E, Pennsylvania Light Artillery, as it dueled with Confederate batteries on the slope of Cedar Mountain. Fears that the battery might be overrun by the Confederates prompted an ill-fated charge by the 1st Pennsylvania Cavalry.

SERGEANT SAMUEL D. BUCK

13th Virginia Infantry, Early's Brigade

Sergeant Buck, a veteran from Winchester, Virginia, recalled the confusion as the Confederate forces to his left crumbled under an unexpectedly aggressive Federal attack. Buck rose to the rank of captain by May 1863. In February 1865 he resigned his commission in the understrength 13th Virginia.

Not over half a mile and just in front of us a brigade of cavalry had formed as if to charge us in open field, this we desired and we laid down to await them with pleasure. Like a stage scene this line of cavalry disappeared and a solid line of blue infantry faced us. "We are in for it now," said the men, and so it was for, at the moment the cavalry got from the front the enemy opened a heavy artillery fire upon us. We lay in an open field under an August sun without shade or water for hours while shell after shell plowed up ground about us. One shell burst almost under Gen. Early's horse covering him with dust. After shelling us terribly, a heavy infantry attack was made on Stonewall's brigade which was on our left outflanking it and driving it back. At the same moment a line in our front moved upon us. The old Thirteenth arose at the sound of Col. Walker's voice and met them half way and with the little Thirty-first Virginia we stayed with our battery which we were supporting, until flanked and fired upon from the rear. While fighting over this battery, Col. Tallefero of Stonewall's Brigade came to the left of our regiment in his shirt sleeves and I heard him call to his men, "Look at the old Thirteenth, rally on her." I was a sergeant but in command of the company in this battle and was horrified when Col. Walker ordered us to fall back. The enemy was all around us and upon our battery. I feared a stampede. We fell back about two hundred yards and rallied. My company, indeed all were badly broken and every effort was needed to form under such a terrible fire. One of my men ran by me and I could not hold him to the line. The next day he came to me and said, "Sergeant, I heard you begging men to rally and heard you say to me 'for God's sake, rally' but indeed I could not stop." This was a fact, he could not stop. We did form a line and looking to our left saw the gallant Thirty-first almost surrounded by Yankees and upon our artillery. With a yell we went to their relief and drove the enemy from their front when the Thirty-first, still game, attached themselves to us and we charged again driving everything from before us and reclaiming our artillery. On we went, strewing the corn field with their dead as their line crowded back.

ANONYMOUS NORTHERN REPORTER

To the rear of Geary's brigade, which was attacking the Confederate center, a Northern newspaper correspondent spoke with a wounded private, 20-year-old William W. Lapham of the 7th Ohio. Lapham's injuries seemed minor, but the wound turned septic and Lapham died in a hospital in Culpeper on August 13.

Just after the firing of musketry became interesting, I noticed a private soldier coming off the field, and thinking perhaps he was running away to avoid danger, I rode up to him, when I found he had two fingers of his left hand shot away, and a third dreadfully lacerated. I saw at once that he had at least a hand in the fight. I assisted him to dress his wound as well as my limited knowledge of surgery would permit, he, in the mean time, propping up my pluck by his quaint remarks. Said he: "I don't care a darn for that third finger, for it warn't of no account, no how; but the 'pinter,' and t'other one, were right good 'uns, and I hate to lose 'em. I shouldn't have come to the rear, if I had been able to load my gun; but I wasn't." After I had dressed his hand, he looked over in the direction of the firing, and stood a moment. Turning to me, he said: "Stranger, I wish you would just load up my shooting-iron for me; I want to have a little satisfaction out of them cusses for spiling my fore paw." I loaded his gun for him, and he started back for the top of the hill at a double-quick, in quest of satisfaction. His name is Lapham, of the Ohio Seventh.

BRIGADIER GENERAL JUBAL A. EARLY

Brigade Commander, Army of Northern Virginia
As the battle raged on August 9, Early, who had been tending to the placement
of troops on the right of his brigade line, returned to the left to find that flank
disintegrating. He called up the 12th Georgia, commanded by Captain William
Brown, and the Georgians opened fire on the flank of the advancing Federals.

t was a most critical state of things, and I saw that the day would probably be lost, unless I could hold the position I still occupied. I could not, therefore, go to rally my retreating men, but sent my Assistant Adjutant General, Major Samuel Hale, to rally them and bring them back, while I rode to the rest of my troops and directed their commanders to hold on to their positions at all hazards. On my giving the directions to Captain Brown of the 12th Georgia, he

replied: "General, my ammunition is nearly out, don't you think we had better charge them?" I could not admit the prudence of the proposition at that time, but I fully appreciated its gallantry. This brave old man was then 65 years old, and had a son, an officer, in his company. The position was held until other troops were brought up and the greater part of the retreating men rallied, and the day was thus prevented from being lost.

Union troops (foreground) press the faltering line of A. G. Taliaferro's Confederate brigade along the Crittenden farm lane. The 12th Georgia and its commander, Captain William F. Brown (left), played a key role in stabilizing Jackson's line. Brown was killed at Chantilly three weeks later.

"A solid shot came jumping over the field like a rabbit, and bounced over our gun, missing everything."

PRIVATE JOHN W. F. HATTON

1st Maryland (C.S.) Battery, Ewell's Division

Student John Hatton joined Snowden Andrews' Maryland artillery company in August 1861. He was slightly wounded in the Seven Days' Battles and re-joined his battery in time to fight at Cedar Mountain. He remained with his severely wounded brother and was captured and later paroled. On June 22, 1864, Hatton was wounded in the leg near Petersburg, Virginia, and was discharged from the service three months later.

*S*aturday—Aug. 9th. 1862. . . . After dashing a while in direction of the right wing of our army, still under cover of the hill, our horses' heads were turned to the left, and we made a rush for the crest of the hill, unlimbered, and commenced a rapid firing. The enemy's balls and shells kept the air torn with deafening roar and buzz, while there was a terrific storm raging on our left and front. Our guns were alined with some of the Chesapeake Battery, in a position to the right of our first section but not in sight to be distinguished by them. In our rear under the hill on a level spot, was located the dwelling house of a lady by the name of Critendon. Yet farther to the rear across the valley, some distance up the side of Cedar Mountain, was stationed a rifle cannon, the balls and shell of which passed nearly over our position. As I raised my right arm up with the rammer in hand, in the act of serving my gun, a fragment of a prematurely exploded shell from that rifle piece passed under my arm. Sergeant Carter, who was standing near our gun, directing its fire, was struck down by a frag-

ment of matter striking him in the face, was picked up by the ambulance detail, and carried from the field, the blood flowing freely from his wound. Many shots were heard striking into Mrs. Critendon's house; and I was told the lady was in the house all the time the Battle was raging. Our gun became so heated by rapid and constant firing that the water on the sponge head would sizz when the gun was being swabbed out; and we had to cease firing awhile to allow it to cool off. I rested the sponge staff against the wheel, and drew my sleeves, first right and then the left, across my face to wipe off the perspiration which was almost trickling into my eyes. I turned my canteen up to my mouth to take a drink of water, but it was empty; a ball of some description, unbeknown to me, had made a hole through the bottom of it. I had to resort to the sponge bucket to quench my thirst, and drank heartily of the water mixed with burnt powder washed from the sponge head. The sponge bucket was a small round iron bucket, holding about one gallon and a half, with a mouth just large enough to insert the sponge head, with a sliding top of iron. It was used to carry water on the Battlefield to dampen the sponge to quench the sparks remaining in the gun after each charge being fired. During this fight our sponge bucket was sent to the branch twice to be filled to quench our thirst as well as to serve the gun. It was a very warm day. While we were waiting for the gun to cool off, the cannoniers were squatting around the gun to protect ourselves as well as we could from flying missiles. A solid shot came jumping over the field like a rabbit, and bounced over our gun, missing everything. By keeping the gun damp with the sponge, it was ready for action in about five or six minutes time, and our work commenced anew. The fury of the engagement had not abated any the least, but if any thing seemed prosecuted with more vigor. Our Boys, with perspiration trickling down their faces, hands begrimed with powder, cheeks flushed to a glow, and eyes sparkling with martial spirit, executed their duties with quickness and vim, apparently neglectful of personal safety. The squeaking, bursting and buzzing of the enemy's shot and shell were only momentarily drowned by the roar of our own guns. The swell of the crest of the hill in front of us, which we had taken advantage of in locating our guns, may be accredited with our fortunate escape.

As the sun still hung in the clear western sky, a little space about the top of the forest we heard to our left a mingled roar and snickering like the noise of a nightly wind-storm, smashing and breaking through the woods on our left flank. An officer road hastily up to us and ordered our guns drawn out. We immediately limbered up, and proceeded to retire in good order along the tracks. We had come under cover of the hill,

Cedar Mountain looms through the August haze in this photograph by Timothy O'Sullivan. Taken from the Federal position, the picture shows the rolling terrain that concealed the Federal right from Jackson's view during the early stages of the battle. Jackson remained unaware that Williams' Federal division threatened his left flank until it was nearly too late. O'Sullivan, who was covering the campaign, visited the battlefield shortly after the Rebels departed.

advancing to the left. Going a few hundred yards, we fell in with our first section, which was also retiring. When we met, one of the men of that section ran to me and said excitedly, "Hatton, your brother is wounded and will likely fall in the hands of the Yankees." "Where?" He pointed to the top of the hill abreast of us whence they had come. I started off at full speed in the direction designated, with a determination to rescue him, or be captured with him. But running about fifty yards on my way, I met an ambulance with a load of wounded. I found him in the ambulance, supporting as best he could his left shoulder with his right hand. "Are you hurt much?" "Yes, I believe I am." was the calm answer. But a reply was not necessary, for I saw his left shattered and cut about the wrist and near the shoulder, the fragments

bleeding and dangling by a few small shreds of flesh and sinews temporarily bandaged with a handkerchief, sufficient merely to stanch the flow of artery blood. He had been struck with a flying shot while he had a shell in his arm, carrying in a run to his gun stationed near that clump of Cedar trees, which was rendered historical by the severe conflict occurring there. As I could render him no assistance at that time, I followed the ambulance to the rear, walking behind rather than adding my weight to the load the horses already had to pull. We travelled near about a mile around Cedar Mountain; and that load of wounded was put out on the green slope in sight of a Dwelling House, and near a little spring oozing from the grassy bank. And the ambulance hurried back for another load of the unfortunate.

"Men, whenever the enemy takes a gun of my battery, look for my dead body in front of it."

PRIVATE ALBERT S. DREWRY

Purcell (Virginia) Artillery, Hill's Division

Albert Drewry joined the artillery in Richmond three days after the Virginia Convention passed an ordinance of secession in 1861. He served until the end of the war, rising to the rank of quartermaster sergeant. At Cedar Mountain, as the Confederate battle line crumbled, Drewry's battery commander, Captain William Pegram, conducted a desperate effort to halt the oncoming Federals.

In a short time an order came to send Pegram's rifled guns to the front. Going forward, we soon came to the open country, where Jackson and our chief of artillery, Gen. R. L. Walker, met us and pointed out the position we were to take and the work we were to do. In an old stubblefield on a little knoll we unlimbered, and Jackson in person directed Pegram to throw shells into a distant woods. We opened fire as directed, using fifteen and twenty second shell—no enemy in sight. Three hundred yards in front of us was a heavy growth of green corn, extending for a mile or more over beautifully undulating ground. To the left was the road by which we had come, and the only

Youthful Captain William J. Pegram directed four guns of the Purcell and Middlesex (Virginia) batteries, firing canister in the face of Geary's attacking Federal brigade and holding his position until the enemy were within yards of his guns. The shy, nearsighted Pegram became a colonel at age 23 and fell mortally wounded at Five Forks, Virginia, eight days before Lee surrendered at Appomattox.

line of retreat in case such an emergency arose.

We had fired only a few shots when over the hill and through the corn we saw at least a brigade of blue infantry coming straight for the guns. Changing from shell to shrapnel and canister, we turned our entire attention to this column, but they continued to come on without a waver. Finally we doubled the charges of canister, and then they broke and went back over the hill. Just then we noticed coming down the road at full speed and in easy shell range a body of blue cavalry. If they passed our flank we were lost. Changing front to the left, we raked the road, first with shell, then with canister. The cavalry came on almost past the danger point, then broke and went back.

Our attention was then called to our old friends, the infantry, who had been reinforced and were coming through the corn as if to take our guns at all hazards. The situation looked desperate, as we had no support near by. Pegram ordered double charges of canister, and seizing the flag he went from gun to gun, waving it in the very faces of the men and begging, "Don't let the enemy have these guns or this flag—Jackson is looking at you." "Go in, men; give it to them."

The column faltered and went back and reformed, only to come again. On they came, and were getting in good canister range when an order came to fall back. The bugle blew. "Limber to the rear; cannoniers mount." Just as this order was executed one of the gun horses was killed, and it looked as if the only prudent thing to do was to leave this gun and save the rest if we could. Pegram did not think so, and he quickly gave the order:

"Action, front! Fire double charges of canister!"

While we obeyed this order under his personal direction the drivers replaced the dead horse, and again the bugle sounded, "Limber to the rear! Cannoniers mount! Retire!" which was instantly obeyed, for the enemy were within less than 100 yards of our guns and in great force.

We galloped away with all of our guns, but reinforcements coming up, we soon had our old position back. After this Pegram heard the men discussing how near we came losing the gun. He merely said: "Men, whenever the enemy takes a gun of my battery, look for my dead body in front of it."

LIEUTENANT WILLIAM P. WARREN

28th New York Infantry, Crawford's Brigade
Although Crawford's attack sent the Rebels reeling, his regiments suffered
severe punishment as they surged across the wheat field. Lieutenant Warren
of Company C, a 30-year-old former civil engineer from upstate New York,
was wounded five times. Left with other Federal wounded at Culpeper, he
was captured by the Confederates and paroled to Fort Monroe, Virginia.
On October 20 he was discharged with the rank of captain.

Colonel Dudley Donnelly was mortally wounded as he led the 28th New York
in action at the wheat field. He died in Culpeper on August 15.

ere was the hardest of the fight. We went back slowly. Our brave Colonel Donnelly had fallen with a mortal wound, and was carried to the rear. Our Adjutant, Sprout, was shot. I saw the color bearer shot down once, twice and three times, and each time a new man sprang forward and caught the flag. Colonel Brown's horse was shot and fell under him. At the same time he received a bullet that shattered his arm. The Rebs came on with a yell, on all sides they seemed. One of the boys, whose name I have forgotten, seeing we were taken, ripped down the colors from the staff and concealed them. A bullet stopped me, and I fell over on a wheat shock, and the rebels rushed on over us. . . .

. . . Just as we were about to start on the charge over the wheat field, a stray ball hit me on the index finger as I was holding up my sword, and carried off the cap of my finger. I did not think much of it at the time. Then as they fired the third volley, I got another in the left arm, below the elbow, that nearly knocked me down. There's not much left of the arm now. I've had thirteen pieces of bone taken from it since. A few minutes after I was struck in the head and knocked senseless for a moment, but the ball came sideways, passing out and carrying away a piece of the skull, where you may see the mark. That side of my face was covered with blood and the eye blinded by the shot. I got up again to do what I could, and pretty soon I caught it once more. This time a Minnie ball struck me in the neck; it passed directly between the carotid artery and the wind-pipe, forcing them apart, but by the greatest wonder did not cut either. If it had cut the artery I should not have been here now, and had it been a round ball it must have done so, but the spiral motion of the Minnie forced the jugular apart from the windpipe. The ball lodged and flattened against the base of my skull. . . .

I had the most peculiar sensation when that shot struck me. There was a sharp pain, and then my head seemed to swell as big as a basket.

I kept up a little longer when I received a settler in the shape of another ball. It struck me in the left leg above the knee, in the very center of the leg. I fell over in the wheat shock done for, and the rebels passed on beyond me after our troops. Most of our boys were killed, wounded or taken prisoners then. . . .

It was about six o'clock when I fell Saturday night, and I was not taken up until Monday afternoon.

"The road was full of Yankees, and there was such a fight as was not witnessed during the war."

PRIVATE JOHN H. WORSHAM

21st Virginia Infantry, Garnett's/Johnson's Brigade

The son of a prominent Richmond clothier, John Henry Worsham enlisted in 1861 and fought with the Stonewall Brigade in most of its battles until a ball shattered his left knee at Winchester on September 12, 1864. Discharged, he returned to Richmond and a career in business. Worsham published his recollections, "One of Jackson's Foot Cavalry," in 1912. He died in 1920.

Col. Cunningham of the 21st, who was sick, came along the line, walking and leading his horse, and said to the men as he passed that the enemy were in our rear and he desired to get us out of the position we were in, and we must follow him. His voice was one of loud compass and great command, but he could hardly speak, and as he passed me he said, "John, help me get the men out of this, I can't talk loudly." I induced all the men near me to face down (southward) the road, and we started. After a few steps, I saw a Yankee sergeant step into the road about fifty or seventy-five yards ahead (south) of us, and at the same time heard the firing of rapidly approaching enemy in our rear. . . . The sergeant, having his gun in his left hand, his drawn sword in his right, turned up the road towards us. . . . the enemy were not only in our front, flank, and rear, but actually had the second brigade surrounded. The Yankee sergeant did not stop his advance towards us until he actually took hold of one of the men of our regiment and pulled him out of ranks, and started towards the rear with his prisoner. One of our men, who was in the act of capping his gun, raised it to his shoulder, fired, and the sergeant fell dead not ten feet away. By this time the road was full of Yankees, and there was such a fight as was

When his command was attacked in the rear by Crawford's Federals southwest of the wheat field, Lieutenant Colonel Richard H. Cunningham of the 21st Virginia was fatally shot as he prepared to lead his men to safety.

not witnessed during the war; guns, bayonets, swords, pistols, fence rails, rocks, etc., were used all along the line. I have heard of a "hell spot" in some battles, this surely was one. Our color bearer knocked down a Yankee with his flag staff, and was shot to death at once. One of the color guard took the flag, and he also was killed; another, Roswell S. Lindsay of F Company, bayoneted a Yankee, and was immediately riddled with balls, three going through him. Four color bearers were killed with the colors in their hands, the fifth man flung the riddled flag to the breeze, and went through the terrible battle unhurt. Col. Cunningham had crossed the road leading his horse, pulled down the fence, passed through the gap into the field, started to mount his horse, his foot in the stirrup, when he was struck by a bullet, and fell back dead, his horse receiving his death wound at the same time. It was a terrible time . . . nearly half of the 21st Va. Regt. lay on the ground, dead and wounded. . . . The remnant was still fighting hand to hand.

CAPTAIN EDWIN E. MARVIN

5th Connecticut Infantry, Crawford's Brigade
With the command "Charge, charge and yell," the 5th Connecticut crossed the wheat field under a deadly fire from Confederate defenders occupying the tree line at the field's western edge. Captain Marvin, who became the regiment's historian, recounted the loss of at least five colorbearers during the attack.

s the line advanced into the field, the fire of the enemy became hotter and Color Sergeant Jones, carrying the stars and stripes, fell on his face, killed outright, and Corporal Crawford H. Nodine, of Company I, fell mortally wounded a little to the left, at the same volley. Captain Corliss, of Company C, caught up and bore on the flag, until he was brought to the ground with a bullet wound in the leg. He, however, planted the flag-staff in the earth, at his side, and bravely upheld the flag after he had fallen. Sergeant Luzerne A. Palmer took it from Captain Corliss and bore it to the front again, until he fell wounded. Color Corporal Daniel L. Smith took it again and he was shot down, killed. Sergeant-Major W. P. Smith is also reported to have carried it on till he, too, was wounded in the leg. Captain Corliss had borne the flag along from the spot where Sergeant Jones fell with it, to near the middle of the field in the hollow, by the brook, before he had fallen with it and by that time the field had become considerably sprinkled with the dead and wounded, and behind were several going to the rear, with wounds less severe in character. Precisely how far this flag was borne by each, and how many, and who bore it and fell with it, cannot now be stated, beyond those who have been named, but it was carried on by some of the brave boys that started with it, and was not captured till the utmost advance had been reached and the regiment had commenced to fall back, when it was captured by the Stonewall Brigade which then came in from the right, probably the Fifth Virginia Regiment.

The 5th Connecticut's national color was captured by Private Narcissus Finch Quarles of the Stonewall Brigade. Quarles reportedly captured three Federal flags and 19 prisoners during the Rebel counterattack against Crawford's regiments.

An unidentified officer, perhaps Jackson himself, presented this captured Federal noncommissioned officer's sword and sheath to Private Quarles to honor his exploits at Cedar Mountain. Quarles was killed three weeks later at Manassas.

LIEUTENANT JOHN M. BLUE

17th Virginia Cavalry Battalion, Robertson's Brigade

Blue, a 28-year-old native of the Hanging Rock region of western Virginia, was temporarily assigned to General Jackson as a mounted courier. At Cedar Mountain the young officer was at Jackson's side when the general rode forward to rally his collapsing left flank.

I was watching the general very closely. He seemed to be getting a little nervous. At length he said, "there is some hard work being done over there," at the same time drew a blank book from a little satchel which he carried, wrote a few lines, tore out the leaf, handed it to a courier, gave him some instructions and away the courier dashed at the top of his speed.

One of his staff then called his attention to a line of Yankee infantry just entering the wheat field on the left of the road and moving in the direction of the firing, which had now become a continuous roar with very little intermission. The general wrote another dispatch, handed it to a courier, gave him some directions and said, "lose no time," as the courier rode away. Then listening a moment said, "that firing is very heavy."

The roar of battle seemed to be getting nearer. I felt sure that the Confederates were being driven back. . . . That they were being hard pressed and could not hold their ground much longer, unless they were reinforced very soon.

The general was sitting with his right leg thrown over the pommel of his saddle, without a word he dropped his leg, pressed his cap on his head, tightened the strap under his chin. This was all done in almost a second of time and would not have been noticed if it had been another than General Jackson. Without a word he wheeled his horse toward the road, pressed the rowells to his flanks and started at a rate of speed

which threatened to leave us far in the rear. His staff was soon close at his heels with a half dozen couriers bringing up the rear.

The general leaped his horse over the fence at the road, which had been partly thrown down. Here he halted a second and ordered some artillery to the rear, which General Winder had ordered placed in position, but which was now in great danger of being captured. Jackson then leaped his horse over the fence on the opposite side of the road into the woods, and had not gone fifty yards when he met his men falling back in considerable disorder. It was here that it has been said that Jackson drew his sword for the first time during the war and called on his men to rally and follow him, that Jackson would lead them.

This may all be true, but how he could have been heard is a mystery to me. The rattle of musketry, the shouting, cheering and yelling was deafening. The smoke of battle and the thick foliage on the timber over head made it impossible to see but a short distance. The leaves and small limbs were falling thick and the bark from the body of the timber flying in every direction, often striking a person in the face leading him to believe that he had run against a load of buck shot or something worse.

It appeared for a few moments as though we had struck a full-grown tornado, loaded with thunder and lightning. This was the most hair-raising fix I had ever struck. When I began to realize the condition of affairs I found that I had lost the general or the general had lost one of his couriers. The confusion and noise at this time was terrible and . . . to me frightful, for a few moments I was almost paralyzed.

Rifle and musket bullets found on the Cedar Mountain battlefield range in size from .58 to .69 caliber. The contending armies carried a wide range of longarms, from up-to-date rifle muskets to old flintlock smoothbores converted to percussion.

CAPTAIN CHARLES M. BLACKFORD

2d Virginia Cavalry, Robertson's Brigade

From his vantage point near the Crittenden farm gate, Blackford, who had already observed the eccentric side of his commanding officer, now saw Jackson the warrior. A fellow Confederate officer witnessed the general rallying his men in the teeth of the Federal onslaught and recalled, "The escape of Jackson from death was miraculous. He was in the thickest of the combat, at very short range."

> "The men would have followed him into the jaws of death itself; nothing could have stopped them and nothing did."

fter what seemed to me a long time the firing on my front and to the left of the road became very sharp and was nearing me rapidly, showing that our men were either being driven or were falling back. I could not see because there were some low bushes in my front, but in an instant a regiment or two burst through into the spot where I was standing, all out of order and mixed up with a great number of yankees. I could not understand it; I could not tell whether our men had captured the yankees or the yankees had broken through our line. In an instant, however, I was put at rest, for Jackson, with one or two of his staff, came dashing across the road from our right in great haste and excitement. As he got amongst the disordered troops he drew his sword, then reached over and took his battle-flag from my man, Bob Isbell, who was carrying it, and dropping his reins, waved it over his head and at the same time cried out in a loud voice, "Rally, men! Remember Winder! Where's my Stonewall Brigade? Forward, men, Forward!"

As he did so he dashed to the front, and our men followed with a yell and drove everything before them. It was a wonderful scene— one which men do not often see. Jackson usually is an indifferent and slouchy looking man but then, with the "Light of Battle" shedding its radiance over him his whole person was changed. His action as graceful as Lee's and his face was lit with the inspiration of heroism. The men would have followed him into the jaws of death itself; nothing could have stopped them and nothing did. Even the old sorrel horse seemed endowed with the style and form of an Arabian.

Just as this scene was being enacted a very handsome and hatless

When Stonewall Jackson (right) rode forward to rally the broken regiments of his left flank, he was unable to draw his sword from its scabbard—the blade had stuck, rusted from long disuse. So he waved the weapon, scabbard and all.

yankee officer, not over twenty-one or two, whose head was covered with clusters of really golden curls and who had in his hand a broken sword, showing he had led the gallant charge which had broken our ranks, laid his hand on my knee as I sat on my horse and said with great emotion, "What officer is that, Captain?" And when I told him, fully appreciating the magnetism of the occasion, he seemed carried away with admiration. With a touch of nature that makes the whole world kin he waved his broken sword around his head and shouted, "Hurrah for General Jackson! Follow your General, Boys!" I leaned over, almost with tears in my eyes and said, "You are too good a fellow for me to make prisoner; take that path to the left and you can escape." He saluted me with his broken sword and disappeared in an instant. I hope he escaped.

Brigadier General Lawrence O'Bryan Branch had enjoyed several careers since his graduation from Princeton University in 1838, including newspaper editor, lawyer, railroad president, and U.S. congressman. In 1861 he was appointed colonel of the 33d North Carolina and rose to command a brigade under A. P. Hill.

LIEUTENANT HENRY KYD DOUGLAS

Staff, Major General Thomas J. Jackson
As the Union attack faltered, Jackson began to throw reinforcements into the breach. He ordered Branch's newly arrived North Carolina brigade to fill the gap opened by the withdrawal of Garnett's Virginians, and the tide of battle shifted.

On the left was a North Carolina brigade that had done the state much service, commanded by an able and gallant officer who afterwards fell at Sharpsburg. General L. O'B. Branch, when in Congress, was an orator of great force, and on this occasion, while waiting orders, he took occasion to give his troops the benefit of it, by making them a speech. It was a dangerous experiment, for I do not believe any general ever made a speech to his troops on the eve of battle who did not do more harm than good. But no harm was done on this occasion for General Jackson hearing of this delay and the cause of it, started with an unfathomable smile and galloped to the spot. As he reached the right of the brigade he took off his hat, rode rapidly along the line looking the men steadily in their faces as he passed along. When he reached their commander, he said curtly, "Push forward, General, push forward!" and then moved to the front. The effect was instantaneous: this was an eloquence the men understood. Forward with quick step and then quicker went the whole line after their illustrious leader and then with an irresistible yell they charged over the field, their wild yell mingling with the rattle of their musketry. Several officers rushed up to Jackson and almost forced him to the rear, but the charging line swept past him with a shout and kept on.

PRIVATE WILLIAM W. PATTESON

21st Virginia Infantry, Garnett's/Johnson's Brigade
On Banks' crumbling right flank, some Federal troops beat desperately against the Confederate counterattack. Brigadier General George Bayard ordered a squadron of the 1st Pennsylvania Cavalry to charge straight into Branch's oncoming battle line. Young Patteson of the 21st Virginia was one of the Rebels receiving the futile Yankee charge.

Just about sundown their cavalry tried to break through our lines on the extreme left. Our lines were very close to the woods in which was the cavalry. Men were ordered to put double charges in their guns. I had shot my gun so often (and wiped it out but once) that when I had rammed down one Minie ball and nine buckshot I thought I would put in some more. I put in nine more buckshot and some paper. In ramming down the extra charge the ramrod stuck fast. I could not move it up or down. Augustine said: "If you fire your gun in that condition, it will burst. Turn it up and drive the ramrod down on that rock." I did so, but as the enemy were about to charge I had to leave the ramrod in. Thinking the gun might kick me over, I knelt down, so I wouldn't have far to fall. It was well I did.

When the enemy came out of the woods, moving straight toward us, I said to my cousin: "Watch that Yankee on the dark sorrel horse." Well, when she went off, I fell one way and the gun another, the horse had no rider, and a gap was cut through their lines. That ramrod, the eighteen buckshot, and the Minie ball did the work. My captain said:

"See here, young man, where did you get that piece of artillery?" I replied that it was a gift from General Jackson. "Well, now," said he meditatively, "General Jackson should have had it mounted on wheels, so it wouldn't kick you over."

That night the boys began to "josh" me about my gun. The captain's joke at my expense had gone the rounds. "Hello, Patteson!" they said. "We hear you have joined the artillery. What battery?" "Stonewall Jackson's Battery." "They say your gun can kick. Is that so?" they asked. "Kick or no kick," I replied, "the Stonewall Jackson Battery got closer to the enemy than some other folks."

"Good for Patteson!" they cried, slapping me on the back.

Captain Jedediah Hotchkiss, Jackson's cartographer, made this rough sketch of the Cedar Mountain battlefield as reference for a more finished map to accompany the official report to be sent to the War Department in Richmond.

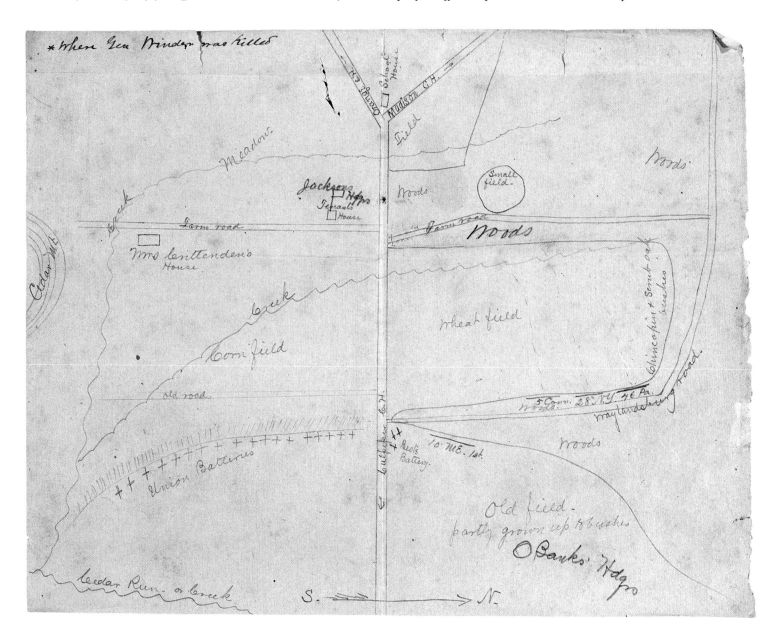

LIEUTENANT JOHN M. GOULD

10th Maine Infantry, Crawford's Brigade Originally the 10th Maine's sergeant major, Gould was commissioned a lieutenant in March 1862. A two-year enlistee, he mustered out in May 1863 but then joined the 29th Maine and rose to the rank of major. Covering the retreat of Crawford's brigade at Cedar Mountain, the 10th Maine suffered 40 percent casualties.

It is a sad thing to refer to, yet in glancing along the line the sight was ludicrous in the extreme. All were excited and were loading and firing in every conceivable way. Some were standing, but most were kneeling or lying down. Some were astraddle their pieces and were ramming the charge totally regardless of the rules on that point. Many had poured their cartridges upon the ground, and were "peddling out" the lead with more speed than accuracy I fear. We all took this occasion to swear at and gibe our friends in gray to the best of our ability. So with the din of musketry and the one common yell of friend and foe, it seemed as if bedlam was loose.

The behavior of those who were hit appeared most singular, and as there were so many of them, it looked as if we had a crowd of howling dervishes dancing and kicking around in our ranks. The bullet often knocks over the man it hits, and rarely fails by its force alone to disturb his equilibrium. Then the shock, whether painful or not, causes a sudden jump or shudder. Now as every man, with hardly an exception, was either killed, wounded, hit in his clothes, hit by spent balls and stones, or jostled by his wounded comrades, it follows that we had a wonderful exhibition. Some reeled round and round, others threw up their arms and fell over backward, others went plunging backward trying to regain their balance; a few fell to the front, but the force of the bullet generally prevented this, except where it struck low down and

apparently knocked the soldier's feet from under him. Many dropped their musket and seized the wounded part with both hands, and a very few fell dead.

The enemy were armed with almost every kind of rifle or musket, and as their front exceeded ours three times, we were under a cross fire almost from the first. The various tunes sung by their balls we shall never forget, and furthermore shall never confound them with any others we have heard. In a moment, when curiosity got the better of fear, I took notice of this fact, and made record of it in my diary a day or two afterward. It was at a moment when probably a fresh regiment had arrived on our right, for the mass of missiles were coming across our

line at an angle of forty-five degrees. The fierce "zip" of the swift Minié bullet was not prominent by comparison, at that particular moment, though there were enough of them certainly. The main sound, or the air of the tune, if I may be allowed the expression, was produced by the singing of slow, round balls and buck shot fired from a smooth bore, which do not cut or tear the air as the creased ball does. Each bullet, according to its kind, size, rate of speed and nearness to the ear made a different sound. They seemed to be going past in sheets, all around and above us.

Edwin Forbes' sketch depicts the Federal attack on Jackson's left flank in the shadow of Cedar Mountain (1). A distant Confederate battle line (2) reels under the assault of General Samuel Crawford's brigade (7) near the wheat field, while the brigades of Augur's division (3 and 4), supported by Knapp's Pennsylvania Battery (6), move against the Confederate center. Forbes also recorded the ominous movement of Ewell's division (11) beyond the Federal left flank.

CAPTAIN SAMUEL M. QUINCY

2d Massachusetts Infantry, Gordon's Brigade

Among the Federals who faced the murderous fire of the reinforced Confederate line was Captain Samuel Quincy, a Boston lawyer. Taken prisoner at Cedar Mountain, he was exchanged and rose to be colonel of his regiment. He was remembered for his eccentricity, falsetto voice, and excessive consumption of cod-liver oil.

Then commenced the furious and incessant roll and crash of musketry, leaving . . . no interval in which a single other shot could have been inserted. We plunged over the ditch and crashed through a wood, out of which came Crane of the Third Wisconsin, covered with blood, and reeling in his saddle, until after about a quarter of a mile we came to a fence with a wheat-field beyond. In this, a brigade of rebels were in line, but what they were firing at we couldn't see. We opened fire and then were ordered to cease—why, I don't know, as I could see no one between us and them. But, as their line advanced, we soon re-opened fire, as the converging storm of balls hailed upon us.

How long this lasted, I could not tell. Their red flags advanced, but large gaps were opening in their lines. Finally, the bullets seemed to come from all sides at once. Pattison, my lieutenant, shouted in my ear that Cary was down, and he had been ordered to take his company; and it seemed to me that the right had fallen back; and I started across the little gap in the fence to see. Yes, the right had gone; but in that instant

Federal soldiers, among those who reoccupied the battlefield after the Confederates withdrew on August 11, lounge in the shade at the edge of the wheat field about a mile from Cedar Mountain. The gently rolling field was the scene of some of the bloodiest fighting on August 9.

I caught it, first in the right leg, then through the left foot, and in that same instant the enemy were upon us, or rather upon me, for what was left of my company had gone with the rest. Though staggering, I had not yet fallen, when one rushed up, aimed at my head with "Surrender, G—d d—n your soul!" which I did. . . .

. . . I gave up my sword and pistol, sat down, borrowed my captor's knife, ripped my trousers open and shoe off, and examined damages. An awful hole in foot and little one in leg, at the bottom of which the bullet was plainly visible. Seeing this, the Confederate gentleman to whom I then belonged was seized with a desire to perform a surgical operation with the knife referred to, but yielded to my remonstrance and request that he would be satisfied with having put it in, and allow some gentleman of the medical staff to undertake the bullet's extraction. Two of them then offered to take me across the wheat-field to where their own wounded were, asking me at the same time what money I had for them. They did not offer any violence or undertake to search me. Had they done so, they would have made a prize of my money-belt, containing over $90 in greenbacks and a gold watch. I gave them some ten or twelve gold dollars which I had in my pocket, reserving one by great good luck, as will presently appear. Then they carried me across the field, with each arm affectionately round a rebel neck. As I passed the fence where the right had been taken, there lay poor Ned,—who half an hour before had joked about being two hours in action without losing a man,—with white, waxen face against the dead leaves. It was just light enough for me to recognize him. Who else of the officers had fallen, I did not know, save that Cary was down, as Pattison had told me, before our lines gave way. With occasional halts, they carried me across the field, and put me down among a groaning mass of wounded of both sides. The men next me gave me water and a knapsack for my head, a man came along with a canteen of whiskey and I got a drink. The moon rose full over the trees, and the cannonade recommenced. I got a piece of the wounded rebel's blanket next me over my shoulder, lay as near him as I could; for, though the day had been blazing, the night mist and loss of blood made me shiver; and I slept. Once I was waked by some one attempting to pull off my seal ring; but he desisted when I pulled my hand away, remarked, "A handsome ring," and went on. Very likely he thought me dead, as my companion under the blanket was by that time.

Before daylight, the pain of my shattered bones brought me again to consciousness. Somehow, I hated to see the sky begin to brighten, knowing how soon the sun would blaze furiously down upon us. . . .

As the sun rose, I gradually dragged myself under trees with the rest of the groaning set, leaving those who had died to sleep it out. A rebel soldier passed with two canteens on. "What will you sell me one of those canteens for?" said I. "I'll give you a dollar." He laughed and was passing on. "A gold dollar," said I. He stopped: "What, Yank! Have you got a gold dollar?" "Yes," said I, "you go to the branch, fill the canteen with fresh water, and here's the dollar." If he had been a wretch, he might have taken it away and left me to die, for there was no one else near except wounded; but, after considering a few minutes, he went off to the stream, filled the canteen, brought it to me, took the dollar, and left. And that canteen, I think, saved my life; for soon the sun rose so that no more shade could be had. I tore up my handkerchief, bound my wounds, and kept them moist, kept the canteen under me and took little sips when my thirst became unbearable, and so got through the day, making the water last until evening. By and by, they began to pick up the wounded by threes and pairs. . . .

. . . After awhile, an ambulance came and picked up the last two of us and carried us to where the hospital flies were pitched. My driver, after making sure that nobody heard him, informed me that he had always been for the Union, and voted against "secesh"; "and when they started this war," said he, "I swore they'd have to fight it out without me; but I was wrong there, for they've got me." He drove me up to a fly under which were some dozen or twenty wounded on hospital cots. At first, they said there was no room; but then somebody discovered that his neighbor was dead, and suggested that the Yankee might take his place. So they moved the dead man under the eaves inside the guys, and gave me the cot. The surgeon examined and bound up my foot, relieving me with the assurance that it would probably stay on, though I should be always lame. The bullet came out of my leg very easily, for, oddly enough, it hadn't pierced my drawers, but had carried them deep into the leg in a sort of bag. A thunder-storm now burst upon us, and with the first gust down came our house, over living and dead. After a long staggering and flapping, they got her set again. The rain thundered on the canvas and cascaded in sheets over the dead man under the eaves, but he was beyond even water cure. The scene was dismal: in the intervals of rain, they took to burying legs and arms upon the hill, and it would not have made a bad slide for a stereoscope, on the whole. But, as night fell, I took my supper with some relish,—a piece of hard-tack and ham, given me by a rebel private on the field,—and with the help of the dead rebel's blanket of last night, which I had sense enough to bag when they picked me up, I slept once more.

CAPTAIN HARRY W. GILMOR

12th Virginia Cavalry, Robertson's Brigade

Maryland cavalryman Harry Gilmor served in two Virginia cavalry regiments before rising to the rank of major. The flamboyant Gilmor made a name for himself as a partisan in the 1864 Shenandoah Valley campaign. He was captured in Moorefield, West Virginia, in February 1865 and spent the rest of the war in prison.

*B*eing the rear guard of the whole army, it was night before we reached near where was the hardest fighting. From our position we could see the flashes of the guns, and hear the shells crashing and bursting amid the trees.

Colonel Harmon having given his consent, I rode to the front, and the first battery I came to was Purcell's (Virginia), where I found young Lieutenant Featherstone, of Baltimore. The enemy were then shelling this particular spot terrifically. Several were killed while I stood there. Not being on duty, I was about to move away, telling Featherstone it was rather warm work, when a spherical case shell came thundering through the wood. I heard it coming, and felt sure that it would strike very near, and in a second I felt the wind of it. It struck Lieutenant Featherstone, taking off the greater part of his head, passed through one horse into the body of another, and then exploded, tearing him to atoms. The first horse fell upon Featherstone, and it was some time before we could extricate his dead body. Before I left four men were killed, three having their heads taken off by one shell.

Photographer Timothy O'Sullivan recorded these dead artillery horses, possibly the ones lost by William Pegram's battery during the nighttime artillery duel that concluded the Battle of Cedar Mountain. One of Pegram's gunners, J. W. D. Farrar, recalled the fight as "one of the hottest actions the battery was ever in."

LIEUTENANT COLONEL DAVID H. STROTHER

Staff, Major General John Pope

A native of Virginia, Strother remained a Unionist and served on the staffs of Generals Banks, Pope, McClellan, and Sigel, ending the war as chief of staff to Major General David Hunter. Breveted brigadier general for meritorious service in 1865, Strother was appointed U.S. consul general to Mexico City, a post that he held from 1879 to 1885. On August 9, 1862, Strother arrived at Cedar Mountain in the late afternoon with General Pope.

The Commanders at length dismounted and seated themselves on the rocky ledges of a gentle eminence, while Staff and escort followed their example, glad to escape the weariness of the saddle. In the mean time the full moon in her glory had risen on our left. We lay here for an hour, probably, during which time I heard at intervals a dropping fire of musketry in the wood in front, and an occasional volley apparently fired by a company. At the same time I had observed numerous stragglers and some organized companies issuing from the wood and moving to the rear by the main Culpepper road and across fields. At length we were startled by the screaming of a shell just over our position, exploding a hundred yards or more beyond. Another and another followed, and then they flew by half dozens, hurtling and crashing in nervous proximity to us. The word was given to shelter ourselves, and we crouched as near the ground as possible on the slope opposite the batteries, with no other advantage that I could perceive than that of avoiding the direct fire by exposing more surface to the fragments of shells, spherical, case, and other deadly missiles which showered around and among us, so close that we were frequently peppered with the dirt and gravel they scattered in their fall.

We lay here holding our horses by the bridles for a half or three-quarters of an hour, watching the fiery tracks of these death-dealing meteors athwart the sky, listening to the thuds of the falling fragments, and making neat calculations as to our chances of being missed. That is, I suppose other people were thus occupied, as there was little said beyond an occasional nervous attempt at a joke. Our respected Chief of Engineers had brought an umbrella to the field, which unmilitary utensil had excited some merriment. In the thickest of the storm a voice was heard desiring him to hoist it for the protection of the company. A stunning explosion near enough to make our ears sing was the only response. Another got up sufficient nonchalance to observe, that the scene, with glorious moon hanging on the verge of that mass of clouds contrasting with the red glare of the bursting shells, was sublime. Quoth a comrade at his elbow, "Yes, sublime as hell!" And the aptness of his illustration was verified by a chorus of demoniac howls that pierced the shuddering air. I had once or twice remarked in the

pride of my heart that I would rather take a shot myself than have my mare hit. Yet when the faithful creature in her tremor put her nose close to my face, and stood over my prostrate body, I experienced a sentiment of involuntary gratitude for the slim protection thus afforded, even considering the probability of being crushed by her falling.

Quartermaster wagons cluster around a house used as a Federal field hospital in a sketch Edwin Forbes drew on the evening of August 9. A Confederate battery (3) fires on retreating Federal infantry while Thompson's Battery C, Pennsylvania Light Artillery, returns fire (4).

"I told him I wasn't a doctor, that I was a priest, and that whereas I could do something for his soul, there was nothing I could do for his leg."

Under a flag of truce, Federal soldiers recover their wounded and dead from the Cedar Mountain battlefield on August 11. Despite protests from Yankee officers, the Confederates, who had already tended to their own casualties, concentrated on picking up as many abandoned Federal weapons as possible. When informed that Jubal Early's men had gleaned more than 1,000 Federal rifles, Stonewall Jackson remarked, "That is the best way to get arms."

CAPTAIN SHEPHARD G. PRYOR

12th Georgia Infantry, Early's Brigade

In 1861 Pryor left his home in Americus, Georgia, to join the 12th Georgia Infantry. Both wounded and commissioned a captain on May 8, 1862, Pryor served with his regiment until October 1863, when he was wounded again and resigned shortly after.

My Dear Penelope

I take the oportunity this morning to write you a fieu lines to let you know something of another battle that wee had here on the road 7 miles from Culpeper Court House. Wee left our camp near [Gordonsville] the 7th. . . . the enemy in force met with the picket pritty soon after starting[.] the fight opened about 4 in the evening[.] oh how hot the weather was[.] great many fell on the road with exaustion[.] some died with sun stroke[.] now for the fight[.] Our reg. acted nobly[.] Stood up square and mantained their place[.] held their position & drove the enemy before them[.] Our loss was 2 killed, 8 wounded[.] Billy Batts & Thos T Linsley killed dead on the field[.] R. J. Browning right arm broken between the elbow and rist[,] McCarthy very slight in the foot[,] Joe Ansley very slight in arm[.] some of the other boys were glanced not hurt at all[.] the fight was not as hot as wee have been in though hot enough for me[.] I am truely thankful that I passed through unhurt[.] there was 8 of our reg killed[.] Leiut. Chambliss killed about 30 wounded[.] wee drove the enemy back about 2 miles[.] they got a strong position[.] wee fell back to our same position from which I am now writing[.] this is the 11th[.] the enemy this morning are getting up their dead & wounded[.] Came up with a flag of truce[.] wee are expecting another hard fought battle dayly[.] Jackson fell back here to draw them from their position. William fainted after the fight was over got so hot[.] he is now well and with the company[.] I don't know when I can mail this to you[.] will as soon as I can. I can't write any more now

I am in good health and company[.] would write more but dont have any dispos[i]tion to write[.] Billy & Tom were buried as soldiers[.] I had their graves marked[.] I guess they will never be moved as they have no coffins

My love to all I am yours

S. G. Pryor

CHAPLAIN LOUIS-HIPPOLYTE GACHÉ

10th Louisiana Infantry, Starke's Brigade

Gaché, a Jesuit priest attached to the 10th Louisiana, described the suffering of the wounded on the Cedar Mountain battlefield in a letter written from Richmond to his friend Father de Carriere. As a Catholic chaplain, Gaché administered last rights to the injured and dying.

The scene which now confronted me was no less horrible than what I had witnessed on the banks of the Chickahominy in the last days of June and the first days of July. There were at least as many dead and wounded as there had been there, and the sight of these unfortunate was no less heartrending. Faced with this carnage, I quite forgot the joy I had experienced when first I heard the sound of cannon and fusillade. All at once I was overwhelmed by a profound sadness: so many men only a few hours before so full of life now lying wounded, mutilated and grotesquely contorted: some dead; some in their last agony; some struggling desperately for life; some still fully conscious and therefore able to suffer more keenly, were calling out for doctors, for wound dressers; for something to drink, for help. One took me for a surgeon and begged: "For God's sake, cut off my leg! Now. Above the knee." He said he could feel the gangrene setting in. And he was right: the lower part of his leg was already purple. I told him I wasn't a doctor, that I was a priest, and that whereas I could do something for his soul, there was nothing I could do for his leg. The poor fellow was a Protestant Yankee; what I was saying meant nothing to him. "But don't you see, if they don't cut it off," he pleaded, "I'll be dead in a matter of hours." "That is quite possible," I replied. "Therefore, all the more reason, my boy, to think about your soul." After a few more words I left him, and went on to see if there were others that I might help.

"In the name of Dixie we bid you welcome to your dreamless couch under the sod that drank your blood. . . ."

CORPORAL GEORGE M. NEESE

Chew's (Virginia) Battery, Robertson's Brigade
Horse artilleryman George M. Neese, a young house painter from New Market,
Virginia, campaigned with Stonewall Jackson's army in the Shenandoah Valley
before his battery was sent to join the Army of Northern Virginia. Neese fought
in all of the major cavalry engagements until his capture at Fisher's Hill, Vir-
ginia, on October 9, 1864. He was released from Federal prison in June of 1865.

August 11—Remained inactive all day. The Yanks came over under a flag of truce, asking permission to bury their dead, which was granted; and their burial parties were at work on the field under the friendly flutterings of a white flag, packing away their comrades for dress parade when Gabriel sounds the great Reveille.

Ah, my silent friends! you came down here to invade our homes and teach us how to wear the chains of subordination and reverence a violated constitution. In the name of Dixie we bid you welcome to your dreamless couch under the sod that drank your blood, and may God have mercy on your poor souls and forgive you for all the despicable depredations that you have committed since you crossed the Potomac.

Federal soldiers view hastily dug graves on the Cedar Mountain battlefield
in a photograph taken by Timothy O'Sullivan. Shortly after the war the
Federal government removed more than 400 bodies to the national ceme-
tery at Culpeper—only one of which could be identified.

LIEUTENANT ROBERT G. SHAW

Staff, Brigadier General George H. Gordon

Three days after the Battle of Cedar Mountain, Shaw wrote to his mother, naming the dead and wounded of his former regiment, the 2d Massachusetts Infantry.

Near Culpepper Court-House, Va.
August 12, 1862
Dearest Mother,

I hope my telegrams and my note to Father reached you, and relieved your anxiety about myself. We have had a hard time. . . .

We hear to-day that the enemy have retired to some distance. If true, we may soon hear more of our missing. Goodwin, Cary, Choate, and Stephen Perkins were all quite ill, but would not stay away from the fight. Choate was the only one of the four not killed. Goodwin couldn't keep up with the regiment, but I saw him toiling up the hill, at some distance behind, with the assistance of his servant. He hardly reached the front when he was killed. All our officers behaved nobly. Those who ought to have stayed away, didn't. It was splendid to see those sick fellows walk straight up into the shower of bullets, as if it were so much rain; men, who until this year, had lived lives of perfect ease and luxury. Oh! it is hard to believe that we shall never see them again, after having been constantly together for more than a year. I don't remember a single quarrel of any importance among our officers during all that time.

Yesterday I went over the battle-field with the General. The first man I recognized was Cary. He was lying on his back with his head on a piece of wood. He looked calm and peaceful, as if he were merely sleeping; his face was beautiful, and I could have stood and looked at it a long while. Captain Williams we found next. Then Goodwin, Abbott, and Perkins. They had all probably been killed instantly, while Cary lived until 2 o'clock P.M. of the next day. His First Sergeant was shot in the leg, and lay by his side all the time. He says he was very quiet; spoke little, and didn't seem to suffer. We found a dipper with water, which some Rebel soldier had brought. They took everything from him after he died, but returned a ring and a locket with his wife's miniature to the Sergeant. His was the only dead body I have ever seen that it was pleasant to look at, and it was beautiful. I saw it again in Culpepper late that night. All these five were superior men; every one in the regiment was their friend. It was a sad day for us, when they were brought in dead, and they cannot be replaced.

The bodies were taken to town, and Lieutenant Francis and I had them packed in charcoal to go to Washington, where they will be put in metallic coffins. I took a lock of hair from each one, to send to their friends. It took almost all night to get them ready for transportation. . . .

Gordon's Brigade was the only one that was kept together, and remained in position all night and the next day. The others scattered,—were collected the day after, and went into camp.

Banks had about seven thousand men, and was greatly outnumbered. We had a good many more in reserve, but they were not brought up for some reason. Whose mismanagement it was, I don't know. Opinions differ. Troops have been coming in pretty fast ever since, and we have a strong position. I have just heard decidedly that Harry was *not* hurt, and I believe it myself,—please let Annie know. I am sorry to send so many different accounts, but it is impossible to get at the truth immediately. Love to all, dear Mother, and God bless you!

Your ever loving son,
Robert G. Shaw

The 2d Massachusetts, dubbed the Harvard Regiment for the high number of Harvard graduates in its ranks, lost six of its officers at Cedar Mountain. Among the dead were Lieutenant Stephen G. Perkins (far left), Captain William B. Williams (left), and Captain Richard Cary (right).

LIEUTENANT HENRY L. ABBOTT

20th Massachusetts Infantry Harvard-educated Henry Abbott served with McClellan's Army of the Potomac during the Peninsula campaign. He was wounded at the Battle of Glendale and rejoined his regiment as it prepared to move to northern Virginia to reinforce Pope. While still at Newport News, Virginia, he received word that his older brother, Edward (Ned), had been killed at Cedar Mountain.

*D*ear Papa,

Untill I got the newspapers & mamma's letter day before yesterday, I thought Ned only wounded. I got your letter yesterday. Today we finished our march & I can answer. It came upon me with terrible force. I could hardly believe it. I thought Ned would surely come through all right. I wish to God I could have seen him on the battle field. Tell me all about it as soon as you can learn. I know how awful the blow is to you, for he was the best son you had & was so sure to have been a great man. It is very hard to think that we will never see him again. If I could only have seen his body. Every time my company is drawn up it reminds me of Ned, for I have been thinking lately of getting it into fine shape to show to Ned when we got up there. Do let me know all you find out about it.

Your aff. son,

H. L. Abbott

Captain Edward G. Abbott of the 2d Massachusetts Infantry was killed commanding his regiment's skirmish line at Cedar Mountain when General Gordon's brigade followed Crawford's attack into the maelstrom of the wheat field.

Stonewall's Daring Sweep

With more of Pope's troops arriving at Culpeper, on August 11 Jackson chose to abandon the hard-won field of Cedar Mountain and pull back across the Rapidan. If less than decisive, the fierce clash had fueled Confederate confidence that the despised Yankee commander could be beaten. "I hope your victory is but the precursor of others over our foe," Lee told Jackson, "which will entirely break up and scatter his army."

In fact Pope's confidence had been severely shaken. With General in Chief Halleck preaching caution and McClellan's reinforcements yet to arrive, Pope feared the prospect of Lee's managing to interpose his forces between the Army of Virginia and Aquia Landing, near Fredericksburg, where the Army of the Potomac troops were expected to disembark.

By August 14 Lee was assured of McClellan's intention to abandon the Peninsula, so he ordered General James Longstreet to begin transporting his 30,000-man corps by rail to Gordonsville. When the revered commander of the Army of Northern Virginia arrived on the 15th to take personal charge of operations, his presence further boosted Southern morale. "Lee has an army great

in numbers and spirit," Lieutenant John "Ham" Chamberlayne wrote; "I believe he will wield it greatly. He is silent, inscrutable, strong, like a God."

Lee's initial design was much as Pope feared: a flank march against Pope's left that would pin the Federals between the Rapidan and the Rappahannock Rivers and bring on a decisive battle before McClellan's troops could arrive. But execution of the plan was poorly coordinated, and the Confederate march was delayed.

On August 18 the 5th New York Cavalry crossed the Rapidan and raided the headquarters of Lee's cavalry chief, Brigadier General James Ewell Brown "Jeb" Stuart, at the hamlet of Verdiersville. Stuart himself barely escaped capture, and dispatches found on a less-fortunate staff officer revealed Lee's intentions to Pope, who began pulling his troops back across the Rappahannock. By the time the Confederates were ready to strike

Federal engineers work to repair a bridge over the Rappahannock River in the summer of 1862 (opposite). General Pope would use the span in his withdrawal across the river in mid-August.

on August 20, the Yankees had slipped away.

By August 21 Pope's army was firmly established along a nine-mile front north of the Rappahannock, where a limited number of potential fords and bridges was favorable to defense. Abandoning his designs on the Union left, Lee responded to the challenge by shifting Jackson's troops upriver, toward Pope's exposed right flank in the vicinity of Rappahannock Station and Beverly's Ford.

Wishing to stir up perennial Federal concern for the safety of Washington, Lee dispatched Stuart with 1,500 troopers on a raid across the Rappahannock to strike at Pope's principal supply line, the Orange & Alexandria Railroad. On August 22 Stuart exacted his revenge for the surprise at Verdiersville by ravaging the Yankee depot at Catlett's Station; his trophies included some of Pope's baggage and the general's dress uniform.

Refusing to be intimidated by the temporary presence of Rebel cavalry in his rear, Pope saw an opportunity to lash out at Jackson's column moving across the river. But when a brigade of Franz Sigel's corps crossed Freeman's Ford, Jackson's troops quickly turned the tables on the Federals, who were driven back over the ford with heavy loss. Jackson followed up his success by shifting Jubal Early's brigade across the Rappahannock near Sulphur Springs, a prewar resort and mineral spa. Heavy rains temporarily stranded Early on the Yankee side of the flooded river, but the downpour also slowed Pope's response to the tempting target, and Early made his escape in the early morning hours of August 24.

Lee was in a quandary. The stalemate along the Rappahannock clearly favored the Union, and Pope's numbers were increasing hourly. The first of McClellan's troops had at last begun to arrive. Major General Samuel P. Heintzelman's Third Corps was heading south by rail from Alexandria, and Fitz-John Porter's Fifth Corps was marching from Aquia and Fredericksburg. The Confederate commander knew he must somehow find a way to pry Pope away from the Rappahannock before the bulk of the Army of the Potomac made its appearance.

On August 24 Lee summoned Jackson to his headquarters and revealed a bold and hazardous new strategy. While Longstreet's forces continued to occupy Pope's attention along the Rappahannock, Jackson would lead his wing of the army on a sweeping march to the west and north, bypassing Pope's left flank and falling upon his supply depots far to the rear. Lee was gambling that the Federal commander would react to such a massive incursion by retreating northward; if in fact Pope decided to attack Longstreet, the Army of Northern Virginia risked disaster. But Lee, the consummate military gambler, was banking on Pope's withdrawal. Once Pope abandoned the Rappahannock line, Longstreet would hasten northward to link up with Jackson's troops.

Jackson, who excelled at independent command, welcomed the challenge, and at 3:00 a.m. on August 25 his 24,000 men got under way. The march proved a grueling test of endurance, even for the famous foot cavalry, as the soldiers slogged northward with only brief halts and little rest. In two days Jackson's troops covered more than 50 miles.

Screened from enemy observation by the Bull Run Mountains, Jackson's column reached the hamlet of Salem and filed right, continuing eastward along the line of the Manassas Gap Railroad and passing through Thoroughfare Gap unopposed. By August 26 Jackson was at Gainesville, where he turned southeast to Bristoe Station on the Orange & Alexandria Railroad, ripping up the tracks and demolishing several Yankee supply trains. That night Brigadier General Isaac R. Trimble's brigade was sent ahead to seize Manassas Junction—John Pope's principal base of supply. The next day Jackson followed with the remainder of his command.

For the lean and threadbare Rebels the well-stocked warehouses and freight cars at Manassas Junction yielded a cornucopia of luxuries. Shoes, clothing, ammunition, and rations were eagerly appropriated before the torch was applied to what remained. When Brigadier General George W. Taylor's New Jersey brigade sallied forth from Alexandria with instructions to clear the junction of what was believed to be an insignificant raiding party, Jackson's troops tore the Federal ranks to pieces. Taylor was mortally wounded and his brigade quickly put to rout.

Lee's instincts had been correct. Alerted to the Confederate presence in his rear, Pope hastily evacuated his line along the Rappahannock. His departure freed Longstreet to follow Jackson's footsteps northward. Lee, who accompanied Longstreet's wing, realized that speed was crucial, lest Jackson be forced to battle alone against the superior might of the Federal armies.

Arriving at Bristoe Station on August 27, General Pope sent scores of couriers riding to the widely scattered elements of his force, urging the senior commanders to concentrate their troops at Manassas. With a two-to-one advantage in numbers, Pope saw an opportunity to trap Jackson, destroy his command, and redeem his own reputation. Scenting blood, Pope exclaimed, "We shall bag the whole crowd."

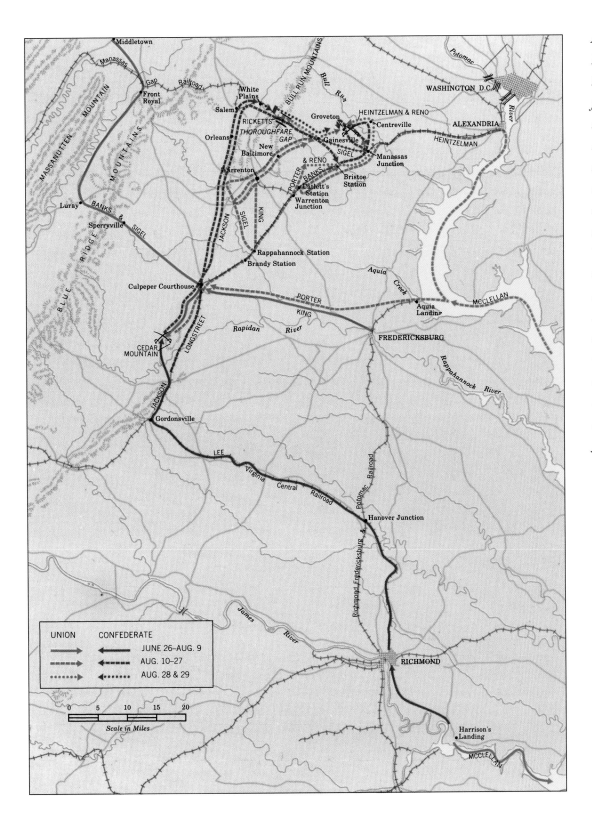

After the Battle of Cedar Mountain, Lee and Longstreet left Richmond to join Jackson, who had fallen back to await reinforcements. Lee's first attempt to get behind Pope failed, and the Federal forces were able to fall back behind the Rappahannock. Over the next 10 days both sides sidestepped up the river trying to gain an advantage, but they found themselves locked in a stalemate. Then Lee sent Jackson circling around Pope's army and into its rear via Thoroughfare Gap. After raiding the Union supply depot at Manassas Junction, Jackson took up positions west of Bull Run. Lee and Longstreet, following the same route, caught up on August 29, uniting the army's two wings. In mid-August, meanwhile, Pope had ordered the scattered corps of McDowell, Sigel, and Banks to concentrate north of the Rappahannock River. Pope also received reinforcements shipped up the Potomac—most notably Heintzelman's III Corps and Porter's V Corps from McClellan's army, which was now withdrawing from the Peninsula. But not until August 26, after Jackson's raid, did Pope come up with a plan. Believing he could destroy Jackson, he ordered his dispersed forces to find and attack the waiting Confederates.

"During the whole of this day a continuous stream of troops, wagons, and other appendages of war poured through the town."

GENERAL ROBERT E. LEE

Commander, Army of Northern Virginia
Lee's decision to leave Richmond and unite his forces to confront Pope came sud-
denly. For the first year of the war, he spent most of his time in and around the
Confederate capital, where his family had relocated after fleeing their Arlington
home. On August 14, he left for Gordonsville with Longstreet's corps, unable to
tender a farewell to his wife, daughters, and son, Custis, who was serving as
a military aide to President Jefferson Davis.

My Dear Custis:
I write a line to say good-bye to you & Mary. I had hoped to have been able to have come in & see you both to night, but I find it impossible to enjoy that pleasure. I have had much to do which with preparation for my departure renders it impossible.

Good bye my dear children. May God bless & guard you both. Tell your mother when she arrives that I was unable to stop to see her. I go to Gordonsville. My after movements depends on circumstances that I cannot foresee.

Truly & affly your father

R. E. Lee

P.S. I send in my straw hat which please give house room to. Also a summer under-jacket which I find out of my trunk. If you have the key put it in, or ask your mother to mend it & keep it for me.

R. E. L.

ANONYMOUS UNION OFFICER

On the evening of August 18, Federal columns withdrawing through Culpeper
created an immense traffic jam that one observer described as "confused and
"ugly." The unknown author of this account probably served on General Franz
Sigel's staff, since his reminiscences, serialized in a Buffalo (N.Y.) newspaper,
disparage all Federal senior commanders except for the German-born Sigel.

The march continued all night, and by day-dawn of the 19th the whole army was again camped in and around the ancient boro' of Culpepper Court House. During this retreat General Pope exhibited a side of character that did not raise him in the estimation of the army. As our poor, dust-covered, foot-sore boys entered Culpepper, they were greeted during nearly the whole night, by a salutation of profanity from their commander-in-chief, of a style that would have graced a Mississippi stevedore much better than a major-general of the United States Army. During the whole of this day a continuous stream of troops, wagons, and other appendages of war poured through the town, and it was not a little humiliating to have a Virginia lady, whose acquaintance we made but a few days before, as she tendered the hospitality of her mansion, add "Ah! you are returning from Richmond, evidently in a very great hurry."

Desperate to avoid a return to bondage, fugitive slaves ford the Rappahannock
River at Sulphur Springs in the wake of Pope's retreating army. Thousands of
blacks abandoned the homes and farms of their masters during the Federal occu-
pation but were suddenly forced to flee north in mid-August. The bridge in the
background was burned once Sigel's troops had crossed over.

"At this the General brought the whip around on the man himself."

PRIVATE STEPHEN E. CHANDLER

24th New York Infantry, Hatch's Brigade
Enlisting in May 1861, Chandler was assigned the following summer to
McDowell's construction corps and spent most of his time erecting bridges and
signal stations. In May 1863 he transferred to the 24th New York Cavalry,
and in action during the last days of the war he won the Medal of Honor.

We reached Culpeper about dark, where we found every street full of wagons of the various armies which had concentrated at that point.

Besides the town being one heterogeneous mass of vehicles there were acres of wagons parked at different places around town. We

The loser at First Manassas, General Irvin McDowell nevertheless managed to earn a new appointment as the commander of Pope's III Corps. As a leader, McDowell's greatest failing was his inability to command respect from his troops. One soldier noted a commonly held suspicion that McDowell's appearance on the battlefield "was a signal to the enemy to cease firing and reserve their ammunition for a more opportune moment."

remained there during the night, sleeping wherever we could catch a nap. It began to rain in the night and continued till near noon of the 19th. There was a stream just to the east of town, which had to be forded, so I posted myself there to wait till our train came along.

Soon Gen. McDowell rode up to the ford to push the thing along. Every team of four or six mules that came to the ford would stop and drink, which took time.

As soon as McDowell took in the situation he procured a large "black-snake" whip, and sat there on his horse, and on every team that entered the ford he would ply the whip till they were out on the other bank. He was protected from the rain by a poncho, which covered any insignia of his rank that he wore.

There were the trains of Pope, Sigel, Reno, Stevens, Augur, Ricketts, McDowell, Banks, and I don't know who else, all jammed and crowded together; wagons enough, when on the move, to reach 30 or 40 miles, and perhaps farther.

All the teamsters belonging to the armies which had been with McDowell knew him, and when he intimated that it would not do to block the train they took the hint and lashed up their mules; but when teams of other trains came to the ford they would pay no attention to the General, supposing him to be a wagon-master, or at most a Quartermaster.

One fellow I remember in particular, one of Sigel's Dutchmen, stopped to let his mules drink, when McDowell began to lay on the black-snake, whereupon the Dutchman commenced swearing at him. At this the General brought the whip around on the man himself, who was sitting astride his nigh-wheel mule. This so enraged the fellow that he jumped from the mule into the water, and made for the General with the butt end of his whip, saying he would "allow no tam wagon-master to hit him mit a whip."

Instantly McDowell threw back his poncho, exposing to the fellow's gaze the grouped buttons and the double-stars of a Major-General. It was amusing to see that Dutchman's face. I don't think it took him 10 seconds to mount his mule and get out of there.

were tied to the fence. I untied them in a hurry, but did not have time to throw the reins over his neck. My pursuers were not more than twenty yards away. Without even taking hold of the reins, I sprang into the saddle and spurred my horse towards the garden gate, which the old woman of the house had opened for me. Here, I came directly upon the major commanding the enemy detachment, who placed his pistol at my breast and ordered me to surrender.

At this moment I grabbed hold of my unbridled horse, and, giving him a slap on the head, turned him in the right direction, dug my spurs into his flanks and thus extricated myself with one powerful leap from the circle that had been forming around me. The Yankee major thought that by this movement I intended to strike at him, and so he drew back momentarily, but soon was by me again. His men, when they saw me escaping, all fired a volley which, somehow, miraculously missed me. Enraged by the trick I had played on them, they dashed after me in wild pursuit. Most of them soon fell far behind, however, owing to the speed of my noble black steed. But the major, with a few of his men, was only a few strides behind me, and from not more than five paces discharged three rounds from his revolver, one of which cut right through my coat, but did not scratch the skin. After a chase of nearly a mile the Yankees gave up, thus allowing me to master the bridle. Until now, my horse had been completely helpless.

That very night, our friend, Fitzhugh, was taken prisoner by this same group. He gave his parole, telling them that he would not take part in the engagement in any way, and thus was able to observe the entire thing. He told me afterwards, when he was exchanged, that he covered his eyes with every shot so that he would not see me fall.

I rode back slowly to the place where I had been separated from the general, and found him with Dabney observing the fleeing Yankees. He was highly indignant over the loss of his hat and haversack, which, with Chiswell Dabney's weapons, had been triumphantly borne away. Both men had watched the Yankees chase me and were concerned that I might be killed or wounded.

General Stuart had covered his head with a handkerchief and tied it as protection against the scorching sun. We could not look at each other without laughing, despite our inner rage. The driver of a sutler's wagon attached to a Georgia regiment, whom we fell in with on our return, gladly gave the general his own hat. Still news of our mishap had spread like wildfire throughout the army, and was quite the sensation.

CAPTAIN WILLIAM W. BLACKFORD

Staff, Major General J. E. B. Stuart

Officially, Blackford served on Stuart's staff as an engineer officer. But like most of Stuart's staff officers, he was often called upon to perform all manner of duties— scout, courier, and above all, front-line fighter. For the raid on Catlett's Station, Stuart ordered Blackford to reconnoiter the Federal depot before taking his place in the first wave of attackers.

I went in with the leading regiment, and the consternation among the quartermasters and commissaries as we charged down the main street, scattering out pistol balls promiscuously right and left among them, made the men laugh until they could scarcely keep their saddles. Supper tables were kicked over and tents broken down in the rush to get out, the tents catching them sometimes in their fall like fish in a net, within whose folds we could trace the struggling outlines of the frantic men within.

One of the line officers captured, an old friend of Stuart's in the U. S. Army, who was there for the night, told us the next day that he and some friends had made some toddy, and were sitting around a table sipping it when one of the party said, "Now this is something like comfort. I hope Jeb Stuart won't disturb us tonight." Just then our yell broke upon their ears, and the speaker, striking the table with his fist, exclaimed, "There he is, by God!" and they never finished their glasses.

At the first alarm the Bucktails sprang to arms and awaited us in the wide doorways and on the platform of the depot. Receiving one withering volley, our men dashed among them with their sabres, leaping their horses upon the low platform and crashing right into the freight room. In less time than it has taken to tell the tale, all was over, and no further resistance was afforded to our work of destruction so far as the enemy was concerned. The tents and wagons were fired and burned merrily, and each moment the light increased as busy hands spread the conflagration, making it the easier to collect the thousands of mules and horses into droves, for there were too many to lead, and to gather in the multitude of prisoners around us. . . .

I now got a detail of men and had the telegraph wires cut in several places, taking out lengths so as to delay repairs as much as possible, and then exerted myself in keeping the men at work burning, and collecting the mules and prisoners. With the rich booty before them there was great temptation to continue plundering too long on their private account. The way they went through the trunks in the tents was amusing; the blow of an ax answered the place of a key and a kick from the foot spread the contents out for inspection. I felt very uneasy for fear

some of the men would get drunk, for there was plenty of liquor in every tent, but the importance of restraint was appreciated, and none took more than they could carry. Numbers of fine saddle horses were eagerly appropriated and led by their halters, and did not escape as so many of the mules did in the latter part of the night from the droves they were formed into. Though so busy superintending what was going on, I captured several dozen prisoners myself as I would come across them singly, or in groups hidden away in a wagon or tent, or making a run to escape; sometimes I would find a man squatting down under a small bush or pine sapling, not higher than his head, for concealment.

All was going on as well as we could wish, when a violent clap of

THE CIVIL WAR IN AMERICA: GENERAL STUART (CONFEDERATE) WITH HIS CAVALRY SCOUTING IN THE NEIGHBOURHOOD OF CULPEPPER COURTHOUSE.—FROM A SKETCH BY OUR SPECIAL ARTIST.—SEE NEXT PAGE.

Jeb Stuart, wearing his distinctive plumed hat, rides at the head of his cavalry in an engraving that appeared in the October 4, 1862, edition of the London Illustrated News. *The sketch is by special artist Frank Vizetelly, who was befriended by Stuart and who was one of the few artists to execute scenes from the Confederate side.*

thunder and a furious wind announced the coming of a storm; then came a deluge of rain; it seemed to come not in drops but in streams, as if it were poured from buckets, and it was driven almost horizontally with such stinging force that it was impossible to keep a horse's head to the blast. Whole regiments of horses would rear and wheel around to get their backs to the storm. Every fire was extinguished and we were left in utter darkness, save where the vivid flashes of lightning came, which served only to make the darkness blacker. It was impossible to light another fire. The rain had beaten through the canvas wagon tops to such an extent that their contents were thoroughly wet. I myself used up a whole box of matches trying to kindle the baled hay with which some of them were loaded, without success. Panic-stricken by the flashes of lightning and crashes of thunder, the mules stampeded and scattered everywhere. The prisoners slipped through the line of the guard under the horses' bodies and sometimes under their necks, unobserved in the inky blackness of the dark. One flash showed the road full of them, but when another came there would be the empty road. . . .

The capture of Pope's headquarters had given us possession of all his papers and among them the morning reports of his army up to the day before, by which we learned as much about his force as he knew himself, for there was the report of the "present for duty" of every command he had. We also secured his army treasure chest which I afterwards heard contained $500,000 in greenbacks and $20,000 in gold. From Pope's private baggage a full dress uniform coat and hat was taken to General Stuart as a trophy, in compensation for his loss at Verdiersville. The General sent them to a friend in Richmond, who placed them on exhibition in the window of a bookstore on the Main Street with a card labeled "Headquarters in the saddle" and "the rear taking care of itself." It attracted much attention from the crowds of amused spectators, as an evidence of the puncture of the inflated and brutal man who had given so much uneasiness to noncombatants, and who now was so easily circumvented when brought in contact with their defenders. . . .

Of the thousands of prisoners we had captured we only brought off about four hundred and some four or five hundred horses and mules. Among the prisoners there was a woman dressed in a man's uniform, and she wanted General Stuart to release her; but he told her if she was man enough to enlist she ought to be man enough to go to prison. So she went on in a state of great indignation.

ANONYMOUS UNION QUARTERMASTER

Identified only with the recipient's name, "Lizzie," and the closing signature "John," this letter from one of Pope's supply officers to his wife relates the chaos and losses that ensued when Stuart's cavalry hit Union-occupied Catlett's Station in a nighttime surprise attack.

While laying there we heard tremendous yelling and shouting, and I remarked to Capt. Johns "that there were reinforcements coming on the Railroad." we both jumped up and went to the opening in the tent, where we heard the tramp of horses, the clashing of sabers and the reports of carbines and pistols and the whizzing balls plainly told us that the Rebel Cavalry were upon us. I immediately *ordered* Capt. Johns to lay down and blow out the candles, and I laid down myself and saw the fiends ride by our tent with drawn Sabers and firing in upon us. The first squad passed by and I got up and went to find Capt. [Goulding,] Neal & others but hearing another charge coming I again retreated to my tent, this time closing the opening and soon the 2nd squad of Cavalry went by blazing away with their carbines right among our tents. after they passed away I told Capt. Johns that we must take to the woods as we were right on the edge of them, and we crawled out of the back side of our tent and came across Col. Clary and others and then took into the woods. we only went a short distance when we heard the cavalry coming back and they soon commenced pulling the teamsters out of the wagons and the badly frightened fellows out of their tents. we laid in the woods and could hear all that was going on, the cursing and swearing, the breaking open of our trunks, boxes, desks & safes. all went on merrily for the poor half clad, half fed Rebels, for they had the ransacking of a "Maj. Gen'ls Baggage Train" and a valuable one it was I can assure you. . . . Wagons and ambulances burnt up, Horses shot, wounded men, one of ours and one Rebel, Trunks, Boxes, Carpet Bags broken open, contents destroyed and taken away, horses, saddles and bridles gone, property scattered all over the ground and everything in the most dire confusion. . . . We lost all our Baggage. Capt. G. lost about $7,000 in his chest. those that had good trunks had everything taken, all that was left for me was my trunk . . . my hair brush, bottle of extract of Dandelion & Hair tonic and a few collars lieing around in the mud. Your likeness, my little studs, sleeve buttons, collar buttons, all, all gone. One of your letters and my likeness was picked up by one of the teamsters. Your likeness is gone & also Frank's cup—such is life and such is the fate of War.

"You have my hat and plume. I have your best coat.
I have the honor to propose a cartel for a fair exchange of the prisoners."

Debris from Stuart's raid still litters the ground in this sketch of Catlett's Station made shortly after the Confederate cavalry withdrew with their booty and prisoners. The depot building at center was the site of the brief stand made by the Pennsylvania Bucktails (13th Pennsylvania Reserves) during the attack. Although the Confederates failed in their principal objective, the destruction of the railroad bridge, the raid was another humiliation for

John Pope. His Federal soldiers made no secret of who to blame—as one disheartened survivor of the raid put it: "This whole loss is entirely due to Genl. Pope's carelessness."

LIEUTENANT HENRY KYD DOUGLAS

Staff, Major General Thomas J. Jackson
In April 1861, Douglas left his law practice in St. Louis and returned east, where he enlisted in the 2d Virginia Infantry. A year later he joined Jackson's staff and served under him until the general's death in 1863. Promoted to colonel and made a regimental commander, Douglas was severely wounded and captured at Gettysburg. After his parole in March 1864, he commanded a brigade and surrendered with it at Appomattox.

Stuart came galloping up next morning to where Jackson was sitting on a fence and to everybody's amusement unrolled from behind his saddle and displayed a beautiful blue uniform coat, inside of which was a tag with the name of its owner, "John Pope, Major General." Our Cavalryman was in one of his jolly humors. He dismounted, and repeating to us what we knew, that a week or two before he was surprised in a house he was visiting by some Federal cavalry, and in his hasty flight left his hat and plume to the enemy, he said he had a proposition to make to General Pope. Taking a piece of paper, he wrote a communication about as follows:

> Headquarters, Cavalry, etc.
> Major Genl. John Pope
> Commanding, etc.
> General.
> You have my hat and plume. I have your best coat. I have the
> honor to propose a cartel for a fair exchange of the prisoners.
> Very Respectfully
> J. E. B. Stuart
> Maj. Genl. C.S.A.

This note amused General Jackson greatly. He was very fond of Stuart, and Stuart could always amuse him. The communication was sent through the lines; whether it amused the Federal General may depend upon the time it reached him. There are times when humor is not humorous—to the other man.

CORPORAL GEORGE M. NEESE

Chew's (Virginia) Battery, Robertson's Brigade
With the two armies facing each other across the Rappahannock, the fighting settled into a prolonged artillery duel. Both sides attempted crossings, but these were all repulsed or called off in the face of enemy countermovements. Corporal Neese's battery was just one of dozens that for four days hurled shot and shell across the river.

August 22—This morning we went to the Rappahannock and drove into a large hilly field that sloped to the river. When we arrived on a rather prominent knoll in the field there was a horseman there who said to Captain Chew: "Put some of your guns in position here and fire a few shell into that piece of woods you see yonder on the other side of the river. I think perhaps there is something in there." The piece of woods referred to was not very large, and somewhat lower in altitude than the hill we occupied, and there was nothing visible . . . that indicated in the least that there was any dangerous game lurking within its peaceful borders. I unlimbered the first gun and landed a shell near about the center of the woods, which waked up the lion sure enough. The shell we fired was a twelve-pounder percussioned, and it exploded near the enemy's lair.

The Yankees had a battery of six or eight rifled guns in position in the innocent little piece of woods, and opened fire on us with all of them immediately after our shell exploded. When I saw six or eight little piles of white smoke rising from the brush and heard the thunder of the guns, and the terrible screaming of the shell overhead, I thought the infernal regions had suddenly opened just on the other side of the river. In the twinkling of an eye our other two rifled guns whirled in battery, and for two hours we fired as fast as we could, and so did the Yanks. Their fire was terrific.

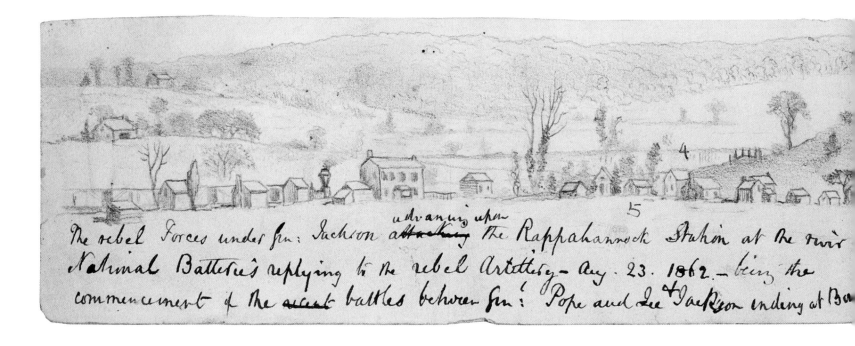

The rebel Forces under Gen: Jackson advancing upon the Rappahannock Station at the river National Batteries replying to the rebel Artillery—Aug. 23. 1862.—being the commencement of the great battles between Gen: Pope and Lee & Jackson ending at Bu

LIEUTENANT COLONEL SAMUEL R. BEARDSLEY

24th New York Infantry, Hatch's Brigade
As the artillerymen furiously worked their pieces, the infantry could do little but hug the ground. Though casualties were relatively light, the wounds inflicted by cannon fire were often horrible. Witness to one of the more gruesome incidents, Beardsley himself was wounded a week later at Manassas; he recovered and returned to command the 24th New York until it was mustered out in May 1863.

ll day Thursday, all Friday and all the forenoon of Saturday, we lay exposed to the most deafening charges of Artillery I ever conceived of. I cannot describe it. On Friday we lay in sort of garden and orchard with one of our batteries of the enemy immediately opposite so that every shot or shell passed immediately over or among us. A great many of our shells burst right over us, the house and out houses near which we lay were completely riddled and torn to pieces, many of our men were hit, but strange to say only one man in our regiment was killed. He, poor fellow, was lying on the ground within a few feet of Levi's company, when as he raised his head to change his position a shell came crashing through the bushes and took his head clean off from his shoulders. His face, with the nose, eyes, moustaches, chin and everything perfect, was blown directly past Levi's company and landed in the grass in front of Capt. Miller's company, the eyes wide open and staring at the men as they lay in the ranks.

The exchange of artillery fire on August 23 was depicted in this sketch drawn at Rappahannock Station by Edwin Forbes. As indicated by Forbes' number key, Union batteries (6) fire across the river (4) at Rebel guns posted on a pair of hills (3). Federal infantry supporting the batteries lies low (8), while in the distance, Longstreet's Confederates (2) march north attempting to outflank Pope.

"What the devil are they sending after us now?"

ADJUDANT EDWARD L. BARNES

95th New York Infantry, Doubleday's Brigade
The infantry of McDowell's corps, defending the crossing at Rappahannock Station, bore the brunt of the damage wrought by shot and shell. For the 95th New York, mustered into service in March, this was a baptism of fire. Barnes, a native of New York City, would have a short career as a soldier. In September he received a disabling hip wound at Antietam and was forced to resign.

On the second or third day we were somewhat startled and puzzled by the change in the tune of the flying missiles. It was a horrible, screeching sound, a combination of the hurtling of spherical shot, the hoarse roar of the solid shot, and the screaming whistle of the shells. We gazed at each other in wonderment, and the query was frequently heard:

"What the devil are they sending after us now?"

An investigation developed the fact that from lack of legitimate ammunition, or from some other cause, the enemy were treating us to a supply of iron rails cut in lengths of from 12 to 16 inches. We were well protected by the sloping side of the hills from any missiles except shells, so that the railroad track thus sent us in sections was not utilized as a medium of travel to the other world.

CAPTAIN HUGH A. WHITE

4th Virginia Infantry, Baylor's Brigade
The Confederates on their side of the river suffered much the same as their foes—forced to endure the constant anxiety caused by shells shrieking overhead and exploding all around. White, whose deep spiritual faith was shared by many of his fellow soldiers, survived the bombardment. But this letter, written on Sunday, August 24, was his last. He was killed in action six days later at Manassas.

My Dear Father: We have not had another battle, though there has been some sharp skirmishing, and the roar of artillery has been almost incessant for several days past. We have moved some distance up the bank of the Rappahannock each day, halting occasionally to throw shells at the enemy and receive some from them. We have had their shells to awake us in the morning, keep us uneasy during the day, and scarcely to allow us to sleep at night. They have sometimes split the trees under which we were lying, but we have thus far escaped without injury. . . .

This has been very little like the Sabbath. With spirits saddened by hunger and fretted by the constant roar of artillery, we have been kept in an uncomfortable frame of mind. The busy preparations for to-morrow prevent any enjoyment of the Sabbath. However, Dr. Stiles is to preach to the Brigade this afternoon, and I hope to hear him. It requires a great struggle to keep the busy scenes around me from driving all devotion from my heart. They ought to have a contrary effect. I ought now more than ever to seek my strength, my happiness, my all, in God. How could I live without him. With him no storm can disturb my peace, no danger can come nigh, no harm can befall which will not do me good.

Odd-shaped shells thought to be lengths of railroad iron by the first Yankees who had to face them were actually the twisted hexagonal projectiles (left) of Whitworth rifled cannon. Imported from England, the guns were favored by Rebel artillerymen more for their accuracy than for their destructive force.

By the second summer of the war, political cartoons lampooning Union military leaders had become a feature in Northern periodicals. This cartoon, from the New York Illustrated News, shows a group of befuddled Yankees watching out for Stonewall Jackson, whose exploits had made him a legend in the North as well as among his fellow Southerners. Newspapers of the day also included more subtle and serious indications of the bloody struggle that was growing steadily more pervasive in the lives of the readers. Among the advertisements on this page are those for stationery and half-priced postage for soldiers, for pills and ointment to fend off sickness for "many a gallant fellow," and for artificial legs and arms, "the best substitutes for natural limbs."

LIEUTENANT HENRY KYD DOUGLAS

Staff, Major General Thomas J. Jackson
When Lee formulated his daring plan to break the stalemate along the Rappa-
hannock, he knew that he had the commander to make it work: Stonewall
Jackson. Douglas was on hand to observe the council of war in which Jackson's
flanking maneuver was devised. True to his nature, Jackson revealed nothing
of his destination when he moved out the next morning.

Jackson's Headquarters were near Jefferson on the 24th. The Rappahannock could not be crossed at Sulphur Springs and a new move must be made. A council of war was held at the General's Headquarters that afternoon. It was a curious scene. A table was placed almost in the middle of a field, with not even a tree within hearing. General Lee sat at the table on which was spread a map. General Longstreet sat on his right, General Stuart on his left, and General Jackson stood opposite him; these four and no more. A group of staff officers were lounging on the grass of an adjacent knoll. The consultation was a very brief one. As it closed I was called by General Jackson and I heard the only sentence of that consultation that I ever heard reported. It was uttered by the secretive Jackson and it was—"I will be moving within an hour."

PRIVATE JAMES M. HENDRICKS

2d Virginia Infantry, Baylor's Brigade
Like the other veterans of the Stonewall Brigade, Hendricks was by now accus-
tomed to marching off at short notice with both destination and purpose a total
mystery. With a string of victories behind them, Jackson's men believed that
wherever he led them, great things would come to pass.

On the evening of the 24th of August, 1862, orders were received to cook three days' rations and be ready to move at any time. We baked our slapjacks, and this finished our preparation, for at this time we never cooked our bacon, but ate it raw. Early on the morning of the 25th sixty rounds of ammunition were issued with the following orders: "No straggling; every man must keep his place in ranks; in crossing streams officers are to see that no delay is occasioned by removing shoes or clothing."

The morning was bright and the men in the best of humor. . . .

The 2d Virginia was in front. There is system in the order of marching as there is in all military movements. The regiment in front to-day is the 2d, to-morrow the 3d, and so on to the last in the bridage. The same rule applies to divisions. . . .

I do not believe that there was a man in the corps that knew our destination except Jackson. Our course was toward the north, and as the day advanced you could hear all kinds of rumors. It looked like madness to march away from our supplies and support with only Jackson's forces; but we had learned to obey and to blindly follow. Each felt that something extraordinary was contemplated, and nerved himself for the expected task. We did not always follow roads, but went through cornfields and bypaths, waded streams, and occasionally we marched right through some one's yard.

AMANDA V. EDMONDS

Resident, Fauquier County, Virginia
For the civilians along Jackson's line
of march, the passing of his troops
promised liberation from the hated
Yankees. The citizens lined the road-
sides, bestowing food, water, and
cheers on the haggard but high-
spirited soldiers. Four days after
this entry, on August 30, Edmonds
would work until midnight making
bandages for the wounded.

We all witnessed the camp fires below here last night, but little did we dream it to be dear "Stonewall" Jackson coming home again! What a glorious and great surprise, just like him. He slips and slides here and there when people are not thinking of him. He stayed in Salem last night with A. P. Hill and Ewell. I am almost afraid I will jump out of my skin.

LIEUTENANT ALANSON M. RANDOL

Battery E, 1st U.S. Artillery
Randol had lost all six guns of his
battery on June 30 during the
Seven Days' Battles outside Rich-
mond. Refitted with four new
12-pounders, he disembarked at
Aquia Landing on August 24 with
orders to join Sykes' division at
Warrenton Junction. Brevetted
several times for bravery, Randol
ended the war as a cavalry colonel.

ere for the first time we saw a part of Pope's Army of Virginia, and the introduction was anything but encouraging, for in contrast with the Army of the Potomac, it seemed to be undisciplined, disorganized and demoralized. I tried to procure some much needed supplies here, but such was the confusion that it was found to be impossible.

Having received orders to march at three o'clock the next morning, the battery left camp at that time, but on arriving at the nearest crossing of Owl creek found it blocked with wagons from Sigel's corps. All the other crossings were in the same condition, so with a detail from my own and Weed's battery, a new crossing was made higher up the creek . . . by which our batteries and wagon train were all crossed. This was not accomplished until some time after daybreak. The delay, although unavoidable on our part, was very annoying and discouraging, for the division had marched without us, and we were constantly receiving orders to hurry up. On resuming the march we found our troubles and delays had only begun, for the roads and the crossings of the various streams along our route were blocked with wagons, the teams of some floundering in the mud, vainly endeavoring to move on, and of others already taken out by the demoralized teamsters, and the wagons left to be plundered by the horde of stragglers accompanying them. New roads had to be constantly sought for, and new crossings made for our columns. We actually fought our way with drawn swords from Warrenton junction to Bristow station.

Exhausted, troops of Pope's army slog through a driving rain toward Manassas Junction, where they would find little but the destruction left by their elusive foe.

CAPTAIN WILLIAM W. BLACKFORD

Staff, Major General J. E. B. Stuart

Around sundown on August 26, Jackson reached the Orange & Alexandria Railroad. Deciding that Manassas Junction might be too heavily defended, he chose to cut the line first at Bristoe Station. Cavalry supported by an infantry brigade attacked and scattered the few defenders. The Rebels then set a trap for the Federal trains due to pass by on their return from Warrenton Junction.

To make all sure for the block of trains expected every moment, the switch beyond the depot was changed so the train could come to the depot without obstruction, but after leaving it would plunge down an embankment near which the switch was situated. All along in front of the depot about fifty yards distant was our brigade of infantry, whose orders were to open fire as soon as the troops in the expected train began to disembark. By this time it was pitch dark. Generals Jackson and Stuart and their staffs were on a small hill on the flank of the brigade, just opposite the open switch. Presently we heard a train coming and soon her headlight appeared coming round a curve. Just then Stuart turned to General Jackson and asked him if he was *sure* the switch was turned this time. He said yes, he supposed so, as he had sent his Engineer officer to have it done. But to make sure Stuart turned to me and said, "Blackford, gallop down there and see if it is all right." I dashed off but on getting to the railroad found the switch was up on the bank and that it was so dark I could not see anything about it from horseback, so I jumped down, leaving Comet unhitched, and ran up the bank. Finding the switch properly arranged for throwing the train off, I started back to my horse.

By some misunderstanding of orders, or by getting over excited, the men in the brigade did not wait for the train to stop to see if it had troops on board; but as soon as it came opposite their flank they opened fire and the whole brigade followed as the train rolled by. The engineer, thinking probably they were only "bushwhackers," as they called

Burned to the wheels, Federal rolling stock lies in ruins on a siding of the Orange & Alexandria line. Both sides were involved in such demolition. Jackson's men set fire to hundreds of cars before departing Manassas Junction, and Pope ordered the destruction of his own supply trains lest they fall into Confederate hands.

our scouting parties of cavalry, opened his throttle valve and came thundering on past the depot at the rate of about fifty miles an hour. When I started to return I found the train was within a short distance of me and if I got on the side of the bank next the troops I would, in another moment, be in front of the fire directed upon the approaching train and would have but a slim chance of escape at so short a range. I barely had time to get back, crossing the track only a few feet in front of the engine, and to run down the bank on the opposite side when the train came rushing on to its doom, the air above the embankment becoming at once filled with the screaming bullets as they tore through and through the sides of the empty box-cars. Down the embankment rushed the engine, screaming and hissing, and down upon it rushed the cars, piling up one upon another until the pile reached higher than the embankment, checking further additions to its confused heap, and arresting the rear half of the train upon the track. The train was a long one, composed mostly of empty cars among which a few sick and wounded were distributed. . . .

On the rear of the captured train were two red lights indicating, according to railway signal laws, another train behind; and these were at once smashed. In a few moments the headlight of another train came in sight around the curve and, seeing no red lights, advanced, entirely unconscious of the presence of either the wrecked train or of our troops.

When it was opposite the flank of our brigade, fire was opened as before, and as before the engineer attempted to run by. Seeing no red lights to warn him, on he came at full speed and into the rear of the wrecked train he went. The locomotive ploughed under the first three box-cars, setting them crossways on its back and on the back of the tender. The impetus having been communicated to the cars, they telescoped each other or got each other crossways on the track, while the jar caused some of the cars in the moving train to leave the track. Many cars were forced out upon the pile over the locomotive, and the general effect was extremely destructive. This train also had some sick and wounded aboard, but for the most part was composed of empty cars. There were red lights on this train also, which were at once extinguished by a blow from the back of a sabre in my hands, and we awaited placidly the coming of the train which they indicated was yet to come.

Presently the light appeared but soon stopped, and then, with a loud, long, protracted scream which lasted until lost in the distance, the train went back, the bearer of the first intelligence General Pope had of our presence. Men from the first trains had doubtless escaped and given this train warning of the fate which awaited it.

CHAPLAIN JAMES B. SHEERAN

14th Louisiana Infantry, Forno's/Strong's Brigade
A native of Ireland, James Sheeran did not enter the priesthood until he was 39, after his wife died and his daughter entered a convent. While he was stationed in New Orleans, he became an ardent Confederate, and when war broke out in 1861 he jumped at the chance to serve as chaplain to the largely Catholic troops from Louisiana.

T was not long . . . in discovering the object of Jackson's visit to Manassa. The storehouses were crowded with provisions of all kinds; on the R.R. was a train nearly a mile in length, laden with commissary stores and supplies of all kinds for Pope's army. I will not attempt to describe the scene I here witnessed for I am sure it beggars description. Just imagine about 6000 men hungry and almost naked, let loose on some million dollars worth of biscuit, cheese, ham, bacon, messpork, coffee, sugar, tea, fruit, brandy, wine, whiskey, oysters; coats, pants, shirts, caps, boots, shoes, socks, blankets, tents etc. etc. Here you would see a crowd enter a car with their old Confed. greys and in a few moments come out dressed in Yankee uniforms; some as cavalry; some as infantry; some as artillerists; others dressed in the splendid uniform of Federal officers. In another place you would see the cavalry helping themselves to new saddles, bridles, spurs, and other necessary equipment. Again you would see our wagoners and ambulance drivers with new sets of harness of every description and curry combs, brushes, sponges, waterpails etc. etc. In another place you would see them distributing canteens. Here you would see the surgeons loading their wagons with medicine of every description as well as surgical instruments, wines, and brandies of the best quality. Here again were our wagoners loading their teams with crackers, bacon, salt, sugar, coffee etc. etc. Again you would see colored servants carrying off bags of oats for their horses and then returning for personal plunder.

I had often read of the sacking of cities by a victorious army but never did I hear of a railroad train being sacked. I viewed this scene for almost two hours with the most intense anxiety. I saw the whole army become what appeared to me an ungovernable mob, drunk, some few with liquor but the others with excitement. I rode frequently through the surging crowd, viewing them sometimes with a smile, again with a look of sadness. As night approached, the thought of the near approach of an enemy four times our number and the disorganized condition of our men filled me with sorrow. Whilst the scenes of which I have given but an imperfect account were transpiring, one Brigade kept the enemy at bay about 1 1/2 miles from Manassas. Between 6 and 7 o'clock orders were given to fall into ranks and to my great surprise the men obeyed with the utmost promptness.

LIEUTENANT JOHN H. CHAMBERLAYNE

Purcell (Virginia) Artillery, Hill's Division
Even the stern Jackson realized the futility of holding his hungry men back when they came upon the vast stores at Manassas. The only precaution he took was issuing an order "to spill all the liquor there," for he feared alcohol more than enemy guns. But as Chamberlayne noted in a letter to his mother, not all the alcohol was wasted.

T was a curious sight to see our ragged & famished men helping themselves to every imaginable article of luxury or necessity whether of clothing, food or what not; for my part I got a tooth brush, a box of candles, a quantity of lobster salad, a barrel of coffee & other things wh. I forget. But I must hurry on for I have not time to tell the hundredth part & the scene utterly beggars description.
. . . we had been living on roasted corn since crossing Rappahannock, & we had brought no new wagons so we could carry little away of the riches before us. But the men could eat for one meal at least, so they were marched up and as much of everything eatable served out as they could carry To see a starving man eating lobster salad & drinking . . . rhine wine, barefooted & in tatters was curious; the whole thing is indescribable, I'll tell you sometime may be.

MAJOR SETH B. FRENCH

Staff, Major General Thomas J. Jackson
In the summer of 1862 French was temporarily assigned to the Army of Northern Virginia as a commissary officer. As he discovered, the enemy depot at Manassas Junction had something for just about everyone, including his unfortunate friend who was mortally wounded on August 28.

T he first thing I did was to get a bag of oats for my horse, and as I had not had a change of raiment, I supplied myself with all that was needed from the hospital stores in the way of clothes, and I gathered in more than would have served out the campaign and put them in the charge of our man Jim, who had secured a barrel of ginger cakes for "Old Jack." Then I pivoted around generally and meeting with my friend, Lawson Botts, Colonel second Vols., I told him of my captures. Poor fellow, he had been sick, ever since the battles around Richmond, from diarrhea, and he told me that one of his great troubles was the fear of being killed and found by friends in the unpleasant condition of his undergarments. I took him to the headquarters wagon and clad him from top to toe and gave him an extra suit. In a few days after, his corpse was delivered to his faithful wife, who came down from Charlestown to receive it. How glad my heart was that he was clad in a decent way.

PRIVATE WILLIAM F. FULTON

5th Alabama Battalion, Archer's Brigade
Jackson's men had barely begun to loot Manassas Junction when Taylor's New Jersey regiments came marching down the track, colors flying, expecting to easily drive off the Rebel "raiding party." Fulton, who two weeks later was promoted to commissary sergeant, would surrender at Appomattox as a lieutenant.

N ow, as we moved on up into the old field encompassing Manassas, looking off toward Washington, we saw a great blue line of men with guns, marching in line of battle, with the Stars and Stripes floating out on the breeze, coming straight toward us. We were drawn up in line to await their coming. Archer's Brigade was here alone; the rest of our division had gone in another direction. As the blue line approached nearer and nearer, the officers of our command were persistent in their orders: "Don't shoot, men. Stand steady and let them come on." And they came briskly on, making right for us, and it seemed that they would walk right over us. Our men began to get nervous and would raise their guns, but the officers were sharp in the command not to shoot: "Put down your guns, and stand steady."

Just to our rear, on a little elevation, a battery of artillery unlimbered. Who they were or where they came from I never knew, but I saw General Jackson sitting on old Sorrel as stiff as a board, with his eyes intent on that blue line. He was right among the cannon, and suddenly every one of those guns blazed away, right over our heads, sending their missiles into that blue line, which by this time was within a stone's throw. As the artillery fired we raised a yell and made a dash forward, our guns blazing away. That line of Yanks melted away like wax in a blaze of fire, and it became a fox and dog chase for quite a distance. They broke without firing a gun. Archer's men were running at good speed, firing as they ran. In passing a house on the way, many of the Yanks entered and began throwing their guns out of the windows, as much as to say: "We surrender." The officer in command of this body of men was killed among the first shots.

LIEUTENANT COLONEL DAVID H. STROTHER

Staff, Major General John Pope
Before the war, Strother enjoyed a notable career as a travel writer and illustrator for Harper's New Monthly Magazine, using the pen name "Porte Crayon." He exercised his talents during his military service, making sketches and keeping an extensive diary to record his role in "that damnable, double-tongued war."

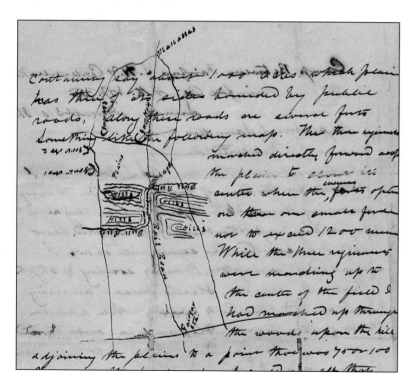

In a letter to a friend, Lieutenant Elias Wright, one of Taylor's officers, included this map showing the railroad surrounded by hills and forts used by the Rebels.

I returned to the Junction by a road running parallel and to the left of the railroad, and found the General and Staff dismounted, and resting under the shadow of one of the old redoubts of Beauregard's engineering. While here I amused myself strolling about observing the débris of the recent rebel carnival. On the railroad track and sidelings stood the hot and smoking remains of what had recently been trains of cars laden with ordnance and commissary stores intended for our army. . . . the plain was covered with boxes, barrels, cans, cooking-utensils, saddles, sabres, muskets, and military equipments generally; hard-bread and corn-pones, meat, salt and fresh, beans, blankets, clothes, shoes, and hats, from bran-new articles, just from the original packages, to the scarcely recognizable exuviae of the rebels, who had made use of the opportunity to refresh their toilets.

Here were scattered quantities of our fine army groceries, salt, sugar, coffee, dessicated vegetables, and the sutler's less genuine supplies of canned fruits, meats, cheese, and ginger-bread. Immediately around the Junction, where the shops and shanties of the storekeepers, sutlers, negro refugee boarding-houses, ambrotypists, Jew clothiers, tract distributors, gamblers, eating and drinking saloons were most congregated, these remains were thickest strewn and most ludicrously commingled. Most of the buildings were burned, and many tents shared the same fate. Other encampments still stood flapping in the breeze, the tents slit into ribbons with sabre strokes. Over this field of wide-spread waste and destruction numerous skulkers and stragglers of our own army were wandering, stuffing their knapsacks or loading their horses with whatever pleased their fancies.

Looking over all this detailed confusion, the grim outlines of the grass-grown earth-works, the solitary chimneys, the broken engines and overthrown gun-carriages, the mouldering graves of former occupants, presented a picture of the waste of war most solemn and impressive.

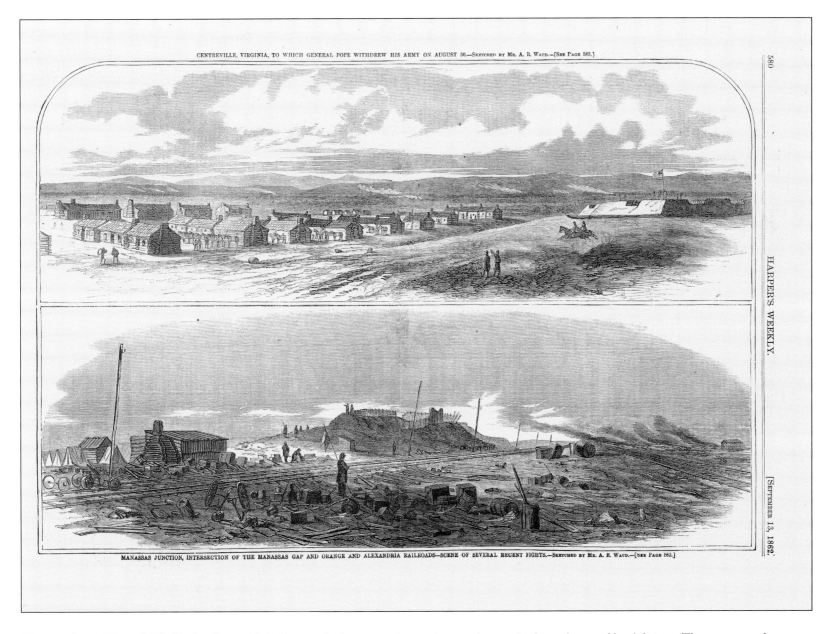

CENTREVILLE, VIRGINIA, TO WHICH GENERAL POPE WITHDREW HIS ARMY ON AUGUST 30.—Sketched by Mr. A. R. Waud.—[See Page 583.]

580

HARPER'S WEEKLY.

[September 13, 1862.

MANASSAS JUNCTION, INTERSECTION OF THE MANASSAS GAP AND ORANGE AND ALEXANDRIA RAILROADS—SCENE OF SEVERAL RECENT FIGHTS.—Sketched by Mr. A. R. Waud.—[See Page 583.]

The same issue of Harper's Weekly that featured John Pope on the front page also ran these two images that bore witness to his misfortune. The upper scene shows Centreville, the site of the Federals' first bloodless conquest in March and to which they returned in defeat five months later. Depicted underneath is the broad plain at Manassas Junction, where smoldering railroad cars provide the backdrop for a scene of vast desolation in the wake of the Confederate raid.

Another Bull Run

As flames from the burning supply depot at Manassas Junction lit the night sky on August 27, Stonewall Jackson made his next move—one that would result in the second climactic battle on the bloodied ground west of Bull Run. Jackson's plan was simple: He would concentrate his three divisions on the old Bull Run battlefield, seven miles to the north, and await the arrival of Lee and Longstreet, who were approaching Thoroughfare Gap.

What began as a short march by Jackson's troops turned out to be a remarkable piece of deception. Evacuating the smoldering ruins that night, each of Jackson's divisions took a different direction. Only W. B. Taliaferro's troops went directly to Bull Run. Ewell's and Hill's columns took wrong turns and headed off toward Centreville before backtracking to their destination. The meanderings of these Rebels, even if by accident, would succeed once again in befuddling Jackson's adversary, John Pope. And the three-pronged march would perfectly fulfill Jackson's own maxim: "Always mystify, mislead, and surprise the enemy if possible."

By dawn on August 28, Taliaferro had reached his objective, and his tired soldiers lay down to snatch what little rest they could—on fields still scattered with debris and shallow graves from the Battle of First Manassas a year before. Seeking a hidden position, Jackson began shifting his troops toward Stony Ridge, a wooded crest just north of Groveton and the Warrenton Turnpike, on the northwestern edge of the old battlefield. It was an ideal point from which to lash out at any Yankee column heading for Manassas, and a position made even more formidable by the presence of an unfinished railroad line that furnished the Southern troops a natural defensive breastwork.

That same morning, General Pope was still hounding his disparate elements toward Manassas Junction, where surely he would corner Stonewall Jackson. Among the forces converging on the junction was McDowell's Third Corps, which was moving eastward on the Warrenton Turnpike—on a route that would take the forces past Stonewall Jackson's hidden Rebels.

This bridge over Bull Run, constructed by Federal engineers in the spring of 1862, was on the main route taken by retreating Federals during their withdrawal on the night of August 30.

Brawner's Farm August 28

McDowell did not march in full strength, however, for he had gotten word from Brigadier General John Buford's Union cavalry that a Rebel force was approaching Thoroughfare Gap 10 miles to the rear. McDowell dispatched one of his three divisions, under Brigadier General James B. Ricketts, to keep an eye on Thoroughfare Gap. What McDowell failed to do was send word of the Rebel advance to his superior, Pope.

That afternoon, when the vanguard of Longstreet's column approached Thoroughfare Gap, the lead troops encountered not only Yankee horsemen but Ricketts' infantry deploying to meet them. For several crucial hours the Federal troops disputed the passage of the narrow defile, until Lee and Longstreet finally managed to outflank their stubborn foe. Evening was fast approaching, and the distant but unmistakable sound of artillery and musket fire alerted the Confederate commanders that Jackson was in a fight.

Jackson himself had picked the fight. He had been watching from cover that afternoon when McDowell's troops on the Warrenton pike approached the old Bull Run battlefield and Stony Ridge, where the Rebels lay concealed just north of the road.

A Confederate detachment screening Jackson's line opened fire on the vanguard of the Yankee column, Brigadier General John F. Reynolds' division. After a brief skirmish, the Rebels pulled off to the north, and McDowell —who considered the affair an insignificant foray by enemy guerrillas—continued his march. Reynolds turned south on the route to

Manassas Junction, and Brigadier General Rufus King's division prepared to follow. McDowell remained unaware of the large Confederate force hovering beyond his left flank.

Before King's division could follow Reynolds', however, General McDowell received orders to abandon the move to Manassas and march due east for Centreville. The nighttime meanderings of Jackson's divisions in the direction of Centreville had Pope convinced that it was there that he would finally snare Jackson. McDowell issued new orders, then rode off to confer with Pope.

When McDowell departed, command of his column fell to Rufus King, who was recovering from an epileptic seizure that he had suffered earlier during the campaign. That afternoon about 6:00, King was again stricken. His division was strung out over more than a mile on the Warrenton pike, and none of his subordinates were aware that their commander was now completely prostrated. Brigadier General John P. Hatch's brigade was in the lead, near the ramshackle settlement of Groveton. Behind Hatch tramped four well-drilled regiments of midwesterners commanded by John Gibbon, followed by the brigades of Brigadier Generals Abner Doubleday and Marsena Patrick.

The unsuspecting Yankees presented Jackson the target he had been waiting for, and with the words "Bring out your men, gentlemen!" Jackson sprang the trap. While Confederate artillery opened on the startled blue ranks below, Taliaferro's and Ewell's divisions emerged from the timber on Stony Ridge and moved forward in line of battle to the fields of the farm of John Brawner.

The sudden rain of exploding shells threw the Federals into confusion. Uncertain of what to do next, Hatch halted his brigade

near Groveton. Patrick's untried units at the tail end of the column fell into disarray and sought shelter in the woods south of the pike. Doubleday and Gibbon shifted their troops off the pike, while Gibbon—the only brigade commander to take the initiative—ordered up artillery and sent his most experienced unit, the 2d Wisconsin, north of the pike to drive off the Rebel batteries. The Wisconsin soldiers collided with the 800 men of the Stonewall Brigade, and as the opposing sides blazed away at a range of 80 yards, Gibbon hurried up his remaining units. Jackson countered by lengthening his own line, but he failed to smash through the gritty Yankees.

With men kneeling, lying prone, or taking what shelter they could behind fence lines and clumps of brush, the opposing ranks slugged it out in one of the most murderous point-blank fights of the entire war. "They stood as immovable as the painted heroes in a battle-piece," Taliaferro recalled. "Out in the sunlight, in the dying daylight, and under the stars they stood, and although they could not advance, they would not retire. There was much discipline in this," Taliaferro concluded, "but there was much more of true valor."

Although he possessed a numerical advantage, Jackson was unable to bring his numbers to bear. The rugged, wooded terrain prevented many reinforcements from reaching the scene of the action at Brawner's Farm. Jackson attempted to mount a general assault at 7:30 p.m., but the troops went forward piecemeal, and the charge was repulsed 30 yards from the Yankee line.

The Confederates suffered a staggering number of casualties, among them many senior officers. Taliaferro and Ewell were wounded. Two regimental commanders of the Stonewall Brigade were killed. One company in the 21st Georgia lost 40 of 45 men, and the 26th Georgia of Lawton's brigade endured a casualty rate of 72 percent.

Frustrated, Jackson made a last effort to roll up the Federal position, shoving a brigade toward the enemy left, but he could make no further headway. Gradually the flashes of musketry subsided in the gloom, and with night the fight at Brawner's Farm ended in stalemate.

Each side had lost some 1,300 men, but Jackson had clearly missed an opportunity to pinch off and destroy a sizable portion of Pope's scattered army. Though initially taken by surprise, the Union soldiers had performed admirably—particularly Gibbon's brigade, which bore the brunt of the fighting.

After the battle, King and his officers decided to avoid a renewed Confederate assault in the morning by obeying Pope's initial directive to retire on Manassas. Though King was unaware of the fact, Pope had changed his mind again. When word of the fight reached the Union commander, he scrapped his plan to unite his forces at Centreville. Instead, the various Federal columns would hasten toward the scene of battle at the Bull Run field. Stonewall Jackson had been found, and once again Pope was determined to trap and destroy him. Pope continued to maintain that the audacious move by Jackson was no more than a large-scale raid before a retreat to the Shenandoah Valley.

In another fateful error on the part of the Union high command, Pope was never told that Lee and Longstreet had fought their way through Thoroughfare Gap and were bearing down on Bull Run with 30,000 fresh Rebel troops. In a few hours, the two wings of Lee's army would be reunited—and poised for the crowning move of Lee's great gamble.

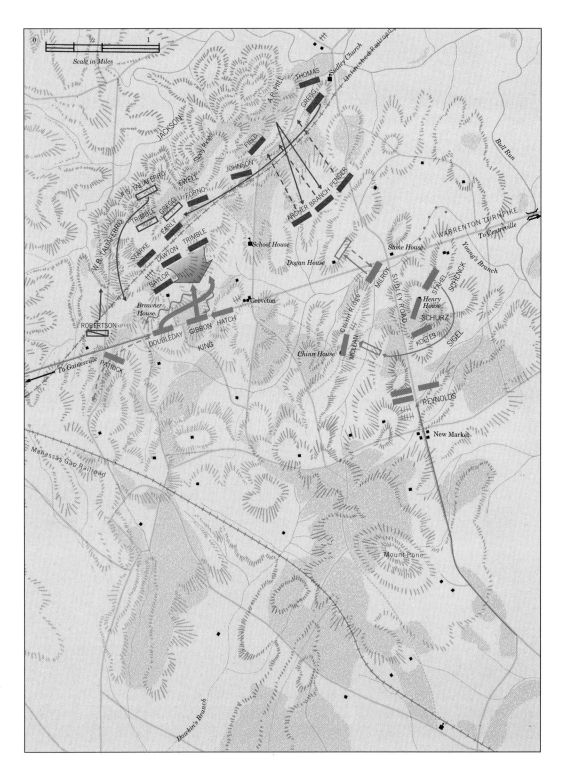

The three-day battle opened with a savage duel between Jackson and King's division at Brawner's Farm.

SERGEANT WILLIAM R. HOUGHTON

2d Georgia Infantry, Benning's Brigade
When Longstreet's vanguard collided with Ricketts' battle line east of
Thoroughfare Gap, the 2d Georgia was ordered to cross Pond Mountain
on the south side of the pass to flank the enemy. Sergeant Houghton served
with the 2d Georgia for the entire war.

This Gap is a natural curiosity. The mountain range has the appearance of having been pulled by a giant hand into two parts, separated by a little space, just sufficiently wide for a little creek, a country road and a railroad to pass side by side through the range. Tomb's brigade was in front that day, and we had gotten well into the defile, when the bullets began to sing through our ranks and some men fell. We had no idea of danger until then.

General Longstreet (above) had to march his corps through Thoroughfare Gap
in the Bull Run Mountains to link up with Jackson's men near the old Bull Run
battlefield. Federal artist Alfred R. Waud made his drawing (right) of Confed-
erate infantry and artillery entering the narrow defile some time after the event.

"As their bright guns dropped down toward me I looked into their muzzles a moment."

PRIVATE BERRIEN M. ZETTLER

8th Georgia Infantry, G. T. Anderson's Brigade
In Thoroughfare Gap, the 8th Georgia extended its battle line to the north,
up the rock-strewn lower slope of Mother Leathercoat Mountain. Zettler was
disabled by a wound at Second Manassas and spent the rest of the war in the
quartermaster's depot at Savannah, Georgia.

PRIVATE RANDOLPH A. SHOTWELL

8th Virginia Infantry,
Hunton's Brigade
In 1861 Shotwell, a Virginian,
returned from a college in Pennsyl-
vania to enlist in the 8th Virginia.
He was commissioned a lieutenant
in 1864 and was captured shortly
before Cold Harbor. His postwar
career as a North Carolina journal-
ist was marked by his imprison-
ment in 1871 for Ku Klux Klan
activities. Pardoned by President
Ulysses S. Grant, he died in 1884.

It was a picturesque spectacle in the narrow gorge . . . the great white moon looking through the notch upon camps of Blue coats at one entrance, and upon masses of Gray coats, or no coats at the other, while in the portion of the pass were ghostly lines of skirmishers whose frequent flashes were not fireflies as they seemed but the deadly explosions of the rifle. Suddenly out of the darkness in front came a dazzling sheet of flame, with deadly hail of bullets. The Yankees had taken post across the path at an old mill where there was a stone fence and great ledges of rock, behind which they were not only safe, but completely concealed. Soldiers will not need to be told that this was an ugly place to stumble into. The advance halted and word was sent to Longstreet who came up—"We must clear them out!"—said he—"Jackson needs us."

It was Thursday, the 28th of August, and one of the hottest days I ever experienced, that we were making this rapid march. I learned afterward that we were hastening to get through Thoroughfare Gap and to the east side of this little range of mountains before Pope should discover the movement. . . .

Two companies were sent out to the left, got to the foot of the mountain and were halted. In a few minutes orders came that skirmishers must be sent up on the mountain to ascertain if it was occupied by the enemy. Companies A and B of the Eighth Georgia were ordered forward and deployed. There were just thirty of us in the two companies.

When the order came for the two companies I have mentioned to deploy and advance, I was standing in front of a cluster of vines and briers well-nigh impenetrable; but soldiers must know no obstacles, so I plunged into the brush and briers. The mountain side was covered with a thick undergrowth of low cedars and vines, and in some places huge masses of rock had broken loose and tumbled down, not only forming a very formidable barrier, but leaving a perpendicular wall of five or six feet that was very difficult to scale. But we clambered up, stopping every few steps to take breath and listen for movements or noises above us that would help us to know who were in our front.

Presently I heard a jingling of canteens in the bushes just above me, and almost at the same moment the man with them exclaimed, "Who's down there?" Stephen Baldy, the comrade four or five steps to my left, threw up his gun with his finger on the trigger. I said, in a low tone, "Don't shoot; it may be one of our men." He replied, "No, I see him; it's a Yankee." Then the man spoke again, "Say, is that Company A?" "What regiment?" said Baldy, his finger still on the trigger. "Eleventh Massachusetts." Baldy fired . . . right between me and where the man was, a line of men in blue rose, and as their bright guns dropped down toward me I looked into their muzzles a moment—a very short moment—and went over backward. I heard a volley, but I was tumbling, rolling, jumping, falling, and had no time or inclination to look behind me.

Colonel Evander M. Law sits surrounded by fellow officers of the 4th Alabama Infantry in this early war photograph.

COLONEL EVANDER M. LAW

Brigade Commander, Army of Northern Virginia
Law, a South Carolinian by birth, founded a military school at Tuskegee, Alabama, and was elected colonel of the 4th Alabama Infantry in 1861. He rose to command a brigade at Second Manassas. At Thoroughfare Gap, Law was given the difficult assignment of scaling the steep slopes of Mother Leathercoat Mountain to attack the Federal right flank.

My brigade was leading the division when it reached the mountain. There I met General Hood, coming from the direction of the gap. He informed me that it was held on the other side in strong force by the enemy, and that Jones' division was unable to force it. He was accompanied by a man living in the vicinity, who, he said, would guide me by a trail across the mountain, a short distance above the gap. His own brigade was to follow mine. The head of my column was at once turned to the left, and striking

a slight trail, commenced the ascent. I had not gone half way up the side of the mountain when my guide either missed the trail or it ran out. At any rate, he seemed to know as little as I did, and told me he could guide me no further. Letting him go, I moved on through the tangled woods and huge rocks until the crest was reached. Here we were confronted by a natural wall of rock, which seemed impassable. Men were sent out on both sides to search for some opening through which we might pass, and a crevice was soon found several feet above our level, where the men could get through one at a time, the first one being lifted up by those behind, and each man as he got up lending a helping hand to the next. As I stood on the crest and heard the fighting in the gap below and the distant thundering of Jackson's battle at Manassas, I felt that the sound of each gun was a call for help, and the progress of the men, one by one, across the rocky barrier was painfully slow. In fact, they got through in an almost incredibly short time.

COLONEL ARMISTEAD L. LONG

Staff, General Robert E. Lee
A Virginian, Long graduated from West Point in 1850 and was assigned to the artillery. He served briefly on the staff of his father-in-law, Union general Edwin V. Sumner, but resigned in June 1861 to join the Confederacy. Long served as military secretary to Robert E. Lee.

Meanwhile, the sound of cannonading was audible from the other side of the range, and it was evident that an engagement was taking place. The moment was a critical one, and the most phlegmatic commander might have been pardoned for yielding to excitement under such circumstances; yet Lee preserved his usual equanimity, and permitted his face to show no indication of the anxiety which he must have felt. That he was lost in deep reflection as he surveyed the mountain-pass in front was evident, yet neither in looks nor words did he show that he was not fully master of himself and of the occasion. And the absence of any overmastering anxiety was shown in another manner. Mr. Robinson, a gentleman who lived near the Gap, invited Lee and his staff to take dinner with him; and this meal was partaken of with as good an appetite and with as much geniality of manner as if the occasion was an ordinary one, not a moment in which victory or ruin hung trembling in the balance.

"From the woods arose a hoarse roar like that from cages of wild beasts at the scent of blood."

CAPTAIN WILLIAM W. BLACKFORD

Staff, Major General J. E. B. Stuart

On the early evening of August 28, the four brigades of King's Federal division crossed Young's Branch and marched along the Warrenton Turnpike, passing the Brawner farm on their left. Undetected by the Federal column, Jackson's corps lay in wait on the high ground just north of the farm.

Presently General Jackson pulled up suddenly, wheeled and galloped towards us. "Here he comes, by God," said several, and Jackson rode up to the assembled group as calm as a May morning and, touching his hat in military salute, said in as soft a voice as if he had been talking to a friend in ordinary conversation, "Bring out your men, gentlemen!" Every officer whirled round and scurried back to the woods at full gallop. The men had been watching their officers with as much interest as they had been watching Jackson, and when they wheeled and dashed towards them they knew what it meant, and from the woods arose a hoarse roar like that from cages of wild beasts at the scent of blood.

As the officers entered the woods, sharp, quick orders to fall in rang from rank to rank, followed by the din of clashing arms and accoutrements as the troops rapidly got under arms, and in an incredibly short time long columns of glittering brigades, like huge serpents, glided out upon the open field, to be as quickly deployed into lines of battle. Then all advanced in as perfect order as if they had been on parade, their bayonets sparkling in the light of the setting sun and their red battle flags dancing gayly in the breeze. Then came trotting out the rumbling artillery to positions on the flanks, where they quickly unlimbered and prepared for action. It made one's blood tingle with pride to see these troops going into action—as light-hearted and gay as if they were going to a dancing party, not with the senseless fun of a recruit who knew not what he had to expect, but with the confidence of veterans who had won every battle they ever fought.

PRIVATE JOSEPH F. KAUFFMAN

10th Virginia Infantry, A. G. Taliaferro's Brigade

Private Kauffman of Page County, Virginia, was a veteran of the Shenandoah Valley campaign. On August 28 he was writing in his diary when he was called into action at Brawner's Farm. He was killed during the fighting and a friend returned the diary to his family.

Thursday [August] 28—We marched all night and camped in an old field at daylight. I had to go on picket and did not get any sleep. We have been marching and countermarching all day and are now drawn up in line awaiting the enemy's advance. It is now sundown. They are fighting on our right. Oh, to God it would stop.

CHAPLAIN FREDERIC R. DENISON

1st Rhode Island Cavalry, Bayard's Brigade

The 1st Rhode Island was in the vanguard of the Federal column as it neared Groveton on the Warrenton Turnpike. When movement was spotted on the left, 1st Rhode Island skirmishers and a battery of artillery were dispatched to feel out the Confederate position. Chaplain Denison, later his regiment's historian, watched from the edge of a grove of trees.

After a little skirmishing near us, we suspected that Jackson had selected a position near the turnpike on the north side, a few miles west of the old battle ground of Bull Run. General Hatch . . . selected our regiment and a light battery with which to feel for the foe, and marched at our head. Lieutenant Waterman commanded the skirmish line. As we cautiously advanced on a slope of ground wholly exposed, near Groveton, Jackson's forces, from their commanding position on the wooded rolling lands to the north, suddenly opened upon us a cross-fire from eighteen well handled pieces of artillery. Their firing was rapid and splendid; we were a fair target and close at hand. Instantly our skirmishers joined the column, and our artillery sprang into position and replied. No imagination was required to understand the poet's phrase, "bombs bursting in air." We could only stand and endure the shower. Over and among and through us, the shell came like a rain of exploding volcanic stones. Five of our horses were killed in a few minutes. When Lieutenant Gove's horse was shot under him and fell, the Lieutenant coolly unbuckled the saddle and took it upon his shoulder. Captain Manchester received a wound in the face from the fragment of a shell, and soberly remarked that he had fears for his mustache (a juvenile, dew-like adornment he had studiously cultivated). Several men were struck, but not fatally. We could do nothing to resist so heavy an attack from well posted batteries. We had drawn their fire and fully revealed the whereabouts of our enemies.

Edwin Forbes exaggerated the elevation of the foreground to improve the perspective in his sketch of the attack by General Gibbon's brigade (4) against the Confederates at Brawner's Farm. A note (1) erroneously reports that Sigel's corps was attacking near the old Bull Run battlefield.

PRIVATE PHILIP CHEEK

6th Wisconsin Infantry, Gibbon's Brigade
The 6th Wisconsin, part of John Gibbon's Black Hat Brigade—so called because
of the full-dress army hats preferred by their commander—advanced to cover the
right of its sister regiment, the 7th Wisconsin. Private Cheek, from Excelsior,
Wisconsin, survived Second Manassas only to be wounded at Antietam in
September. He was discharged three months later.

Just as we looked ahead from the cut in the road, we saw a light battery going into position on the double quick. (There is no prettier sight in any military movement.) One of the boys marching beside Gus Kline remarked to him, "That don't look like any of our batteries." Gus replied, "See here! we have been in the service over a year and except a few skirmishes, we have never been in a fight. I tell you, this d—n war will be over and we will never get into a battle!" Just as he concluded his remarks a twelve pound shell came from that battery over the heads of our regiment. . . .

. . . Colonel ordered the 6th to lie down. We all dropped in place and the shells came thick and fast and we hugged the ground, then we heard to our left a rip-rip-rip of a heavy infantry fire. . . . Adjt. Gen. Wood of Gibbon's staff rode up and saluted our Colonel, saying so our company could hear it, "Col. Cutler, with the compliments of Gen. Gibbon, you will form your regiment by battalion front, advance and join on the right of the 7th, and engage the enemy.". . .

The regiment advanced in line of battle across a field. Soon we heard a rip-rip, but did not fully realize the situation until the boys began to fall. "Halt! Right dress! Ready! Aim! Fire!" and the old 6th gave a volley that awoke a cheer from the other three regiments and a corresponding yell from the other side. And that yell. There is nothing like it this side of the infernal region and the peculiar corkscrew sensation that it sends down your backbone under these circumstances can never be told. You have to feel it, and if you say you did not feel it and hear the yell you have never been there.

MAJOR RUFUS R. DAWES

6th Wisconsin Infantry,
Gibbon's Brigade
Dawes attended the University of
Wisconsin before graduating from
Marietta College in Ohio, his
home state. Elected captain of the
6th Wisconsin in 1861, he fought
in most major battles of the Civil
War and won the rank of brevet
brigadier general in 1865. Dawes
returned to Ohio, was elected to
Congress in 1881, and died in 1899.

General Hatch, in advance, sent the 14th Brooklyn regiment as advance guard and flankers. I remember seeing the line of their red legs on the green slope of the same hill from which the enemy fired upon us, but they discovered no enemy. Our brigade moved along the turnpike on that quiet summer evening as unsuspectingly as if changing camp. Suddenly the stillness was broken by six cannon shots fired in rapid succession by a rebel battery, point blank at our regiment. The shell passed over the heads of our men, and burst in the woods beyond. Surprise is no sufficient word for our astonishment, but the reverberation had not died away when gallant old Colonel Cutler's familiar voice rang out sharp and loud, "Battalion, halt! Front! Load at will! Load!" The men fairly jumped in their eagerness, and the iron ramrods were jingling, when—"Bang! Bang!" went the rebel cannon again. Again they overshot our men, but a poor horse was knocked over and over against the turnpike fence. "Lie down!" shouted Colonel Cutler. Fortunately a little bank along the roadside gave us good cover. Battery "B," 4th U. S. artillery, now came down the turnpike on a gallop. Quickly tearing away the fence, they wheeled into position in the open field, and the loud crack of their brass twelve pounders echoed the rebel cannon. Thus opened our first real battle.

General Gibbon ordered the 2nd Wisconsin and 19th Indiana regiments to move forward upon the enemy. This attack of General Gibbon was made upon the theory that a comparatively small force of the enemy was present. . . . No sooner had the 2nd Wisconsin shown its line in the open field, than there burst upon them a flame of musketry, while Confederate batteries distributed along about a mile of front opened with shell and round shot. Under this terrible fire the second was obliged to change front before they could return a shot. We could not see them nor the 19th Indiana, owing to the intervening woods, but we heard the awful crash of musketry, and we knew there was serious work ahead. Captain J. D. Wood, of Gibbon's staff, came galloping down the turnpike with an order for the sixth to move forward into action. . . . Our regiment, five hundred and four men in ranks, pushed forward rapidly in perfect line of battle, field officers and Adjutant E. P. Brooks mounted and in their places, and colors advanced and flying in the breeze. Colonel Cutler was on a large dark bay, well known to all the men as "Old Prince." Colonel Bragg rode a pure white horse of high mettle, which was skittish and unmanageable. My own sturdy old mare was always steady under fire.

The regiment advanced without firing a shot, making a half wheel to the left in line of battle as accurately as if on the drill ground. Through the battle smoke into which we were advancing, I could see a blood red sun, sinking behind the hills. I can not account for our immunity from the fire of the enemy while on this advance. When at a short range, Colonel Cutler ordered the regiment to halt and fire. The seventh Wisconsin now came forward and passed into the ranks of the second Wisconsin. Our united fire did great execution. It seemed to throw the rebels into complete confusion, and they fell back into the woods behind them. We now gave a loud and jubilant cheer throughout the whole line of our brigade. . . . It was quite dark when the enemy's yelling columns again came forward, and they came with a rush. Our men on the left loaded and fired with the energy of madmen, and the sixth worked with an equal desperation. This stopped the rush of the

Colonel Lysander Cutler of the 6th Wisconsin, part of Gibbon's Black Hat Brigade, was wounded in the leg as he led his regiment against Jackson's Confederates in the gathering dusk of August 28. The shattered flagstaff (right) of one of Gibbon's other regiments, the 2d Wisconsin, was struck by at least four Rebel bullets.

Captain George H. Brayton's bloodstained gloves were preserved by his family after he was killed commanding a company of the 7th Wisconsin at Brawner's Farm. Brayton had been a teacher in Aztalan, Wisconsin.

enemy, and they halted and fired upon us their deadly musketry. During a few awful moments, I could see by the lurid light of the powder flashes, the whole of both lines. I saw a rebel mounted officer shot from his horse at the very front of their battle line. It was evident that we were being overpowered and that our men were giving ground. The two crowds, they could hardly be called lines, were within, it seemed to me, fifty yards of each other, and they were pouring musketry into each other as rapidly as men could load and shoot. . . . Men were falling in the sixth, but our loss was small compared to that suffered by the regiments on the left. I rode along our line and when near Colonel Cutler, he said, "Our men are giving ground on the left, Major." "Yes, Sir," said I. I heard a distinct sound of the blow that struck him. He gave a convulsive start and clapped his hand on his leg, but he controlled his voice. He said, "Tell Colonel Bragg to take command, I am shot." Almost at the same time "Old Prince" was shot; but he carried his master safely from the field. I rode quickly to Lieut. Colonel Bragg and he at once took command of the regiment. There was cheering along our line and it was again standing firmly. . . . But soon the enemy came on again just as before, and our men on the left could be seen on the hill,

in the infernal light of the powder flashes, struggling as furiously as ever. I could distinctly see Lieut. Colonel Fairchild, of the second Wisconsin and Lieut. Colonel Hamilton of the seventh Wisconsin, and other officers whom I recognized, working among and cheering up their men. Men who had been shot were streaming back from along the whole line. Our regiment was suffering more severely than it had been; but, favored by the low ground, we kept up a steady, rapid, and well aimed fire. . . . Our line on the left gradually fell back. It did not break but slowly gave ground, firing as savagely as ever. The rebels did not advance. Colonel Bragg directed our regiment to move by a backward step, keeping up our fire and keeping on a line with our brigade. But one of the companies of the right wing ("C") became broken by the men marching backward into a ditch. Colonel Bragg halted the regiment to enable them to reform their line, and upon this ground we stood until the enemy ceased firing. The other regiments of the brigade fell back to the turnpike. After an interval of quiet, Colonel Bragg called upon the regiment to give three cheers. No response of any kind was given by the enemy. It was now about nine o'clock, and the night was very dark.

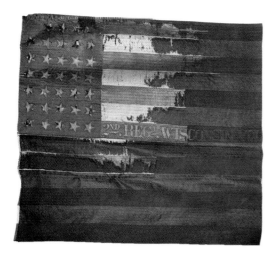

Officers of the 2d Wisconsin (right) enjoy a meal at their camp near Arlington, Virginia, in the spring of 1862. Colonel Edgar O'Connor (second from right) was mortally wounded at Brawner's Farm. The regiment's tattered flag (above) bears witness to the intensity of the fighting.

PRIVATE WILLIAM A. MCLENDON

15th Alabama Infantry, Trimble's Brigade
McLendon enlisted in Abbeville, Alabama, in July 1861. Promoted to sergeant
in July 1863, he was elected to the post of lieutenant the following November.
McLendon survived the war to be paroled at Appomattox.

Our march, in line of battle which was preceeded by a line of skirmishers, led through this clump of rocky woods until we reached an old dilapidated fence that skirted it on the opposite side. Our skirmishers had halted at the fence and were firing on the enemy, which were only a short distance in front. The space in front was clear, but the night was so dark that the "Boys in Blue" could not be seen or located only by the flash of their guns. . . .

My position in line at this fence was in the immediate rear of Alonzo Watson. We were both on our knees, he firing through a crack, and I firing over the top of the fence. I stood as high on my knees as possible in order to rest my gun on the top rail, my left elbow was at one time resting on his shoulder when all at once I heard a "thud" and felt a jar and poor 'Lonzo began to relax and sink, exclaiming in a low tone, "Oh Lordy, I am a dead man." These were his last words, life soon became extinct, but I didn't move but kept loading and firing until the fight was over.

PRIVATE T. A. COOPER

60th Georgia Infantry, Lawton's Brigade
As the 60th Georgia pushed forward through a "blaze of fire," Private Cooper
was struck in the head by a bullet and wandered dazed behind the lines until he
was rescued by a passing cavalryman. Cooper deserted from the 60th Georgia
near Woodstock, Virginia, in October 1864.

Just before sunset we were in line of battle skirmishing in our front. There seemed to be an old abandoned field between us and the enemy, partly grown up in pine, with occasional gullies. About dusk we were ordered to cast off knapsacks. When a Sergeant of our company took from his a small, fine pocket Bible and requested me to take and return it to his sister, I said:

"Why not take it yourself?"

He said: "Do you know you will be killed to-night?"

"I do not, but my chances are the same as are all others."

He said: "I will never see the sun again. Do me this last favor."

I took his Bible. We were ordered forward, Gen. Jackson riding in our rear, exhorting us to hold fire till ordered to begin: that he expected much of that body of men. I think there were between 5,000 and 6,000 in our brigade that night. The enemy had got busy, and seemed a blaze of fire belching from their entire front.

Soon the comrade on my right fell, pierced thru the head. Then the comrade on my left was shot thru both arms. Then I was lifted from my feet by a ball hitting me high in the forehead. I aroused to consciousness prone on my face, gun clasped in both hands, and hot blood flowing copiously from my head. I tried to see if I could reach my brains with my finger, finding only the outer strata of skull shattered by a glancing ball. I decided it was no use to die from that, and arose, dizzy, and saw the column busy a few rods in front, while the roar of cannon and musketry was deafening.

I think they were in a railroad cut. An officer grasped my shoulder and pushed me in a gully with other wounded, and said, "Stay there. Up here is no place for men in your condition."

I had been in the depression but a few moments when a cannon ball about buried us with earth. I crawled out, and the same man said, "Get down there. You will be killed up here."

"Yes, sir, and buried down there before I am killed, which I fail to appreciate."

Colonel John Francis Neff's dress frock coat was returned to his family after he was killed in action at Brawner's Farm. Neff, a Virginia Military Institute graduate who had practiced law in Memphis and New Orleans, commanded the 33d Virginia Infantry, part of the Stonewall Brigade.

CAPTAIN G. CAMPBELL BROWN

Staff, Major General Richard S. Ewell

Brown, General Richard Ewell's future stepson, served on the general's staff from 1861 until his capture at Sayler's Creek in 1865. Brown attended Ewell when the general suffered a bone-shattering wound at Brawner's Farm. Ewell was struck by a bullet in the left knee as he knelt to peer beneath some low pine branches at the approaching Yankees.

We rode to the extreme left of the line, then back towards the right & up to the batteries on the hill, looking for the Gen'l. By this time the enemy had yielded more ground, & we had stopped firing. It was 8:00 P.M. & quite dark. . . . Very soon, in answer to my calls, made every now & then for fear of passing him in the dark, somebody ran out & called that Gen'l. E. was there. I found him lying in a little opening among the brush pines, quite conscious, but in considerable pain. I rode off at once to find a surgeon—letting Trimble know, on the way, what had happened & that he was in command of the Divn. Finding a surgeon, I returned & met Gen'l. E. being brought off in a litter. So broken down was he by his exertions in the campaign that he actually slept while being carried off in the litter. He told me, before his leg was cut off next day, that one of the things which had touched & pleased him most in his life was the devotion of some of the men who lay near him on the field. He heard two who were badly hurt themselves call out to passers-by that Gen'l. Ewell was wounded & refuse when the litters came up to be carried off before him. But being anxious himself to have the amputation performed before he was moved, he had them carried off, sending for the surgeons to come & operate on him there if practicable. They refused to do it, considering the case not free from doubt & thinking it possible to save the leg. He was carried back to the gate I have mentioned, where a field hospital was established & after resting there a short time was taken by a road thro' the woods to Sudley's & across the Run to a house just below the Ford, where was a Field Hospital. . . . While under the influence of the chloroform he gave several orders to troops, spoke hurriedly of their movements, &c. only appearing to feel conscious of pain when the Doctor (Surgeon Hunter McGuire) began to saw the bone, at which he stretched both arms upward & said: "Oh, My God!" Dr. Robertson of La. opened the leg along the back of the ball, in order to show me that they were justified in taking it off. . . . When the leg was opened we found the knee-cap split half in two, the head of the tibia knocked into several pieces & that the ball had followed the marrow of the bone for six inches, breaking the bone itself into small splinters & finally had split into two pieces on a sharp edge of bone. These pieces I took out & gave to my Mother, but have always avoided letting the Gen'l. know that I had them. The leg [was] wrapped in an oil cloth & it was decently buried in a corner of the garden.

Major General Richard S. Ewell, affectionately dubbed "old bald head" by his men, commanded one of Jackson's divisions until a severe wound at Brawner's Farm put him out of action for nine months.

CORPORAL THERON W. HAIGHT

24th New York Infantry, Hatch's Brigade

Haight joined the 24th Infantry, the Oswego County Regiment, as a private in May 1861 and was promoted to corporal the following January. Captured at Second Manassas, he was quickly paroled and returned to duty. He was promoted to lieutenant in January 1863 and mustered out with the regiment in May.

The woods were between us and the unseen combatants, and I could not then realize that bright young lives were going out at every instant like tapers in a wind, and that the passing moments were carrying sorrow and gloom to hundreds of northern and southern homes. . . . we could only lie there and listen so long as the daylight lasted, not venturing to withdraw ourselves so as to visibly uncover the flank of our line. But when darkness was over us, and we could change position without attracting the attention of the enemy, we were called to our feet, and moved back to that part of the road directly in the rear of the field where the fighting had been going on, but had now subsided, the surgeons' knives being busy by the flickering light of candles in the old orchard in our front.

CAPTAIN WILLIAM W. BLACKFORD

Staff, Major General J. E. B. Stuart

When darkness and exhaustion finally ended the two-hour battle at Brawner's Farm, Captain Blackford rode across the battlefield while soldiers from both armies combed the terrain to recover their wounded. Blackford served with Stuart until 1864, when he transferred to the 1st Confederate Engineers as a major.

In one place I heard through the darkness the shrill voice of a boy apparently not over fifteen or sixteen years old sobbing bitterly. I started towards the place to render him some assistance but as I reached the place his father, who it seems was the captain of his company, came up and said, "Hello, Charley, my boy, is that you?" "Oh, yes," said the boy, "Father, my leg is broken but I don't want you to think that is what I am crying for; I fell in a yellow-jackets' nest and they have been stinging me ever since. That is what makes me cry—please pull me out." The stings and the wound proved too much for the plucky boy and he died in his father's arms soon after.

"And the faces of these brave boys, as the morning sun disclosed them, no pen can describe."

ADJUTANT FRANKLIN A. HASKELL

Staff, Brigadier General John Gibbon

Haskell left a law practice in Madison, Wisconsin, in 1861 to accept a lieutenant's commission in the 6th Wisconsin. Assigned to Gibbon's staff in spring 1862, he was promoted to colonel of the 36th Wisconsin for gallantry at Gettysburg. He was killed leading his regiment at Cold Harbor on June 3, 1864.

At a little past midnight, we were ordered to leave the scene of our terrible battle, and having cared for the wounded as well as we could, and taking as many as the ambulances would hold with us we silently took up the line of march for Manassas Junction. As the day light came on the next morning, none of us could look upon our thinned ranks, so full the night before, now so shattered, without tears. And the faces of these brave boys, as the morning sun disclosed them, no pen can describe. The men were cheerful, quiet, and orderly. The dust and blackness of battle were upon their clothes, and in their hair, and on their skin, but you saw none of these,—you saw only their eyes, and the shadows of the "light of battle," and the furrows plowed upon cheeks that were smooth a day before, and now not half filled up. I could not look upon them without tears, and could have hugged the necks of them all.

Federal Attacks August 29

Fearing that Jackson might again slip away, Pope spent the early hours of August 29 trying to unite his scattered forces at Groveton. King's division was ordered to retrace its steps from Manassas Junction, along with Ricketts' division, which had arrived following the fight at Thoroughfare Gap. Porter's Fifth Corps had also arrived at Manassas, and those Army of the Potomac troops would join Hatch and Ricketts in a movement toward Gainesville, where they would be in a position to sever Jackson's probable line of retreat. Sigel's corps and Reynolds' division would strike at Jackson's right and center, while Heintzelman's Third Corps and Jesse L. Reno's Ninth Corps would move on Jackson's left flank from their positions near Centreville.

Jackson knew a Federal assault was likely, and he counseled his subordinates to avoid battle pending the arrival of Lee and Longstreet, whose troops were fast approaching from the west. Jackson's wing was firmly ensconced along Stony Ridge and the line of the unfinished railroad: Hill's division on the left, Ewell's division (now led by Brigadier General Alexander Lawton) in the center, and W. B. Taliaferro's division (commanded by Brigadier General William E. Starke) on the right, near the Warrenton Turnpike, where Longstreet would make his appearance.

The first Union threat came in late morning, when Sigel's 9,000 men fanned out from their staging area on Henry Hill and moved west across a two-mile front. Two elements of Sigel's force tangled with Jackson's line; Brigadier General Carl Schurz's division engaged Brigadier General Maxcy Gregg's South Carolinians, who held a rocky crest on the Southern left, and Milroy's brigade impetuously advanced across the Groveton-Sudley road to strike at a partially filled gap in the unfinished railroad grade known as the Dump. Both Yankee attacks were thrown back, but Jackson's troops had been unavoidably drawn into a rapidly escalating battle. To Jackson's great relief, Lee and Longstreet appeared on the field at about 10:00 a.m., and the vanguard of Longstreet's column—Brigadier General John Bell Hood's division—began deploying astride the Warrenton pike.

Lee narrowly escaped death while reconnoitering the Federal line, when a bullet from an enemy sharpshooter grazed his cheek. The episode barely seemed to faze the stoic commander. Lee exuded confidence. He would soon have more than 50,000 men in position to blunt his opponent's continued assaults and, possibly, to launch an attack of his own.

Pope reached the battlefield at 1:00 p.m., single-minded in his desire to destroy Jackson. Incredibly, he was still unaware of Longstreet's arrival. McDowell, who had learned of Lee's approach from the defenders of Thoroughfare Gap, had unaccountably failed to inform his commander of the new danger.

Pope relieved Sigel's bloodied troops with elements of the Third and Ninth Corps, and the fresh units lashed out at Jackson's position. At 3:00 p.m. Major General Joseph Hooker ordered Cuvier Grover's 1,500-man brigade forward over the ground Milroy had earlier failed to carry. Grover astutely avoided the open terrain where Milroy had come to grief, and sidled his five regiments northeastward in order to strike Jackson's line from the cover of woods adjoining the railroad grade. With a cheer Grover's men launched a bayonet charge toward a cut in the unfinished railroad—a portion of the Rebel line between Gregg's and Thomas' brigades that was largely void of defenders. Within minutes Thomas' Georgians had given way, and Gregg was desperately striving to shift his South Carolinians to plug the break as Grover forged ahead. But no Federal supports were forthcoming, and A. P. Hill was able to stem the Yankee breakthrough with Pender's brigade. With more than a third of his men down, Grover had no choice but to order a retreat.

The next Union advance on the unfinished railroad came southwest of Grover's charge, where Colonel James Nagle led three regiments from the Ninth Corps against the line held by Lawton's division. Nagle's little brigade also penetrated the Rebel position, but initial success quickly gave way to disorderly retreat when Colonel Bradley T. Johnson's Virginia brigade slammed into Nagle's exposed left flank. Colonel Nelson Taylor's brigade of Hooker's division came up too late to help Nagle and was in turn thrown back, with two Confederate brigades in hot pursuit. A Federal battery was nearly overrun and two guns lost before Hooker could restore order and repulse the Southern counterattack.

The largest Federal attack of the day came at 5:00 p.m. when Pope directed Major General Philip Kearny to lead his division against Jackson's left. Kearny, who had lost his left arm in the Mexican War, was a striking figure with a reputation for battlefield heroics. But his performance on August 29 had been marred by a dilatory march to the battlefield and his unwillingness to cooperate with Sigel's earlier assaults.

Kearny hurled 10 regiments against a portion of Hill's line that had already been sorely tested and was low on ammunition. Despite their stiff resistance, Gregg's and Thomas' Rebel brigades were driven from their positions behind the unfinished railroad. On Kearny's left, two regiments from Brigadier General Isaac Stevens' division also managed to punch through the Southern defenses. In response Jackson committed his only available reserves—Jubal Early's brigade—and yet again the Federals were repulsed without being able to exploit their breakthrough.

With night coming on, Pope was forced to call off his assaults on the Confederate left. He was baffled and enraged that Porter's expected offensive had failed to materialize against the enemy right. In fact Porter had not even received Pope's order to attack until after 6:00 p.m., and he had decided not to risk a night assault against what was clearly a large enemy force—Longstreet's troops.

It was not until after 7:00 p.m. that the truth dawned on Pope. McDowell ordered Hatch's division west on the Warrenton pike toward Groveton, where the movement of enemy troops and wagons appeared to confirm Pope's unwavering belief that Jackson was preparing to quit the field. But instead of a retreating force, Hatch's men collided with elements of Longstreet's newly arrived wing, and the Federals were locked in a confused battle that sputtered out in the darkness.

Finally willing to accept the fact that Longstreet had arrived, Pope woefully misjudged his opponents' intentions. Lee, Pope thought, would merely feed Longstreet's men into Jackson's line, or else use the fresh troops to cover his withdrawal from the battlefield. It never occurred to the Union commander that Lee would use Longstreet to extend the Southern line southward, and that the Confederates were contemplating a grand offensive strategy of their own.

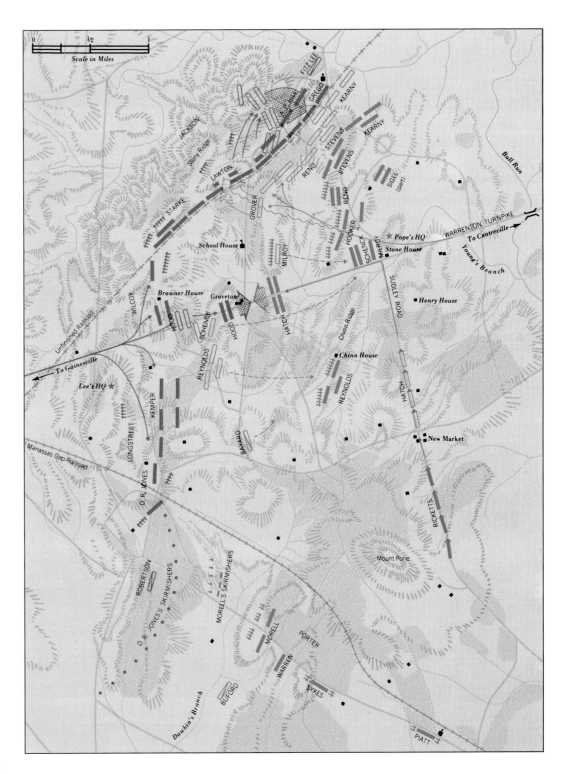

From late morning until after sunset, Pope launched repeated attacks but failed to break Jackson's line.

LIEUTENANT COLONEL DAVID H. STROTHER

Staff, Major General John Pope

In the early hours of the 29th, Pope remained convinced that Jackson was still intent on escaping west. The fight at Brawner's Farm, he reasoned, had been only a rearguard action, and victory lay within easy reach. Pope spent most of the morning issuing another spate of countermanding orders, this time calling for all units to converge on Groveton and the "retreating" Confederates.

Meanwhile the head-quarters breakfast had been served, and I sat down with the Staff officers to partake. The General, who was busy writing dispatches on the corner of the same table, looked up and asked, How do you spell "chaos?" I spelled the word letter by letter c-h-a-o-s. He thanked me, and observed, smiling, that, by a singular lapse of memory, he often forgot the spelling of the most familiar words. . . .

The anxiously-expected order to mount was at length given, and we rode rapidly by the Warrenton turnpike toward the field of battle. Hundreds of stragglers were toiling along the hot and dusty road, apparently actuated by the desire of rejoining their regiments in the engagement, while hundreds of others were shamelessly skulking, plundering, cooking, or sleeping by the way-side. At every house and under every convenient shade parties of these *tricoteurs* were picking chickens, roasting corn, and making themselves comfortable generally—neither orders, threats, nor scorn had the slightest effect on these recreant hogs. We at length saw quite a large body of men approaching us unarmed and marching in a disorderly manner. I was quite shocked at this apparition, and perceived by their countenances that others were equally bewildered. General Pope halted the column, and in a stern voice demanded what this meant? He was answered that they were prisoners taken by Jackson at Manassas Junction, now liberated on parole, and returning home. There were between five and six hundred, chiefly made up of officers having had charge of the supplies at Manassas, with their train of clerks, assistants, sutlers, invalids, and bummers. There were mutual recognitions between them and individuals of our cavalcade, and in passing they cheered, hoping that we would make a finish of Jackson this time.

MAJOR RUFUS R. DAWES

6th Wisconsin Infantry, Gibbon's Brigade
After the clash at Brawner's Farm, the battered troops of King's division marched back toward Manassas Junction. They had left the field but had every reason to be proud, for even Jackson, always stingy with compliments for Yankees, wrote in his report that they "maintained their ground with stubborn determination."

A fresh beef ration has been issued and hot coffee has been made, and at nine o'clock all are listening to the sounds of battle that come from the old Bull Run field. There is a heavy sound of cannon and an occasional ripple of musketry. We were near the railroad track, which branches off at Manassas Junction. I was myself aroused from a sleep by the heavy tramp of hurrying feet. I arose to see the corps of General Fitz John Porter passing by us toward the battle field. At the time they were passing, the cannon were roaring so loudly that the men fully believed they were marching directly to battle. They appeared fresh and in good spirits and the corps was a remarkably fine body of troops. The men marched rapidly, appeared to be well fed, and there was a great contrast between them and our own exhausted troops. As things are in a battle campaign they were in excellent condition. They showed quite a contempt for us as of "Pope's army." They said: "We are going up to show you 'straw feet' how to fight." The lesson did not prove to be impressive. All through the ranks of Porter's Corps was a running fire of disparagement of us as "Pope's" soldiers, something quite inferior to the Army of the Potomac. Of course our men retorted. There was one regiment of Zouaves with baggy trousers (Duryea's I think). I remember one of our men said: "Wait till you get where we have been. You'll get the slack taken out of your pantaloons and the swell out of your heads."

Pope established his first headquarters on the battlefield around 1:00 p.m. near the John Dogan house (left) that stood just north of the Warrenton Turnpike. The Dogan farm boasted a fine orchard, which in the week after the battle was used as the main assembly point for Federal wounded waiting to be evacuated.

"Wait till you get where we have been. You'll get the slack taken out of your pantaloons and the swell out of your heads."

PRIVATE EDWARD A. MOORE

Rockbridge (Virginia) Artillery, W. B. Taliaferro's Division
In one of the first engagements on the morning of the 29th, Captain James Cooper's Pennsylvania battery drew up near the Brawner house and opened fire on the Confederate guns on Jackson's right. Responding quickly, Captain William T. Poague brought up his Virginia battery to within 600 yards of the Yankee guns and, after a vicious hour-long duel, drove them off.

While quietly awaiting developments, we heard the sound of a horse's hoofs, and, as a courier galloped up to General Jackson, to announce Longstreet's approach, the cloud of red dust raised by his vanguard in the direction of Thoroughfare Gap assured us that he would soon be at hand. Before he reached the field, however, and while we were enjoying the sense of relief at his coming, one of the enemy's batteries had quietly and unobserved managed to get into one of the positions occupied by our battery during the morning. Their first volley, coming from such an unexpected quarter, created a great commotion. Instantly we galloped to their front and unlimbered our guns at close range. Other of our batteries fired a few shots, but soon ceased, all seeming intent on witnessing a duel between the two batteries of four guns each. Their position was the more favorable, as their limbers and caissons were behind the crest of the hill, while we were on level ground with ours fully exposed. Each man worked as if success depended on his individual exertions, while Captain Poague and Lieutenant Graham galloped back and forth among the guns, urging us to our best efforts. Our antagonists got our range at once, and, with their twelve-pound Napoleon guns, poured in a raking fire. One shell I noticed particularly as it burst, and waited a moment to observe its effects as the fragments tore by. One of them struck Captain

Poague's horse near the middle of the hip, tearing an ugly hole, from which there spurted a stream of blood the size of a man's wrist. To dismount before his horse fell required quick work, but the captain was equal to the occasion. Another shell robbed Henry Boteler of the seat of his trousers, but caused the shedding of no blood, and his narrow escape the shedding of no tears, although the loss was a serious one. Eugene Alexander, of Moorefield, had his thigh-bone broken and was incapacitated for service. Sergeant Henry Payne, a splendid man and an accomplished scholar, was struck by a solid shot just below the knee and his leg left hanging by shreds of flesh. An hour later, when being lifted into an ambulance, I heard him ask if his leg could not be saved, but in another hour he was dead.

Practicing law in Missouri when war came, Captain William T. Poague (above) returned to his native Virginia and signed on as a lieutenant in the Rockbridge Artillery. In April 1862 he was promoted to captain and given command of this celebrated unit. One of the South's finest artillery officers, Poague ended the war as a lieutenant colonel.

GENERAL SIGEL AT THE

-YORK ILLUSTRATED NEWS.

LL RUN.—Sketched by an Officer of the Division. See page 307.

The first Federal attacks of the day were made by General Franz Sigel's I Corps. In this engraving, Sigel (center, astride his horse) points his sword toward the enemy as he sends in another wave of attackers. A native of Germany, where he received his military training, Sigel rallied his fellow German immigrants to the Northern cause, an effort that earned him his general's stars. Although he was a mediocre field commander, Sigel nevertheless had pluck and an unassuming air that earned him the affection and trust of his troops.

MAJOR THEODORE F. LANG

3d West Virginia Infantry, Milroy's Brigade

Lang was promoted to major and given command of his regiment just nine days before he was called upon to lead it into battle. In a matter of minutes his unit was cut to shreds, along with the other three regiments of Milroy's brigade.

In the midst of this slaughter, Milroy came to the writer and with all the enthusiasm of his nature, said: "Major Lang, now is the opportunity for you to distinguish yourself. I want you to charge the railroad embankment just in front of our position, and see what is behind it." There was but one reply to such a command, and that was to charge.

While arranging the companies that I was to guide, an incident in illustration of premonition of death on the battlefield was forcibly presented to me. Capt. David Gibson of Company H, 3d W. Va., approached me with a face as calm and spiritual as if he had been pre-paring for the march to the bridal altar, and said to me, "Major, I shall be killed in this charge." I endeavored to quiet his apprehension in some by-play of pleasant words, but he did not heed them, but forcefully said, "I tell you I am going to be killed in this charge, I knew it last night, I have known it all morning." The captain was as brave a man as ever drew sword, but on this occasion his voice and manner were so changed, that I begged him not to make the charge, but he would not listen to that. So, the charge began,—out of the wood, across the field, and before we had passed half the distance, a bullet struck him in the forehead, and brave Captain Gibson fell dead, face to the foe. The charging column continued, only a few scattering shots from the railroad met our advance until we were within 150 feet of the embankment, when immediately a deluge of bristling muskets poured over the embankment and sent such a crash of leaden hail into our ranks, that we beat a hasty retreat, leaving many of our men dead or wounded on the field; we had met "Stonewall" Jackson's own command.

The unfinished railroad bed is barely visible as a light-colored line on the horizon of this photograph taken some years after Second Manassas. Intended as a bypass of the Orange & Alexandria, the rail line was left incomplete in 1860 because of lack of funds. Two years later, its overgrown cuts provided cover for Jackson's men.

LIEUTENANT HENRY N. BLAKE

11th Massachusetts Infantry, Grover's Brigade
A 22-year-old lawyer, Blake enlisted as a sergeant in June 1861, only to be wounded a month later at First Manassas. When he returned to the battlefield in 1862, this time as a lieutenant, he was quick to notice "the familiar scenes of the first battle." Blake was wounded again in May 1864 and left the service shortly afterward.

A member of West Point's class of 1850, Brigadier General Cuvier Grover (left) spent most of his pre-war service in the West. He returned from New Mexico when the war broke out and in April 1862 was given command of a brigade in McClellan's army. He performed admirably during the Peninsula campaign, only to lose nearly 500 men at Second Manassas. Grover saw distinguished service in both the Gulf Coast and the 1864 Valley campaign.

member of the staff, dressed like an officer of the day . . . arrived, and gave a verbal order to the brigade commander; after which the regiments were formed and marched, unmindful of the cannon-balls, towards the right of the line, and halted in the border of a thick forest, in which many skirmishes had taken place.

"What does the general want me to do now?" Gen. Grover asked the aide who again rode up to the brigade.

"Go into the woods, and charge," was the answer.

"Where is my support?" the commander wisely inquired; for there were no troops near the position.

"It is coming."

After waiting fifteen minutes for this body to appear, the officer returned and said that "the general was much displeased" because the charge had not been made; and the order was at once issued, "Fix bayonet." Each man was inspired by these magical words; great enthusiasm arose when this command was "passed" from company to company; and the soldiers, led by their brave general, advanced upon a hidden foe, through tangled woods which constantly interfered with the formation of the ranks.

"Colonel, do you know what we are going to charge on?" a private inquired.

"Yes: a good dinner."

The rebel skirmishers were driven in upon their reserve behind the bank of an unfinished railroad. . . . "We will stir up these fellows with a long pole in a minute," one of the company said when the bullets began to sing; and he welcomed the fatal shot which cut him down in his youth. "Victory or death" were the last words of another humble hero. The awful volleys did not impede the storming party that pressed on over the bodies of the dead and dying; while the thousands of bullets which flew through the air seemed to create a breeze that made the leaves upon the trees rustle, and a shower of small boughs and twigs fell upon the ground. The balls penetrated the barrels and shattered the stocks of many muskets; but the soldiers who carried them picked up those that had been dropped upon the ground by helpless comrades, and allowed no slight accident of this character to interrupt them in the noble work. The railroad bank was gained, and the column with cheers passed over it, and advanced over the groups of the slain and mangled rebels who had rolled down the declivity when they lost their strength. The second line was broken; both were scattered through the woods; and victory appeared to be certain, until the last support, that had rested upon their breasts on the ground, suddenly rose up and delivered a destructive volley, which forced the brigade, that had already lost more than one third of its number in killed and wounded, to retreat. . . . The horse of Gen. Grover was shot upon the railroad bank while he was encouraging the men to go forward; and he had barely time to dismount before the animal, mad with pain, dashed into the ranks of the enemy. The woods always concealed the movements of the troops; and at one point a portion of the foe fell back, while the others remained. The forces sometimes met face to face, and the bayonet and sword—weapons that do not pierce soldiers in nine-tenths of the battles that are fought—were used with deadly effect in several instances. A corporal exclaimed in the din of this combat, "Dish ish no place for de mens," and fled to the rear with the speed of the mythical "flying Dutchman." In one company of the regiment, a son was killed by the side of his father, who continued to perform his duty with the firmness of a stoic, and remarked to his amazed comrades, in a tone which showed how a strong patriotic ardor can triumph over the deepest emotion of affection, "I had rather see him shot dead as he was, than see him run away."

The victors rallied the fugitives after this repulse, and their superior force enabled them to assault in front and upon both flanks the line which had been contracted by the severe losses in the charge; and the brigade fell back to the first position under a fire of grape and canister which was added to the musketry. The regimental flag was torn from the staff by unfriendly limbs in passing through the forest, and the eagle that surmounted it was cut off in the contest. The commander of the color company saved these precious emblems, and earnestly shouted when the lines were re-formed, "Eleventh, rally round the pole!" which was then, if possible, more honored than when it was bedecked in folds of bunting.

PRIVATE MARTIN A. HAYNES

2d New Hampshire Infantry, Grover's Brigade
Using the woods as cover, Grover's men, with the 2d New Hampshire in the front rank, closed within a few yards of the railroad embankment before drawing Confederate fire. Haynes survived the rush up the bank and the fight that followed unscathed. Mustered out in 1864, he later wrote his regiment's history.

The dash was evidently a surprise to the rebels, as most of them, having delivered their fire, were closely hugging the ground under cover of the bank. They were expecting a return volley, apparently, but had not anticipated looking into the muzzles of the guns that delivered it. Those who made a fight were instantly shot or bayonetted, and in less time than it has taken to write it the rebel first line was disposed of. Some threw up their hands and cried for mercy; some, doubtless, "played possum," lying as if dead and making no sign; while others, as soon as they could realize what had happened, made a break for the rear, closely followed by the men of the Second, now wild with the rage of battle. There was a desperate dash for a stand of rebel colors, but they were saved by the fleetness of their bearer and the devoted bravery of the color guard.

Yet in this wild turmoil of murder there were not wanting instances of man's humanity to man. One fleeing rebel, tripped by a bullet or some other obstruction to locomotion, and cumbered by two or three rolls of blankets (probably spoils from Manassas), pitched headlong; and down in the same heap went Sergeant Wasley. Quick as a flash Wasley yanked from the Johnny's belt a ferocious looking "Yankee killer," fashioned from a huge flat file—such as many of that regiment seemed to carry for side arms—and swung it aloft for the finishing blow. The poor fellow's eye caught the glint of the vengeful steel just in season, and in a piteous tone he gasped out: "Oh, for God's sake—don't!" The blow was suspended. "All right, Johnny!" said Wasley, as, pushing the weapon into his own belt, he scrambled to his feet.

The national flag of the 11th Massachusetts (left) was almost lost to "unfriendly" tree limbs during the retreat of Grover's brigade. Recovered by the color sergeant, it barely escaped capture at Gettysburg, survived the hard fighting at Wilderness and Spotsylvania, and was finally retired in June 1864.

Photo by R. N. Keely, 4th & Coates St., Philada.

PRIVATE MARION H. FITZPATRICK

45th Georgia Infantry, Thomas' Brigade
Writing to his wife, Amanda, on September 2, Fitzpatrick began with the most important news that "I am well at this time and through the mercy of God am alive." He then went on to relate his role in the fighting on August 29, when Grover's assault sent the Georgians running.

We got a strong position behind a railroad embankment fought them for about an hour and drove them back. Before a great while they charged our position and flanked us at the same time. Gen. Hill had sent a curior previous to that for us to get out from there but we failed to get it. Our brigade fought like heroes. Our Regiment in the centre. The first thing we knew both wings had given away and the 45th was nearly surrounded the last fire I made I stood on the embankment and fired right down amongst them just as they were charging up the bank about fifteen ranks deep. I turned and saw the whole Reg. getting away, and I followed the example in thribble quick time. They charged over the road and fired on us but were met by Branch's Brigade and were driven right back over it and about a mile the other side. I went to where I fired last and three of the devils were lying there. I got me a good Yankee zinc canteen which fortunately was nearly filled with water.

In the second line of the attack, the 26th Pennsylvania Infantry "did not have the opportunity of showing its mettle," as General Grover stated in his official report. But the regiment still suffered 53 casualties, including six killed. Among the dead was Lieutenant David Potts (above) whose broken sword (below) was recovered from the battlefield.

By midafternoon on August 29, hard fighting and a hot day had left many soldiers with a powerful thirst. Canteens, like this battered Rebel model (right), became precious items and were often stripped from prisoners and the dead.

"Webster and Calhoun had exhausted the argument in the Senate and now the soldiers of the two States were fighting it out eye to eye, hand to hand, man to man."

LIEUTENANT COLONEL EDWARD MCCRADY

1st South Carolina Infantry, Gregg's Brigade

The most sorely tried of the Confederate defenders on August 29 were the South Carolinians of Gregg's brigade, posted on the far left of Jackson's line. First they had to fight desperately for more than an hour to beat back an entire Federal division. Then, during Grover's Federal attack, they found themselves locked in a ferocious struggle with the 1st Massachusetts Infantry.

The struggle, indeed, was a memorable one. It was the consummation of the grand debate between Massachusetts and South Carolina. Webster and Calhoun had exhausted the argument in the Senate and now the soldiers of the two States were fighting it out eye to eye, hand to hand, man to man. If the debates in the Senate chamber were able and eloquent, the struggle on that knoll at Manassas was brave and glorious. Each State showed there that it had the courage of its convictions. . . . But it was too fearful if not too grand, to last. Slowly at first the New Englanders began to give back, and step by step we pressed on them every inch gained by us, until Colonel McGowan, with the Fourteenth of our brigade and the Forty-ninth Georgia, coming up to our assistance, Grover's men at last broke, and then followed the awful and pitiful carnage of brave men who have failed in an assault. Grape and canister cruelly tearing to pieces in their retreat those whose lives had escaped while fighting hand to hand with their foes.

PRIVATE JOHN H. WORSHAM

21st Virginia Infantry, Garnett's/Johnson's Brigade

Jackson skillfully deployed his reserves to turn back the Federal penetrations. Both Grover's and Nagle's assaults were stopped cold, and Rebel counterattack-ers, including the men of the 21st Virginia, threatened the main Union line until concentrated artillery fire drove them back.

The whole field seemed to be full of Yankees and some of them advanced nearly to the railroad. We went over the bank at them, the remainder of the brigade following our example. The enemy now broke and ran, and we pursued, firing as fast as we could. We followed them into the woods, and drove them out on the other side, where we halted and were ordered back to the railroad. We captured two pieces of artillery in the woods, and carried them back with us. As we returned a Yankee battery of eight guns had full play on us in the field, and our line became a little confused; we halted, every man instantly turned and faced the battery. As we did so, I heard a thud on my right, as if one had been struck with a heavy fist. Looking around I saw a man at my side standing erect, with his head off, a stream of blood spurting a foot or more from his neck. As I turned far-ther around, I saw three others lying on the ground, all killed by this cannon shot. The man standing was a captain in the 42d Va. Regt., and his brains and blood bespattered the face and clothing of one of my company, who was standing in my rear. This was the second time I saw four men killed by one shot. The other occurred in the battle of Cedar Run, a few weeks earlier. Each time the shot struck as it was descend-ing,—the first man had his head taken off, the next was shot through the breast, the next through the stomach, and the fourth had all his bowels torn out.

CAPTAIN HENRY H. PEARSON

6th New Hampshire Infantry, Nagle's Brigade
After fighting their way over the railroad embankment, the troops of Nagle's three regiments were pinned down and soon forced to withdraw when no support came. Pearson, promoted to lieutenant colonel two months later, was killed in action on May 26, 1864.

Discovering that our Reg. was alone and that the bullets began to come thick and fast from the rear the Col. sent me back to see why the other two regiments did not follow us and to tell them they were firing upon us. As I approached the ditch I heard loud cheering on the other side and thought that we were about to be supported. But as a number of bullets whistled by my ears, I quickened my pace to inform them that we were ahead. Mounting the opposite side of the ditch the bullets flew by me so thick that I quickly jumped back again and peeping up over the bank could hardly trust my eyes when I saw yellow legs standing as thick as wheat not more than 25 paces from the ditch. I instantly called to the Reg. to retreat to the ditch which was done at a run. Taking a second look to see if I could see a flag I saw one, their battle flag, with a red cross worked in it and a swarm of rebels following it at double quick towards our left, as we were now faced, so as to surround us. The Col. still doubted whether it could be rebels took our flag and waved it above the ditch. It was instantly riddled with bullets.

CHAPLAIN JAMES B. SHEERAN

14th Louisiana Infantry, Forno's/Strong's Brigade
The Confederates that surged forth on the heels of Nagle's brigade came under galling fire from the four guns of a Pennsylvania battery, placed well in front of the rest of the Federal artillery. Enraged, the Rebels rushed the guns, capturing two and driving off the rest of the battery.

Now occurred one of the most laughable incidents of the war. The Yankees had placed a mountain howitzer opposite the 15th La. Reg. which very much annoyed the boys. Having repelled the attack of the N.Y. infantry the gallant 15th boldly charged this battery which they captured with a large squad of Yankees. Desirous of securing their booty and the horses of the battery being killed, they harnessed the Yankees and compelled them to haul the artillery into our lines. The sight of some fifty Yankees hitched to a piece of artillery, with the 15th charging bayonets, coming across the battle-field at a double quick drew forth a burst of laughter from our Confederate boys.

The 15th Louisiana saw many hard fights, as the regiment's tattered battle flag reveals. On the third day of Second Manassas, men of the 15th Louisiana threw stones from atop the embankment when they ran out of bullets.

PRIVATE JOHN O. CASLER

33d Virginia Infantry, Baylor's Brigade
By his own admission a scourge to his superiors, Private Casler indulged in straggling, petty thievery, and unauthorized leaves. Still, he was as good in a fight as any in his regiment and no shirker when it came to shouldering the more dismal duties that befall a soldier.

My Captain told me to get Lieutenant Earsome, who was shot through the bowels, into an ambulance and take him to the hospital at Sudley church, which I did. After going a short distance, he said he could not stand the jolting of the ambulance and wanted us to take him out. We did so, and, making a stretcher out of two rails and a blanket, four of us started to carry him on our shoulders, but soon met the ambulances and wounded coming back in a hurry, saying the enemy was at Sudley and we would have to go in another direction. . . . but we soon saw a yellow flag hoisted to denote a hospital, and we went to it. I then got a surgeon to examine the Lieutenant's wound. When he had done so, he said that he was shot through and through and his entrails were cut; that he could not live and he could do nothing for him.

As I was a particular friend of his, he asked me to remain with him and take care of him until he died, as he knew he could not live.

I told him I would like to do so, but could not do it without permission from the Captain. He begged me to go and see the Captain, as he knew his dying request would be granted.

I immediately did so, when my Captain said: "Certainly, remain with him; and when he dies bury him and join the company."

I went back to him and did all I could for him, but he suffered terribly; he could not lie still, but was up and down continually, and I worried with him all day and all night. The next morning he died, when I buried him as decently as I could and then joined my regiment.

In this March 1862 photograph, Sudley Church perches on a small rise overlooking Bull Run at the northern end of the battlefield. In the first clash at Manassas, Federal troops had streamed past the church on their way around the Rebel flank; during the second battle it served as the main Confederate field hospital.

CAPTAIN OLIVER C. BOSBYSHELL

48th Pennsylvania Infantry, Nagle's Brigade
As Nagle's beaten men tumbled back out of the woods east of the unfinished railroad, they encountered their long-overdue reinforcements. At the head of these fresh troops rode General Kearny, who was stirred to furious action by the sight of panic-stricken soldiers and oncoming Rebels.

It is not meant to say that the regiment got out of the woods in perfect order; the men were scattered some, in fact a good deal. Kearney was exceedingly anxious to promote those retiring near where he was. All engaged can remember the occasion well, Kearney riding in with his troops—the reins guiding his horse, in his teeth, and sword in one hand, hissed through his clenched teeth: "Fall in here, you sons of bitches, and I'll make major-generals of every one of you!" Some of the men under the lamented Gilmour returned to the fight with a Michigan regiment, but the commissions promised by Kearney never were forthcoming.

Called by one of his superiors "the bravest man I ever knew, and a perfect soldier," Major General Philip Kearny was one of the most dynamic commanders in the Federal army. Despite inheriting great wealth, his only interest was soldiering, a career he pursued with unflagging zeal. He fought with the French army, lost an arm in the Mexican War, and was one of the few bright stars during the Peninsula campaign. His attack during the late afternoon of August 29 was the largest of the day and nearly broke the Rebel line.

LIEUTENANT HENRY KYD DOUGLAS

Staff, Major General Thomas J. Jackson

By the late afternoon, Jackson's line had been stretched but so far unbroken. Eight hours of combat had, for many of the Confederate defenders, "exhausted all the romance of battle," but there was to be no rest yet. Pope, aware that his only success had come against the Rebel left, ordered General Kearny to attack this beleaguered flank with 2,700 fresh troops.

It was a fearfully long day. Jackson's staff was unusually small, several being absent, the invaluable Pendleton among them, and upon those who remained the labor was unceasing. On that day I acted in every capacity from Assistant Adjutant General to courier, and our Medical Director was most effective as an aide-de-camp. For the first time in my life I understood what was meant by "Joshua's sun standing still on Gibeon," for it would not go down. No one knows how long sixty seconds are, nor how much time can be crowded into an hour, nor what is meant by "leaden wings" unless he has been under the fire of a desperate battle, holding on, as it were by his teeth, hour after hour, minute after minute, waiting for a turning or praying that the great red sun, blazing and motionless overhead, would go down.

Late in the afternoon I had occasion to visit A. P. Hill. The last two attacks had been directed particularly against him and the last of the two barely repulsed. One of his brigades was out of ammunition, and details were out on the field collecting cartridges from the boxes of the dead and wounded—friend and foe. He requested me to ride to General Jackson and explain the situation and say if he was attacked again, he would do the best he could, but could hardly hope for success. Such a message from a fighter like Hill was weighty with apprehension. I quickly found the General and delivered the message. It seemed to deepen the shadow on his face, and the silence of the group about him was oppressive; but he answered promptly and sharply, "Tell him if they attack him again he must beat them." As I started off, he followed. We soon met General Hill on the way to General Jackson and he repeated his fears. The General said calmly, "General, your men have done nobly; if you are attacked again you will beat the enemy back."

A rattle of musketry broke along Hill's front. "Here it comes," he said and galloped off, Jackson calling after him, "I'll expect you to beat them."

Major General Ambrose Powell Hill (above) directed his division with great effectiveness at Cedar Mountain, and his six brigades would prove their worth for a second time on August 29. A West Pointer and future corps commander, Hill staunchly defended Jackson's left flank at Manassas.

The attack was fierce and soon over. The Rebel yell seemed to follow and bury itself among the enemy in the wood, and we knew the result. A staff officer rode up, "General Hill presents his compliments and says the attack of the enemy was repulsed."

"Tell him I knew he would do it," answered Jackson with a smile.

LIEUTENANT ENEAS N. LAMONT

101st New York Infantry, Birney's Brigade

Lamont's regiment, along with the 40th New York, formed the left wing of Kearny's attack. After trading a couple of volleys with Gregg's sorely depleted brigade, they "resorted to cold steel to drive them out." Within minutes, the Carolinians broke, and the New Yorkers surged forward to make the deepest Federal penetration of the battle.

It was about 5 o'clock on that beautiful autumn evening, as the brigade of General Sickles retired broken and dispirited, that we saw our General riding rapidly toward us. "Fall in, men," cried the warning voice of the Colonel, and we stood to our arms. We knew that our turn had come. A few moments before I had been conversing with one of my sergeants, as we lay and smoked our pipes philosophically in the fading sunlight. He remarked that he had a peculiar presentment that his time had come. There was a tinge of sadness in tone as he spoke of his wife and little ones far away in the Susquehanna Valley. "Ah, well!" said he, "I guess some one will look after them when I am gone." The order came. The angry volleys reared in front of us. The wounded were coming out in threes and fours, borne upon blankets and stretchers. The Colonel dismounted, placed himself in front of the regiment and in a clear and manly voice gave forth the command: "Now, boys, keep cool and fire low. Forward, march!"

Forward we went across a green meadow, where the children had played and the sheep gamboled in the peaceful past, into the dark and dreadful woods, reeking with blood and sickly with the scent of death. Every mouth was firmly set, every heart beat faster, and perhaps across the war-worn faces there came a shadow, and may be a little prayer just whispered its half-forgotten mutterings in some sinful ear. On we went. One fell. We were in the midst of it, and above the deafening roar from every quarter the voice of the Colonel sounded clear and full, "Fire!" and we sent a volley into the enemy's front so steady and so sure that we afterwards heard it was the settler of the day. Their fire slackened and it was then that our Colonel, like the gallant fellow that he was, went right in front, waved his cap and shouted, "Forward, boys; we're driving them." On we went at the double, through the brushwood, toward the railway cutting, on with the enthusiasm and excitement of—the Lord knows what.

There they were sure enough, ready, waiting for us dear fellows.

Away to our left their gray figures crouched among the trees, and as far as we could see for the few seconds it took us to dash across were the mingled bodies of blue and gray, dotting the ravine like locusts. A faint cheer came from a wounded blue coat and the bullets whistled past my ear with their peculiar "fiz" as I rushed up the steep bank on the other side. There we stood and let them have it hot and heavy. Whether it was that we were fresh and they somewhat exhausted I know not, but their fire at this moment almost ceased. We had lost a good many men and as the shadows now began to gather over the tall pine trees the order was given to retire. Back we went across the well-known death-pit, sending a parting shot as we advanced up on the other side. Short as the affair appeared from the time we entered these woods until we fired our last shot, an hour must have elapsed. It did not seem five minutes.

Lieutenant Simon Brennan (right) of the 3d Michigan was wounded during Kearny's attack, his blood staining the hymn book (below) that he was carrying. He survived but was captured at the Wilderness two years later.

CAPTAIN JOSEPH J. NORTON

1st South Carolina Rifles, Gregg's Brigade

Within minutes after Kearny's attack rolled into Norton's regiment, the two senior officers were shot down and Norton found himself in command. Shortly afterward, his father, a company commander in the same regiment, also fell. Four months later at Fredericksburg, Norton lost his left arm and was forced to resign.

While this fire was going on Col. M & Lt. Col. Ledbetter were both shot down (Col. died in an hour or two) (Lt. Col. was removed to the hospital) & the command devolved on me—Genl. Gregg ordered me to charge, which I did. Just after ordering a retreat my father was mortally wounded & I & Lt. Reid carried him from the field—By permission of Genl. Gregg I accompanied him to rear—B. L. Lowery, H. A. Powell, Joseph Alexander & John J. Ansel bore him to Hospital on creek Saturday 30th removed my father to Alexr. J. McMullen's 4 miles from Haymarket, with the assistance of B. L. Lowery, Jos. Alexander, John J. Ansel & John C. L. Knee, at 5¼ P.M. he expired—The four men last named remained with me & we interred him on the side of a (crooked forked) persimmon tree next to the battlefield near to Mr. McMullen's house on Sunday 31st.

Captain Norton's diary (right), open to the pages describing the events on August 29, exhibits the terse style typical of many diaries carried during the war. Many soldiers saved their more colorful, descriptive language for letters, in which they shared their thoughts and experiences with friends and loved ones.

August

I did, just after ordering a retreat my father was mortally wounded & J. H. St. Reid carried him from the field. By permission of Genl Gregg I accompanied him to rear. R. L. Lowry, H. A. Porter, [ ] Alexander & John J. Ansel bore him to Hospital on creek Saturday 30th [ ] removed my father to Mrs J. McMullen 4 miles from Haymarket, with the assistance of R. L. Lowry for Alexander, John J. Ansel & John C. Lewis, at 5¾ P.M. he expired. These four men last named remained with me & we interred him

During the most critical phase of the battle, General Gregg shouted, "Let us die here, my men, let us die here." A hundred of his men did die there, and more than 500 were wounded. Among the dead were three officers of the 1st South Carolina Rifles (right, top to bottom): Colonel J. Foster Marshall, the regimental commander; Lieutenant Colonel Daniel A. Ledbetter, his successor for a few moments; and Captain Miles M. Norton, the father of Joseph J. Norton.

SURGEON SPENCER G. WELCH

13th South Carolina Infantry, Gregg's Brigade
During the early summer of 1862, Surgeon Welch had gotten his first look at "the shocking results of the battlefield"—the wounded of the Seven Pines battle. This letter to his wife, like so many others, bears testimony to the grim life of a military surgeon.

Married just a few months before the war, Spencer Welch corresponded faithfully with his wife, Cordelia Strother Welch (left). In December 1863 their only son, George, died at the age of two, moving Spencer to write, "I could forget the loss . . . much sooner if I could only be with you."

Next morning (Friday) we had breakfast, and I ate with Adjutant Goggans. Our command then took position in the woods near the cut of an unfinished railroad and sent out skirmishers, who soon retreated and fell back on the main line. The Yankee line came up quite near and fired into us from our right, and Goggans was shot through the body. I remained some distance in rear of our line and saw Mike Bowers, Dave Suber and two other men bringing someone back on a litter, and I said: "Mike, who is that?" and he said: "Goggans," just as they tumbled him down. I looked at him as he was gasping his last, and he died at once. Then the wounded who could walk began to come back, and those who could not were brought to me on litters. I did all I could for them until the ambulances could carry them to the field infirmary, and this continued until late in the afternoon.

I saw an Irishman from South Carolina bringing a wounded Irishman from Pennsylvania back and at the same time scolding him for fighting us. Colonel McGowan came limping back, shot through the thigh, but he refused to ride, and said: "Take men who are worse hurt than I am." Colonel Marshall and Lieutenant-Colonel Leadbetter were brought back mortally wounded. . . .

Our brigade was not relieved until about four o'clock. They had been fighting all day and their losses were very heavy. I saw General Fields, commanding a Virginia brigade, ride in on our left to

Colonel of the 14th South Carolina, Samuel McGowan (left) rose to become one of the finest brigade commanders in the Army of Northern Virginia. During the height of Kearny's attack, McGowan's regiment found itself in the midst of "a semicircle of smoke and flame." A thigh wound late on the 29th put him out of action—the first of four wounds he sustained in the war.

relieve us, and I then went back to the field infirmary, where I saw large numbers of wounded lying on the ground as thick as a drove of hogs in a lot. They were groaning and crying out with pain, and those shot in the bowels were crying for water. Jake Fellers had his arm amputated without chloroform. I held the artery and Dr. Hout cut it off by candle light. We continued to operate until late at night and attended to all our wounded. I was very tired and slept on the ground.

Colonel Oliver E. Edwards (left) of the 13th South Carolina was in the front of the battle line during the morning action, "cheering the men, directing their fire, and even supplying them with cartridges." Edwards was one of four of Gregg's five regimental commanders to be hit on August 29. He recovered but was mortally wounded at Chancellorsville.

LIEUTENANT GEORGE C. PARKER

21st Massachusetts Infantry, Ferrero's Brigade
Parker witnessed the final action on the 29th when the Federals of Hatch's division collided with Hood's Confederates along the Warrenton pike sometime after sunset. He left the war as a captain soon after sustaining a wound at the Wilderness on May 6, 1864.

While we were going back I saw the most beautiful sight I think that I ever saw. One of our Batteries had taken a position close to the woods away off on our left, at the other end of the valley a mile and a half. The Rebs attacked it just as it was dark and we could see the flash of every gun, but could hear no report. I guess as many as six thousand men were in the muss, and I could only think of a meadow full of fire flies on a summer evening. The novelty of the thing gave it a charm. I never heard who got licked because the next day was the great fight of all and we had enough to think of for that day. But after watching that fight at night, we went to a supperless bed on the bare ground and no blankets, for our things were all in the woods in a pile. How many times did I get up that night and walk and run and sing "who wouldn't be a soldier" till some of the boys left off shivering and took to laughing. I thought of you and home that night, for on the morrow we were told that we must try those woods and I knew what that meant: "death in the pot" to 2 out of 3 of us.

CAPTAIN WALTER W. LENOIR

37th North Carolina Infantry, Branch's Brigade
The first reinforcements sent in to bolster Gregg's faltering line were the North Carolinians of Lenoir's regiment. Swept up in the desperate fight with Kearny's Federals, they in turn were saved by the arrival of Early's brigade. Lenoir resigned at the end of the year after losing his lower right leg at Chantilly.

On Sunday the day after the battle closed, I went over the ground we had fought on Friday. At the place where we made our first stand I picked a minie ball with my knife from the bark of a hickory tree where it had struck near my head as I stood by it. I believe that before reaching the tree the ball had passed through the head of William Weaver, a brave soldier of my company who fell dead at my feet and seemed to look me in the face with an expression that I cannot forget, a gentle smile on his lips and a look from the eyes that seemed to ask for aid. The blood gushing from his forehead and from the back of his head gave too plain evidence that the look was unconscious. At the railroad cut at the spot where my company fought I counted where 20 balls had struck a white oak not much larger than a man's body, and nearly all within six feet of the ground. Not a bush had been missed. Most of the trees had been struck many times. There was other fighting here in the three days besides that in which my company took part; but it seems marvelous how many of us escaped being killed.

Longstreet's Assault August 30

Late on August 29, the last of Longstreet's troops—6,100 men of Major General Richard H. Anderson's division, plus the 18 guns of Colonel Stephen D. Lee's artillery battalion—arrived on the battlefield from their rearguard duty along the old Rappahannock line. The artillery occupied a prominent knoll on Brawner's Farm, providing much-needed firepower on Jackson's right flank. Uncertain of their whereabouts in the darkness, Anderson's tired soldiers marched a considerable distance toward the Federal lines before being recalled to the Confederate positions at Groveton just before sunrise. When Pope was advised of this retrograde movement by the enemy, he took it as one more sign that the Rebels were preparing to abandon the field.

On the morning of August 30, the Federals launched several probes and reconnaissances along the line that encountered stiff resistance. Pope chose to interpret the Rebel response as a mere rearguard action, and at noon he ordered a two-pronged pursuit by Porter and Ricketts against what he believed to be a retreating enemy. The advance had barely begun before Confederate artillery fire stopped the Yankees in their tracks.

Exasperated, Pope determined to launch an all-out assault by Porter's Fifth Corps and Hatch's division on the right of Jackson's line. By shear weight of numbers he hoped to smash a way through the stubborn defenders of the unfinished railroad, then exploit the breakthrough with all the forces at his disposal.

Preoccupied with his plans for the grand offensive, the Union commander was in no mood to listen when General Reynolds rode up to headquarters with dire warnings of a massive Rebel presence opposite the Federal left. Reynolds requested reinforcements, but only a brigade and a battery of artillery were sent to join him south of the Warrenton Turnpike atop an open crest called Chinn Ridge. Thus a mere 8,000 Federals were facing Longstreet's 25,000 Southern troops.

In the meantime, Robert E. Lee was debating whether or not to seize the initiative from his indecisive opponent, perhaps by sending Jackson on a sweeping maneuver around the Union right flank. But at 3:00 p.m. Lee's decision was made for him when the 10,000 Federal soldiers of Porter and Hatch emerged cheering from the woods north of Groveton. With bayonets fixed and flags flying, they headed toward Jackson's line.

Porter had massed his units in compact columns, many ranks deep, which deployed into lines of battle as the attackers came out into the open fields west of the Groveton woods. Brigadier General Daniel Butterfield led his troops forward on the left, while Hatch swung his division into action on the right. Porter held Brigadier General George Sykes' division of Regular Army troops in reserve, ready to follow up the initial assault. But unfortunately for Porter, Sigel's corps, in line atop Dogan Ridge, was too far in the rear to offer any immediate support should the attack not go according to plan.

Porter's charging columns ran into difficulty as soon as they emerged from the woods. All day long S. D. Lee's artillery had been harassing Porter's troops from their commanding position on Brawner's Farm, and now Lee's 18 guns had a target they could not miss. With Jackson's artillery joining on their left, Lee's gunners raked the tightly packed Yankee formations with shot and shell, tearing gaps through the oncoming ranks. As the attackers pushed across a little stream called Schoolhouse Branch, the Southern infantry opened fire from the grade of the unfinished railroad.

The brunt of the Federal assault fell on Starke's division, which lay along the railroad in two lines of battle—one hunkered down behind the embankment and one to the rear, in reserve. Bradley Johnson's Virginia brigade defended a stretch of the railroad that sliced through Stony Ridge to form the so-called Deep Cut, while Colonel Leroy A. Stafford's Louisiana regiments defended the Dump on Johnson's left. Stafford's men savaged the oncoming enemy ranks but could not prevent some of Hatch's troops from gaining a foothold on the embankment.

As two New York regiments from Colonel Timothy Sullivan's brigade battled Stafford's Louisianans at point-blank range, a number of Butterfield's units managed to fight their way alongside them on the left. Johnson and Stafford committed their reserves and called on Jackson for reinforcements. The Stonewall Brigade, now down to fewer than 500 men, started forward but was driven back with the loss of their commanding officer, Colonel William Baylor. Under Jackson's stern eye, the Virginians rallied and succeeded in plugging a widening gap in the embattled Southern line. For nearly an hour the opposing troops grappled along the unfinished railroad, with neither side willing to retire. Their ammunition exhausted, desperate Southern soldiers began tossing rocks at their assailants.

When Lawton and Hill shifted units to bolster Starke's line, the tide began to turn in favor of the Confederates. The open ground to Porter's rear was raked and torn by Rebel shellfire, and no Federal regiment was able to pass through the ordeal without demoralizing loss. Unable to blunt the enemy counterattacks with reinforcements of his own, Porter could only watch as the Union survivors began falling back from their positions along the railroad, losing still more men as they recrossed the shell-torn fields.

With Porter and Hatch continuing to retreat toward Sigel's position on Dogan Ridge, General McDowell made a fateful decision. Acting in his capacity as commander of Pope's left wing, McDowell ordered Reynolds' division north from Chinn Ridge, across the Warrenton pike, to bolster the crumbling Federal center. With Reynolds' departure, only two small Union brigades remained to face Longstreet's five divisions.

Lee and Longstreet knew that the decisive moment had come, and at 4:00 p.m. Longstreet's 25,000 troops swept down on Pope's denuded left flank. Hood's division, astride the Warrenton pike, with the Texas Brigade in the lead, collided with the 5th and 10th New York—a scant 1,000 men commanded by Colonel Gouverneur K. Warren. Two hours earlier Warren had moved his troops alongside Lieutenant Charles E. Hazlett's battery, partially filling the gap Reynolds had left when he retired to Chinn Ridge. Hazlett managed to get his guns safely away when Hood struck, but in less than 10 minutes Warren's brigade was virtually annihilated.

The tail end of Reynolds' division had yet to cross the pike when Longstreet struck. Those Yankee troops were shattered and put to flight. Screaming the fearsome Rebel yell, the Texas Brigade overran the guns of Captain Mark Kerns' Pennsylvania battery and surged on for Chinn Ridge. Longstreet's Rebel onslaught seemed unstoppable, and a Union disaster imminent.

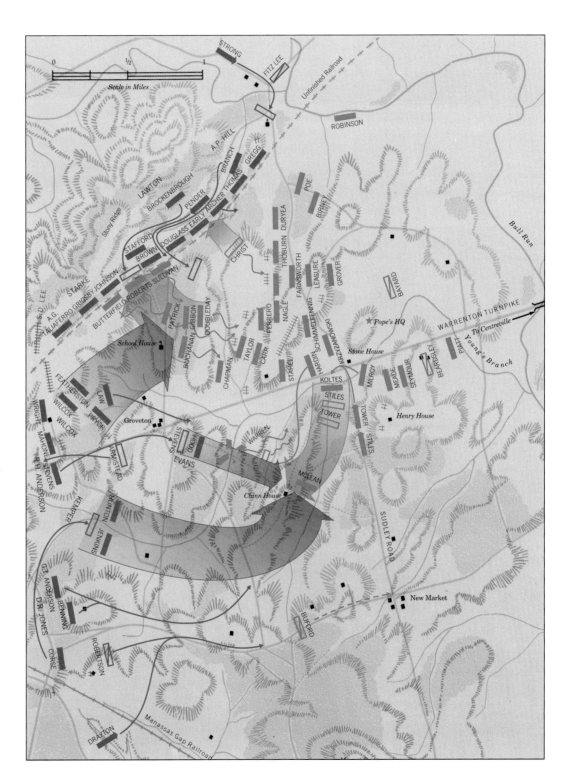

After the collapse of Porter's attack, Longstreet unleashed his corps against the Federal left.

PRIVATE WILLIAM MCLEOD

104th New York Infantry, Duryea's Brigade

Canadian-born William McLeod was a 21-year-old farmer when he enlisted in Company G, 104th New York. While advancing with his unit's skirmishers on the morning of August 30, he was shocked to discover a woman on the battlefield. Later that day McLeod was severely wounded and suffered the amputation of his right arm.

SERGEANT GEORGE N. WISE

17th Virginia Infantry Corse's Brigade

As Longstreet's corps approached Thoroughfare Gap, Sergeant George Wise visited his family's nearby home, which he had not seen since signing up with the Old Dominion Rifles (Company H, 17th Virginia) a year earlier. Wise's regiment would play a conspicuous part in Longstreet's assault on the afternoon of August 30.

My astonishment at seeing here, a woman, in such a place, can be better imagined, than described. Who the men were, and who the woman was, and what she was doing there, was more than I could understand, until I was now within rifle range. I saw an officer approach them from the direction in which the woman had come.

I was now near enough them to see that the officer had on a suit of "blue," and as I could now make out the same to be the case with the men, I saw that my caution had been unnecessary; so I walked boldly up to them, and there I saw what had been such a mystery to me.

On the ground lay a young man, a rebel, he was wounded. A bullet had passed through his body, close under his heart, and he had lain there on the ground since the day before; unable to help himself, for he was also wounded in his left arm.

The first man had stopped when he came to him; so had the second, and the woman, going round the field, like a good spirit, as she was, looking for wounded men, had come across him, and having her apron full of bandages, was doing what she could toward dressing his wound and easing the severe pain which was raking his body. . . .

Words cannot express the admiration with which I regarded her as she knelt besides this wounded man, utterly regardless of the bullets that had been flying round there, ten minutes before, and might be again at any moment.

Saturday 30th August. The morning broke upon the Confederates brightly, finding them in position of night before. Not a ripple broke the quiet of the dawn & all was still as death. Not a shot. Not a sound broke the stillness of the morning & many thought that the enemy had fallen back. Our Brigade enjoyed corn from the neighboring fields & potatoes & other vegetables in plenty, which was a great treat. Many of the men strayed off a mile in front to gather corn. About noon the sound [of] moving artillery was heard on the enemy's side & clouds of dust arose at several points on their line, showing that a move was going on either forward or backward. We had not long to wait, the sounds came nearer & then a shot & the bursting of a shell gave us notice that our lines were about to be attacked.

This officer's sword and bloodstained sash belonged to Lieutenant Henry C. Arnold of Company K, 1st Michigan Infantry, killed during Porter's attack.

CORPORAL THERON W. HAIGHT

24th New York Infantry, Hatch's Brigade
On August 30, the men of the 24th New York charged forward in the vanguard
of Porter's assault against the Confederate defenders of the unfinished railroad.
The New Yorkers managed to fight their way onto the railroad embankment,
where they battled at point-blank range with Stafford's Louisianans.

Just in front of ourselves was an old-fashioned rail fence, such as I had been familiar with in northern New York. On the other side of the fence was an open field, and beyond that, forty or fifty rods from us, was the railroad embankment, of which I have spoken before, apparently twelve or fifteen feet high, directly in front of the place where I was standing. This grading lay at an angle of forty-five degrees, I should think, from the right of our brigade. Above it, at the rear, was a rather abrupt hill. Between us and the grading were a few dead bodies in blue uniforms, but otherwise there were no signs of war immediately visible. More careful scrutiny, however, revealed things entirely at variance with the first aspect. Along the top of that railroad embankment there was a gleam of musket barrels, as they were aimed towards us and resting upon it. Behind each musket was a slouch wool hat, and a pair of eyes under its brim. That was all we could see of the enemy, but it was enough to afford us reasonably correct information of what we were to encounter. Quick as a flash every one appeared to comprehend what it was necessary for him to do, as well as the general object of the impending charge. The embankment of broken stone and gravel had been reconstructed into a most formidable work of defense by cutting the other side of it down straight for about five feet, leaving a ledge there for standing room, so that those aiming over the top of the grade exposed nothing of their persons below their shoulders. We were to rush across the open field through the fire of the enemy, drive them from their lodgment, and capture the position.

We leaned hard against the fence and pushed it down sufficiently to enable us to jump over, and leaped into the open meadow. For half a mile or more to the left of us a long line of men in blue was marching forward with the same object. Now the bullets began to fly about our ears, and men to pitch forwards or backwards, out of the line, to the earth. Artillery from unseen locations back of the enemy's infantry line opened upon us, and the shouts and yells from both sides were indescribably savage. It seemed like the popular idea of pandemonium made real, and indeed it is scarcely too much to say that we were really

transformed for the time, from a lot of good-natured boys to the most blood-thirsty of demoniacs. Without my being in the least degree conscious of any such thing, the bottom of my haversack had been torn away by a fragment of shell, and a bullet had pierced my canteen, relieving me of the weight of all my provision and drink, and my hat had somehow been knocked off my head on my way from the woods to the railroad grade, while a comrade at my side had been shot through the sole of his foot by a bullet which cut the flesh clear across just above the lower cuticle (a very sensitive place, as everybody knows), and was surprised, after we had reached the embankment, to see blood flowing from the bullet hole in his shoe. . . .

. . . Comparatively few of our number arrived at the embankment—probably not a dozen of my own company. Some of those who had been shot less seriously than the young man of whom I just spoke, were not endowed with his fighting enthusiasm, and had run back to the woods on feeling the sting of bullet or of broken iron. But many, very many, were lying on the ground behind us, dead, or yielding up their young lives with the blood that was oozing from their gaping wounds. Those of us who were on the embankment were too few to even attempt to drive out the troops on the other side of it, and accordingly lay as flat to the slope as we could, crawling occasionally to the top, and discharging our muskets, held horizontally over our heads, in the direction which seemed to afford a chance of hitting somebody on the other side . . . and the din instantly became so infernal that I desisted from the feeble efforts I had been making against the enemy, in order to see what was happening in our rear.

As I looked back, I saw our line making a grand rush in our direction, many of the men holding their arms before their faces, as though to keep off a storm. Bullets were pouring into them from the infantry beyond us, but worst of all, Longstreet's batteries, freshly posted on a rise of ground a mile or so to our left, were enfilading the approaching troops with solid shot, shell, and sections a foot long or more, of railroad iron, which tore up the earth frightfully, and was death to any living thing that they might touch on their passage. Our second line gave way before this terrific storm, and ran back to the cover of the woods, leaving us on the embankment to our fate. As for ourselves, we still kept up the desultory fire that I have described, with no serious effect, I presume, after the brief intermission mentioned. But shortly there came an unlooked-for variation in the proceedings. Huge stones began to fall about us, and now and then one of them would happen to strike one or another of us with very unpleasant effect. By this time all my friends on the rebel work at my side were badly wounded, and I had received a few scratches and bruises for my own part. The enemy kept up the showers of stones, and we were returning the favors to such extent as we were able, and bullets intended for the rebels from our soldiers back in the woods were striking the ground about us, and at least one of them struck a comrade at my elbow, wounding him in the back, and fatally. . . .

It was a puzzle to decide upon any course of action . . . before finally deciding to try running over the embankment in the hope of obtaining a cessation of hostilities at that point, in case of my getting over alive. I was fortunate enough to be permitted to jump down from the top into the rebel line before anybody got a successful shot at me, and made

bold to ask the further favor of being allowed to bring my wounded friends over the work. This request was not granted, and I probably owe my life to the refusal. The stone-throwing ceased there, however, and I helped bandage up the wounded arms of a few of their soldiers who had been retired into the ditch at the foot of the grade. Shortly afterwards an officer seized me by the collar, drew me to my feet, and bade me look at the greatest soldier, he said, that ever lived. It was indeed Stonewall Jackson, who was riding down the line, a stalwart figure, in rusty uniform, his slouch hat in his hand, and accompanied, of course, by a retinue of mounted officers. He was greeted with hearty cheers, but his own aspect was rather pre-occupied, as though he were thinking of something out of the range of present vision.

A stretch of the unfinished railroad called the Deep Cut, seen here in a photograph made 20 years after the battle, provided the Virginians of Colonel Bradley Johnson's brigade a formidable defensive position. Firing from the cover of the improvised entrenchment, Johnson's men devastated Porter's Yankees.

Minutes before he was killed, Colonel Horace Roberts of the 1st Michigan Infantry reminded his men of what "our friends at home expect of us."

Lieutenant James Wheaton, 1st Michigan, was struck in the left eye, leaving a scar that he carried until he was killed in 1864.

it was impossible to miss them. Cicero Kirkland, of my company, who is living today, in his enthusiasm and reckless bravery, mounted on top of our breast-work and poured buck and ball into them as fast as some of the boys could load and hand him a musket. I expected to see him shot down every second. The Louisianians ceased firing and threw cobble stones over the embankment at them. I saw them going over lighting upon the heads of the Yankees just as thick as I ever saw corn go into a pen at an old time "corn shucking." It was more like that than anything that I can compare it to. . . .

What a slaughter! what a slaughter of men that was. At first bombshells, shrapnel shells, then grapeshot, and as they came nearer canister was poured at them which mowed them down, but still those that lived would close the ranks and press forward.

PRIVATE WILLIAM A. MCLENDON

15th Alabama Infantry, Trimble's Brigade
Captain W. F. Brown's units were posted along the unfinished railroad just to the north of the hundred-yard gap known as the Dump. William McLendon and his comrades in the 15th Alabama volleyed into the front and flanks of the Yankee columns, but despite terrible losses the Federal soldiers kept coming.

When I reached the embankment I just naturally fell over among our men and about faced. "Look out boys, they are coming, lots of 'em." The boys were ready, but by some cause unknown to me they failed to attack all the front of the 15th Alabama, but seemed to have divided, a part obliqueing to the left and a part to the right. That which went to the left could not be seen, but on the right they were in an old field in plain view, and the whole of the 15th Alabama got in some deadly work at a right oblique. They just simply jammed up against the embankment, opposite the right of the 15th Alabama and one of the Louisiana regiments. They were so thick that

Private Boling Williams of the 2d Louisiana was among the troops defending the Dump. When their ammunition ran out, they began heaving rocks, eventually beating back the Union assault. Williams was wounded during the action.

LIEUTENANT STEPHEN M. WELD

Staff, Major General
Fitz-John Porter
Weld, a 20-year-old Harvard
graduate, left law school to join
the 18th Massachusetts. Serving
on General Fitz-John Porter's
staff, Weld was captured at the
Battle of Gaines' Mill, spent a
month in prison, and was ex-
changed in early August. His
diary entry refers to the sketch he
made at Manassas (below).

In regard to my being rash in going out so far that day, I wish to say a few words. I have always made it my intention to do everything the general has told me to do, and not come back and tell him that I could not find any one I was sent for or do anything I was sent to do. So this time I did not want to come back and tell him that I could not find the rear guard. The position of some of our troops and of the enemies' batteries confused me, and made me go out too far.

I will try and give you the position of our forces on the 2nd Bull Run field. *A* was where the enemy had a battery placed during the day, that fired at us and finally withdrew, leaving only two pieces there. We advanced from the hills, *B*, and went across the plain into the woods *A'*. The enemy had a strong force in the woods *C*, and in the railroad gap in which they were posted. We tried to advance from the woods *A'* across to *C*, and were repulsed by a terrible fire of grape, canister and musketry which mowed down the men like sheep. They had their batteries posted along the edge of woods *C*, and got a cross fire on us. The railroad gap served as a breastwork for them.

Major General Fitz-John Porter, who
directed the final Federal attack, was
courtmartialed after the Battle of Sec-
ond Manassas, when Pope made him
the principal scapegoat for the defeat.

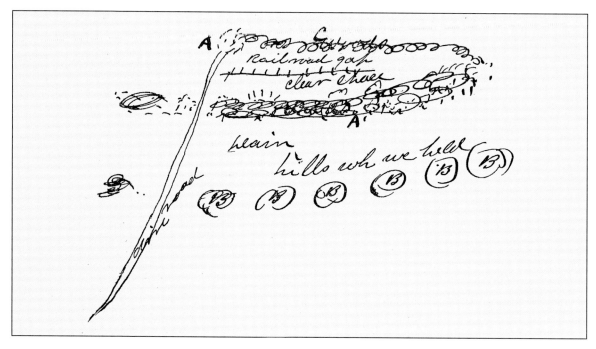

In a letter to his father written a day after the battle, General Porter's aide, Lieutenant Stephen Weld, sketched his perspective of the V Corps assault against Stonewall Jackson's line.

Federal soldiers load and fire furiously, trying to contain the surging Confederate line just visible in the distance. The repulse of Fitz-John Porter's attack left the Federal troops wallowing in confusion and ripe for General Longstreet's massive counterstrike.

CAPTAIN JOHN W. AMES

11th U.S. Infantry, Chapman's Brigade
When the Federal assault of Fitz-John Porter collapsed north of the Warrenton Turnpike, the First Battalion of the 11th U.S. Infantry came up from a reserve position to cover the withdrawal of Porter's troops. Captain Ames served until the war's end, becoming colonel of the 6th U.S. Colored Infantry.

The wounded came streaming past us—all very jolly and full of enthusiasm. "Look at that," said an officer, holding up an arm which showed a clean bullethole through it; "that's good for thirty days! just the prettiest little wound a man could ask for. I wouldn't take a hundred dollars for it." And our own officers looked envious, and called him "mighty lucky." Then came a fellow with a very slight hurt, but with the bloodiest face imaginable, who mopped away at the crimson gush, saying, "Whaled 'em like h——, boys; no show for you to-day." They were all merry at first as they came limping by, swearing very cheerfully and heartily, and quite sure it was all up with the "Johnnies." But as the crowds multiplied, it began to look more dubious; and when I saw the well-known broken squads of un-hurt men, I knew the Johnnies had not been dislodged.

PRIVATE ALFRED DAVENPORT

5th New York Infantry, Warren's Brigade

Davenport, a 25-year-old Zouave in Company G of the 5th New York, served in every battle of the colorful unit's two-year term of service. His dramatic account of the Zouaves' doomed stand south of the Warrenton pike on August 30 appeared in one of his wartime letters, which he later used in writing a regimental history.

It was not long before a Company of the skirmishers came in on our left all much excited, huddled together in a heap & much scared & said that the Enemy were coming on & were right on top of us, on the left flank, but before any orders could be given to change position, the balls began to fly from the woods like hail. It was a continual hiss, snap, whizz & slug.

Pvt. Brady who used to live opposite us in Lexington Ave. in the wooden house, was the first one hit—he stood a few files from me. He fell without saying a word, struck in the body. He was dragged a few paces to the rear to be out of our way by our Lieut., when he undid his body belt himself. He died there. On account of part of the 10th being drawn up in the woods in front of our right wing only the companies on the left could fire. We commenced, but the Rebel's fire was now murderous, our men falling on all sides. The 10th had already broken & were flying to the rear. We had not fired more than two rounds, before they were on us in front & flank, their object being to surround us.

The order had been given to retreat—& save ourselves, every man for himself, but we did not hear the order. The recruits began to give way & then the whole Regmt. broke & ran for their lives. The Rebels after us with their yells, meant to represent an Indian war whoop. They

Struck in front and flank by Hood's Texas Brigade, and caught in a deadly cross fire, the 5th New York Zouaves were able to unleash only two or three volleys before being overrun by Longstreet's onslaught. Artist Alfred Waud sketched the moment when the decimated regiment began to break for the rear.

Sergeant George W. Wannemacher (left) of Company C, 5th New York, was a 21-year-old Philadelphia native who left college to sign up with the Zouaves. At the Second Manassas he was shot through both arms and the left hand, but he recovered from his injuries and went on to finish the war as a lieutenant.

"The balls began to fly from the woods like hail. It was a continual hiss, snap, whizz & slug."

were Mississippi & Texan Riflemen & were six to one of us, they were in their shirt-sleeves & came charging on, yelling for Jeff Davis & the Confederacy, there was no hope but in flight—of saving a man, all the time they were pouring in their deadly shots at short range picking out their men. The battery we were supporting got off safe, leaving Capt. Smead, its commander & one of our best artillery officers, a graduate of West Point, dead on the field. Col. Warren, & Capt. Winslow, who was acting in command of Regmt., being mounted got off safe, but it is a miracle.

While running down the hill towards the small stream at its foot, I saw the men dropping on all sides, canteens struck & flying to pieces, haversacks cut off, rifles knocked to pieces, it was a perfect hail of bullets—I was expecting to get it every second, but on, on, I went, the balls hissing by my head. I felt one strike me on the hip, just grazing me & only cutting a hole in my pants. I crossed the Run in the wake of Warren, he being about 100 yards ahead of me, with his red cap in his hand, his horse running at the top of his speed. I turned around to look behind once & only once, that was enough to let me know, there was not time to stop. I saw two or three Rebel officers, on horseback, their swords drawn & waving their men on. It occurred to me to turn & fire on them, but as quickly decided that it was folly, as I could not stop long enough to take any kind of aim, & I would become a mark for a score of rifles, so I kept on.

SERGEANT THOMAS C. ALBERGOTTI

Hampton (South Carolina) Legion, Hood's Brigade
Attached to the famed Texas Brigade, the Hampton Legion of South Carolina participated in the destruction of Colonel Warren's units. Albergotti (who mistakenly refers to Young's Branch as Bull Run in his account) had enlisted at Charleston in June 1861. He spent much of his last year of service in a Richmond hospital being treated for dysentery.

The Yanks were in a piece of pine woods. Our skirmishes were forced forward as far as they could go and brought to a standstill. General Hood passed word down the line when he gave the order to charge, he wanted the whole line to charge, and the Yanks heard the order to charge, but I think misunderstood it, thinking the order was for the skirmishes to charge, instead the whole line charged and we ran right on top of them, and we there met the Red Britches Zouaves, and had a hand to hand fight, shooting them down at the point of the gun. They retreated across Bull Run, a small stream, and that was just full of dead and dying Yankee soldiers. It was pitiful to hear the poor devils crying from pain and drowning, leg, arm, and some mortally wounded and unable to get out; terrible, terrible, to be placed in this predicament. Just as I ascended the Hill on the other side of the Run, I was shot in the face just below my nose on the right side. Fortunately, it did not penetrate very deep. The ball glanced from the cheek bone, knocked me down, however, and bled a great deal.

This battle flag was issued to the 18th Georgia of Hood's brigade in the early summer of 1862. It is said that the lock of hair attached to the top edge of the banner was taken from a New York Zouave slain in the rout of Warren's brigade.

PRIVATE ANDREW COATS

5th New York Infantry, Warren's Brigade

Born in Glasgow, Scotland, in 1840, Andrew Coats was working as an orderly at Saint Luke's Hospital in New York City when the war broke out. He was among 330 casualties the 5th New York sustained on August 30. Struck in the right shoulder and left leg, Coats eventually returned to duty and attained the rank of Brevet Major.

As soon as the skirmish line of the Tenth came rushing through our ranks the enemy's line of battle had reached the edge of the woods, where they halted and began pouring in a withering fire upon us. For a short time the Regiment tried to fight back the overwhelming force that was pouring in a fearful stream of destruction and death upon it, but the stream became a torrent, as the right and left flanks of the enemy almost surrounded us. War has been designated as Hell, and I can assure you that where the Regiment stood that day was the very vortex of Hell. Not only were men wounded, or killed, but they were riddled.

Brothers Rufus (left) and Miers Felder fought at Manassas with the 5th Texas Infantry, on the right of Hood's brigade during the attack. Miers was wounded and later discharged, but Rufus soldiered on until Appomattox.

The colorful garb of the 5th New York (right) was modeled on the Zouave uniform worn by French colonial troops. The short, collarless jacket and baggy trousers were designed to permit freedom of movement.

CORPORAL JOSEPH B. POLLEY

4th Texas Infantry, Hood's Brigade
Slightly wounded at the Battle of Gaines' Mill in June 1862, Joseph Polley recovered in time to join Hood's assault on August 30. A more serious wound during the siege of Petersburg in 1864 required the amputation of his right foot. In later years Polley served in the Texas legislature.

Looking up the hill, a strange and ghastly spectacle met our eyes. An acre of ground was literally covered with the dead, dying, and wounded of the Fifth New York Zouaves, the variegated colors of whose peculiar uniform gave the scene the appearance of a Texas hillside in spring, painted with wild flowers of every hue and color. Not fifty of the Zouaves escaped whole. . . .

The Zouaves, it seems, were posted just under the crest of a hill, and a hundred feet from the edge of the timber, and fired the moment the heads of the Texans showed above the crest. Of course they aimed too high, and before they could reload the Texans poured such a well-directed and deadly volley into their closely formed ranks that half of them sank to the ground, and the balance wheeled and ran. Not waiting to reload, the Texans rushed after the fugitives, and, clubbing their muskets, continued the work of destruction until every enemy in sight was left prone upon the ground. Then, as General Hood said, the Fifth Texas "slipped its bridle and went wild." Had they not been recalled, they would have gone right on to the Potomac.

Graduating second in the West Point class of 1850, Gouverneur Kemble Warren went to war as second in command of the 5th New York Zouaves. Promoted to colonel and placed in command of a brigade composed of the 5th and 10th New York, Warren made a valiant but futile stand against Longstreet's assault at Manassas. Elevated to the rank of general, he distinguished himself at Gettysburg and commanded the V Corps in the last year of fighting.

SERGEANT WILLIAM E. DOUGHERTY

First U.S. Infantry, Chapman's Brigade
Irish-born William Dougherty, among the Regular Army troops shifted south to counter the Confederate onslaught, encountered the pitiful band of survivors of the once proud 5th New York Infantry. More than half of the regiment was left behind, dead, wounded, or captured.

Warren sat immobile on his horse, looking back at the battle as if paralyzed, while his handful of men, formed in files of four, blackened with dust and smoke, stood under the colors silent as statues, gazing vacantly at the tumultuous concourse trudging by. A murmur of surprise and horror passed through the ranks of our Regulars at the fate of this brave regiment, for they had a special fondness for the Zouaves on account of their superior discipline and bravery, and they had fought side by side since the siege of Yorktown.

Federal Collapse

On the afternoon of August 30, Longstreet's juggernaut rolled up the Federal left flank, crushing all resistance in its path. As it approached Chinn Ridge, the Rebel spearhead encountered a single brigade—Ohio men under Colonel Nathaniel C. McLean. The colonel had only four regiments—some 1,200 men—but he was determined to buy enough time for Pope to respond to the emergency. McLean's men made a valiant stand, staving off the attack by the Texas Brigade and Brigadier General Nathan "Shanks" Evans' South Carolinians for a crucial half hour.

In that precious 30 minutes, General McDowell was able to rush the brigades of Brigadier General Zealous B. Tower and Colonel John W. Stiles across the Warrenton Turnpike and onto Chinn Ridge. Tower arrived first, just as McLean's men were finally collapsing in the face of Brigadier General James L. Kemper's division, which had wheeled north and was sweeping past the Chinn house. Tower's regiments came into line beside the guns of the 5th Maine Battery and opened a heavy fire on the Southern masses. But with Colonel Montgomery D. Corse's brigade in the lead, Kemper's troops linked up with Hood's battered brigades and fought their way through Tower's line, overrunning the Maine battery. Stiles' brigade came to Tower's support but was struck on the left flank by two more of Kemper's brigades and began to give way in turn.

General Pope, who had at last realized the extent of the disaster to his left, ordered McDowell to continue shuffling units to shore up the collapsing left flank. Meanwhile Pope would try to patch together a defensive position atop Henry Hill, some three quarters of a mile east of Chinn Ridge. If the new line could hold until dark, Pope would stand a good chance of avoiding the total destruction of his force. In a last effort to hold onto the strategic crest of Chinn Ridge, two of Sigel's brigades were shifted from Dogan Ridge and thrown into the fray south of the Warrenton pike.

Had Jackson sallied forth from his line on Stony Ridge, Sigel would not have been able to carry out this maneuver. But Jackson was slow to commit his decimated units to support Longstreet's great offensive. Sigel's troops pushed onto Chinn Ridge through a hail of artillery fire that killed the commander of the leading Federal brigade, Colonel John A. Koltes, and tore gaps through the blue-clad ranks. But the Yankee reinforcements halted the Southern advance only briefly, until yet another of Longstreet's divisions—Major General David R. Jones'—further extended the Southern line. Again the Federals were flanked on their left, and this time there would be no stopping the Rebel juggernaut.

By 6:00 p.m., as still more of Longstreet's brigades swung into action against the Yankee line, the defenders of Chinn Ridge were at last compelled to yield. With their formations shattered, thousands of soldiers streamed eastward in chaotic retreat.

Pope's left wing had been crushed, and only Jackson's reluctance to press the Union right enabled the Federal commander to stave off total disaster. Free to shift still more troops to the left, Pope and McDowell patched together an improvised line on the formidable crest of Henry Hill. There, for the next two hours, the divisions of Reynolds and Sykes, along with Milroy's and Schurz's brigades, joined fragments of the decimated left wing in repulsing a series of disjointed Confederate attacks. The sunken bed of the Manassas-Sudley road at the bottom of the slope provided a measure of protection for the Federal defenders, while reserves and artillery batteries blazed away from the crest. Neither Jones' nor R. H. Anderson's divisions were able to penetrate the stubborn Yankee line, and as darkness settled over the battlefield Pope began withdrawing his defeated army toward the banks of Bull Run.

At 7:00 p.m. the Federals were finally yielding the southern portion of Henry Hill. But Lee's last chance to destroy Pope's army had passed. Jackson had finally begun moving four brigades against the retreating Union right, but the Federal troops north of the Warrenton pike still preserved good order, and Jackson's advance was tentative at best. A greater threat to Pope's line of retreat came when Southern cavalry led by General Robertson fought their way through Buford's Yankee horsemen guarding the southernmost portion of the Union line.

Buford's stiff resistance intimidated Robertson, however, and the Rebel troopers failed to continue their advance into the rear of Pope's army and to the crossings of Bull Run. In a retreat depressingly reminiscent of the Battle of First Manassas a year earlier, the beaten Union forces disengaged and retired across the creek to take up a new defensive position at Centreville. As the survivors of Pope's debacle shuffled onto the heights of Centreville, they were jeered by the men of Major General William B. Franklin's Sixth Corps, whose tardy arrival bore witness to McClellan's unwillingness to hasten Army of the Potomac forces to the front. At that moment Lee was sending glorious news to Richmond—that the Army of Northern Virginia had won a "signal victory" on the plains of Manassas.

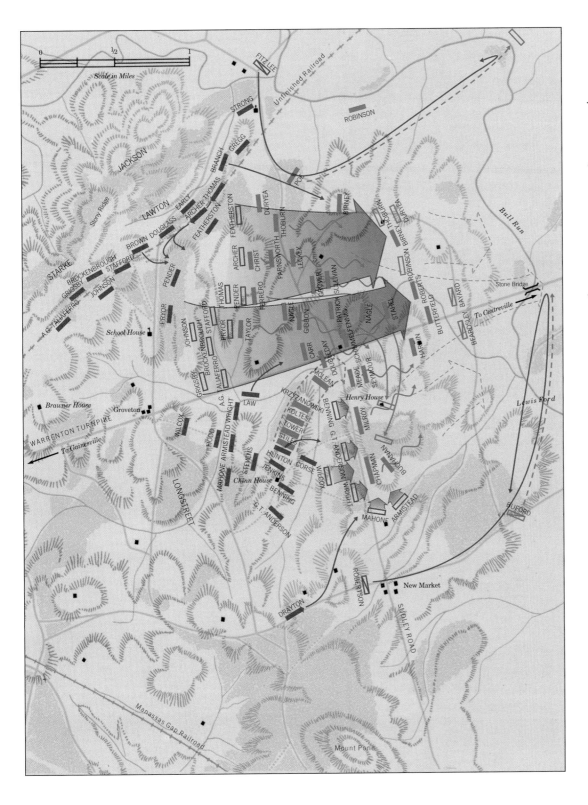

Shortly after 5:00 p.m. on the 30th, most of Longstreet's corps hurled itself against the weak Federal line that had been hastily formed on Chinn Ridge. Despite a dogged Federal defense, the Confederates captured the ridge in less than an hour. At about 6:00 p.m., Jackson's troops attacked the center and right of Pope's line. Federal troops on Pope's left began withdrawing toward the Warrenton Turnpike, while a stubborn rearguard action by a few Federal units along the Manassas-Sudley road and on Henry Hill held the Confederates at bay. Confederate cavalry managed to get around the Federal flanks, but exhaustion and the onset of darkness finally stalled the Rebel advance. As night fell, Pope's army made an orderly retreat. By midnight all but a few stragglers had crossed Bull Run. The Federals destroyed the bridge and fell back into the defenses around Centreville.

PRIVATE SAMUEL C. LOWRY

17th South Carolina Infantry, Stevens' Brigade
Wounded on the last day of fighting at Manassas, Lowry was discharged as underage in December 1862 and joined a cadet corps in South Carolina until he was old enough to return to his regiment in January 1864. Commissioned a lieutenant that summer, he was killed at Petersburg on July 30.

On entering a little clump of black-jacks, grape, canister, shrapnel, fairly rattled amid the trees. Here we lost very heavily, the man by my side was killed dead on the spot; our gallant Colonel, Ex-Gov. Means, fell pierced with a ball through the breast while gallantly cheering us on. It seemed strange how a man could escape, still we pressed resolutely on, and, on clearing the woods at Mrs. Chinn's house, we came in full sight of the enemy drawn up in good line . . . with a shout that sounded loud above the cannons roar, we charged forward on the run, firing and loading as fast as possible. The Yankees did not await to lock bayonets with us, but turned and fled precipitently, still keeping up a desultory fire. While giving our whole attention to the fleeing foe, a regiment of Yankees suddenly drew up in line, in a few yards from us on our left, and poured in a destructive fire. And now my turn came, for it was here, while busy loading my rifle, that a ball from the enemy came whizzing through my thigh. My first thought was to look at it, but there was so much blood on my leg that I could not distinguish the wound. The balls continued to fly around me, knocking up the dirt all around me, and I was in eminent danger of getting another one. I got up and found I could walk a little, and hobbled about five steps back and lay down (Hors de Combat). The battle continued with unabated fury, grape shells, shot, and Minnie Balls were plowing the air around me, and at that time I was suffering acute pain from my leg. My leg seemed to be numbed all over. Still, with a dull kind of pain thrilling through it. Several other wounded were lying near me. It was while lying here that someone came and lay down beside me saying, "We are friends now if we have been enemies." I did not understand him, in fact, I did not take any notice of him, but I saw he had on a Yankee uniform, which a great many of our men wore, and I supposed him one of our men. I lay still sometime without speaking to him, examining my leg, but having

Colonel John H. Means (left), commander of the 17th South Carolina Infantry, was wounded as he led his men toward the Chinn house in the wake of the Texas Brigade. The 50-year-old former governor of South Carolina died two days later, one of 189 casualties suffered by his regiment. Means' death was, reported his successor, "lamented not only by every man in his command, but by every good citizen of South Carolina."

finished I asked him to what regiment he belonged. He replied, "I belong to the 24th Ohio." You are a Yankee then, says I. "Yes," he replied, "but I am tired of this D——d War, and won't fight any-more." I told him I would not trust a Yankee no further than I could see, and demanded his gun, which he complacently delivered, re-marking, "It is loaded." I turned him over to our soldiers on their return. I lay here where I was wounded until the battle ended.

PRIVATE WESTWOOD A. TODD

12th Virginia Infantry, Mahone's Brigade
Private Westwood Todd and his fellow veterans of William Mahone's brigade crossed the blood-soaked ground below Chinn Ridge where Hood's Texans had encountered the 5th New York. Todd was wounded in the left hand later in the day. In July 1863 he was transferred to the army's ordnance department.

The line was moving forward in beautiful order when we were suddenly marched by the right flank and carried over to the right wing commanded by Longstreet. We were again formed in line of battle and went forward. We soon came upon one of the most interesting and stirring scenes of war. A Texas Brigade had just charged a line of Federals uniformed as Zouaves—red skull cap, blue jackets and red breeches with white gaiters. Those red clothes must have inflamed the Texans, as the red flag is said to inflame the wild bull, for I never but once during the war (Mayre's Hill) saw such slaughter as we witnessed while advancing over this ground. From the line of battle where the Texans first struck them, all along the grassy slope down which they were driven, these red-breeched troops lay scat-tered in every direction. A little further on we saw the Texans who had stopped the pursuit. They were in high spirits, and cheered us as we swept rapidly on. Their loss had been slight, but they had gotten into great disorder in the chase. I remember seeing all their battle flags in a huddle. About this time a very excited individual made his appearance on horseback. He looked like an old farmer. He was in his shirt sleeves, and had on a beaver hat. He was throwing his arms about wildly, and he hallooed to us, "Go on, my boys, and you'll end this war. The Yankees are running like hell." I never exactly understood what that old cock was doing there, for it was an "unhealthy" latitude for a peaceful citizen.

Artist Edwin Forbes made this sketch from a vantage point near the northern end of Henry Hill on the afternoon of August 30, just as Longstreet's Confederates began their attack on the Federal left flank. The artist showed McDowell's columns (9) moving along the Manassas–Sudley road (10) past the Stone House toward the Federal left. In the center, the massed troops of Pope's battle line (8) maneuver on the east side of Dogan Ridge, while on the left, dense smoke still rises from Porter's clash with Jackson's line (2).

PRIVATE ALEXANDER HUNTER

17th Virginia Infantry, Corse's Brigade
Montgomery Corse's Virginia brigade, along with the rest of Kemper's Con-
federate division, struck northward up Chinn Ridge. Private Hunter and his
comrades were stalled for a time by Federal reinforcements sent in to hold the
ridge. Soon, however, the Confederate attackers overwhelmed McDowell's
hastily organized Federal defense.

Seeing right in front of me two or three large brigades advancing with cheers, their burnished arms glittering in the sun, their stars and stripes fluttering in the breeze, and their line superbly dressed—I could not resist an involuntary cry of admiration—even tho enemies. Yet their martial appearance was truly terrific. At their front were the drummers beating the pas-de-charge, the first, and the last time I ever heard the inspiring roll on the battlefield. I began to think that it was time for me to get away from there—and I was just turning around when right behind me I heard a shout—a savage yell, from hundreds of throats—and turning I saw a brigade in gray coming in a terrific pace, their line irregular and broken—the red cross shaking to and fro. Forming with them I kept on at the top of my speed—and the two opposing forces met in full career. A heavy volley on one side —accompanied by a hearty hurrah—a scream of rage—with the dropping fire on the other. We got within ten yards of them—and they broke—and in a second they were running without order or form for the rear. Their guns were thrown away. They would unstrap their knapsacks as they ran—their hats would fly off—but nothing stopped them. The Brigade did not suffer much—the balls generally flew over our heads—but it seemed as if every shot told. The progress of their flight could be traced by the blue uniforms. . . .

I fired until my shoulder was sore—and had just rammed home my last cartridge when a hearty cheer and the many tramping of feet was heard behind us. And a brigade—or a division, I could not see which—

Colonel Orlando Smith's 73d Ohio, shown here parading behind their band in
the streets of Chillicothe, Ohio, early in 1862, served in McLean's brigade, part
of Brigadier General Robert C. Schenck's division. Nearly half of the 312 men
that the 73d took into action on Chinn Ridge became casualties.

advanced to our relief. In a second we were on our feet and going with them—kept on with a real rebel cheer. A hasty volley met us—the enemy broke and ran—we after them firing as we ran. Grasping a gun and accoutrements that lay near, my gun being too hot for use, and ammunition expended, I followed. And the excitement was now so intense that I am in the dark as to what happened next. The first definite thing that I remember was lying behind a small group of trees in company with eight or twelve men—nearly all from different regiments. I heard a childish voice say, "Boys, if you say so, I'll take command of this squad." Looking up I perceived a boy—for assuredly he was not a man—with his beardless cheek and fresh rosy face—with the two bars of a lieutenant on his jacket collar. "What regiment are you?" "—— Georgia," I did not catch the number. "But look, here comes a whole regiment;" sure enough some six hundred yards in front of us was a whole regiment of Federals—marching directly towards us. I look behind—I could not see any other troops. I called out, "Lieutenant, we will have to fight! We can't run." "I don't intend to" was his reply. He ordered the men to bring in plenty of spare rifles, to load them, and keep them by our sides. As the place we were had, during the evening, been the scene of the fiercest carnage, hundreds of guns lay scattered about—and soon each man had nearly a dozen muskets, all loaded and cocked, lying beside him. By this time the enemy were not a hundred yards off—"Steady men" cried the gallant Georgian—"Don't fire yet— and when you do, every man fire at the colors." We had not long to wait—and simultaneously a dozen rifles cracked—and the colors fell.

"Hurrah!" cried our improvised commander. "Keep cool—don't get flurried boys—Gently! Gently—lie close." A perfect storm of bullets whistled over us—and tore up the ground in every direction, causing the dust to rain like little miniature bullets, but we were in a small hollow—the ground dipped some three or four feet—and we were so safe from minnie bullets as if we were in the most elaborate bomb proof. A second time—resting our guns on the earth—we all took careful aim at the colors—fired—and a second time they fell. Another volley hurtled harmlessly by. Throwing on one side our discharged guns, we grasped the loaded ones and returned the volley. A third time their flag came down—they now advanced at a charge. The sight was a bad one for us—several turned to leave—but the gallant boy placing himself in full view of the enemy, and waving his sword around his head—burst in a hurrah. The contagion was infectious—turning around he exclaimed, "Men—for the honor of your states—Don't run—keep cool—and try again. Don't run—be men—and another volley for the Sunny South."

"I beheld a sight which I can never forget—it is daguerreotyped indelibly on my memory. I saw the grand final charge of all our reserves . . . with heart-exulting cheers they dashed forward at a run."

There was fire in every eye as they discharged their pieces. The colors fell—on came the enemy—again we fired at pistol range, aiming at the color guard—and the *fifth time* it was grounded. We turned then to run—but what was our astonishment to see the regiment right about-face, and leisurely retire. A cheer of exultation burst simultaneously from each soldier's lips as they beheld that proud evidence of their prowess. The young Georgian turning said, "Boys—this is an event which you ought to be proud of all your life—but it is a needless sacrifice of life for us to stay here. Let's go back."

We accordingly started. The battle in the various portions of the field was still being fought—all around the flash of the cannon could be seen—and the awful thunder of the guns and still more horrible rattling of the small arms. Where we were it was strangely quiet. We fell in soon with a battalion of our troops who had halted out of reach of the fire to get fresh ammunition. I was painfully reminded though of the long range of the new rifles by a ball tearing two holes through my jacket, and just grazing the bone of the elbow. I took off my jacket and rolling up the sleeve, with an averted eye, expecting to behold the mangled remains of a stump—imagine my surprise—I may say too mortification—when I perceived only a crease of the passage of the bullet—it going no deeper than just breaking the skin.

. . . It was now evening—the sun had set—but the shades of night had not yet fallen, when I arrived at the top of the hill where the Washington Artillery had been posted in the early part of the day. From here I had a good view of the surrounding country, and at this moment I beheld a sight which I can never forget—it is daguerreotyped indelibly on my memory.

I saw the grand final charge of all our reserves, numbering many thousands [of] men, as with heart-exulting cheers they dashed forward at a run. It was a glorious sight, and one that repaid me for all the hardships that I had heretofore endured. On they dashed, passing on their way many wearied & cut up regiments who were returning slowly to the rear, but the contagion was infectious—grasping their muskets with a firmer grip—and in their noble excitement forgetting their wounds and weariness, the gallant men turned about—and swept onward with them. I was carried away like the rest & kept on, every step we took our line was augmented, until it was an army flushed with victory, not reserves hurrying to retrieve some disaster.

Leading his men, Lieutenant Colonel Frederick G. Skinner (above) of the 1st Virginia spurred his horse into the guns of the 5th Maine Battery on Chinn Ridge. Striking out with his sword, Skinner routed a gun crew before he fell severely wounded. His French heavy cavalry saber (below) had been presented to him by the Marquis de Lafayette for his support of the 1830 Paris revolt.

LIEUTENANT WILLIAM J. RANNELLS

75th Ohio Infantry, N. C. McLean's Brigade

In the cauldron of Chinn Ridge, Lieutenant Colonel Joseph McLean, commander of the 88th Pennsylvania, was knocked off his horse by a bullet. Rannells, whose 75th Ohio was retreating under withering fire, went to help the wounded officer. Rannells was captured trying to assist McLean from the field; later he took upon himself the mournful duty of informing McLean's widow of his death.

Lieutenant Colonel Joseph A. McLean, dubbed Uncle Joe by his men in the 88th Pennsylvania Infantry, wrote to his wife on August 22, asking her to "kiss the little ones for me, and assure yourself I will do all I can to save myself consistent with honor." On August 30 he was mortally wounded and died on the field. His body was never recovered.

I have just arrived home from Richmond. I was taken prisoner while attending to your dear husband's wounds, it is my painful duty to inform you dear madam that your Husband is dead. He fell near me while doing all that a brave man could do to hold his men to the support of a battery. He fell from his horse, his foot fasting in the stirrups, his horse was about to run with him in this condition, but I caught him and took his foot out of the stirrup laid him on the ground. I found him to be severely wounded high up on the thigh, the ball rupturing the main artery. With a strap the Lt. Col. gave me I succeeded in stopping the hemorrhage of the wound. with the assistance of three of the 88th men, we was about to carry him to the hospital, when the Col. saw the charging foe. he said, "Boys, drop me and save yourselves for I must die. the three men became excited and let him fall and ran. this caused the strap to slip below the wound. it commenced to bleed as freely as ever. I again placed the strap above the wound, and was in the act of tightening it when I looked behind me I found the rebels had charged past our battery and were within two rods of us. these passed over us without noticing me, [perhaps] taking me for a surgeon. they fought over us for about 15 minutes, in which time your husband was wounded again in the same leg below the knee. They would not help me take him to some surgeon, they made me leave him, when he said "tell my wife she will never blush to be my widow. I die for my country and the old flag." One of my [men] was detailed to bury the dead, and he reported having buried a Liet. Col. J. A. McLean of the 88th P.V. this convinces me that your husband is dead. I sympathize deeply with you in your loss, and hope God! will bless you and aid you in raising your little ones.

The flag of the 12th Massachusetts Infantry (left) was a gift to the regiment in 1861 from the Ladies of Boston. After the regiment's commander, Colonel Fletcher Webster, was killed at Second Manassas, the flag was presented to his widow.

COLONEL FLETCHER WEBSTER

12th Massachusetts Infantry, Stiles' Brigade
Rushed to the northern end of Chinn Ridge in a vain attempt to stem the Rebel tide, Stiles' brigade was soon overwhelmed by the charging Confederate infantry. Colonel Webster was fatally wounded. He had penned a last letter to his wife on the morning of the battle.

We got here last night—to-day a great and decisive battle is expected—Forrester Devereaux has just called & here sits by me, on the grass under a tree while I write. He was again in action the day before yesterday & has lost nearly all his company. He is unhurt. If a fight comes off, it will be to-day or to-morrow & will be a most dreadful & decisive one. Both sides are preparing, some three hundred thousand men are on the eve of conflict & Washington depends upon the issue. This may be my last letter, dear love; for I shall not spare myself—God bless and protect you & the dear, darling children. We are all under his protection.

Love to 'Don' & Charlie. I have not means to write more. You must show this letter to the girls with my love.

Good bye, my own dear wife, darling Carry. Love to Bertie & dear Kori. I hope to have many a good gallop with them on nice horses. Bye bye dearest.

Yours
Fletcher

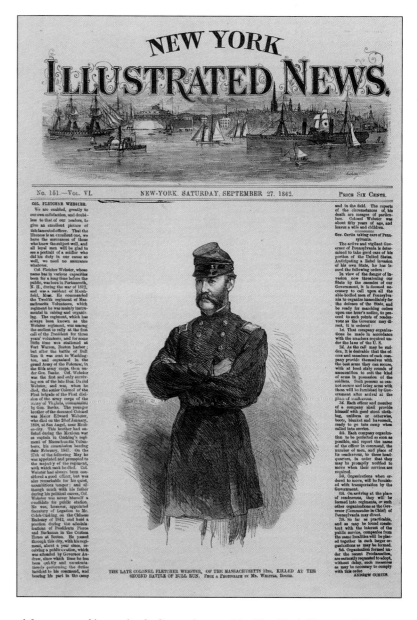

A front-page obituary in the September 27, 1862, New York Illustrated News mourns the death of Colonel Fletcher Webster, only son of Daniel Webster of Massachusetts. Webster was struck in the arm and chest by a bullet as he rode behind the faltering line of the 12th Massachusetts. Captured, he died shortly afterward. Two days later, friends found his body on the field, stripped of everything but vest and underclothing. Between the vest buttons they also found a card on which Webster had scrawled his name as he waited for death.

PRIVATE AUSTIN C. STEARNS

13th Massachusetts Infantry, Stiles' Brigade

Austin Stearns, a boot maker from Hopkinton, Massachusetts, enlisted in the 13th Massachusetts in July 1861. Promoted to corporal after Second Manassas, Stearns mustered out with the rank of sergeant in the summer of 1864. He vividly recalled the disaster that overtook his regiment on Chinn Ridge.

Everything to our hasty glance seemed in confusion. Batteries were going at a breakneck speed and taking positions farther in the rear, and the infantry was moving in all direction. Wounded men were everywhere; some were being helped away, others were striving with all their strength to get away to a safe distance. A wounded man begged piteously for us to take him to the rear; he was wounded in the neck, or head, and the blood flowed freely; everytime he tried to speak the blood would fill his mouth and he would blow it out in all directions; he was all blood, and at the time I thought he was the most dreadfull sight I ever saw. We could not help him, for it was of no use, for he could not live long by the way he was bleeding, so we turned away, and went over a hill where there was a stone house. . . .

We went along not entirely alone, for there was a goodly number of soldiers to keep us company, not going in the same direction however, but all having the same object in view, viz, to get out of the range of the shells. I have no idea how far we went, but should think it was more than a mile and perhaps two, when we came to a road, and such a sight as we saw there I shall never forget, for there, regardless of any order, or organization, but going pell mell, as fast as they could possibly go, were all branches of the service in inextricable confusion, intent only upon one object, and that was to get to the rear.

Their position on Chinn Ridge having collapsed, Federal soldiers flee in panic past one of their own batteries, ignoring the entreaties of a mounted officer. "You can imagine my feelings at this moment," wrote one Federal officer. "Mortification, shame, and indignation were all commingled."

CAPTAIN JOHN W. AMES

11th U.S. Infantry, Chapman's Brigade
Realizing that a firm stand was vital to the survival of his army, Pope rushed reinforcements, including the U.S. Regulars of Colonel Samuel Chapman's brigade, to the crest of Henry Hill. Ames was breveted for gallantry and meritorious service first at Gaines' Mill and later at Gettysburg.

On we went over hill and hollow, running till we panted like dogs, and I thought we should all fall from sheer exhaustion. Stumbling over the remnants of a fence, we found ourselves, finally, in a country lane, and almost as soon as we struck it we came to a halt. There was a partial lull in the firing, just then. For a few minutes, we seemed to have found a quiet retreat in that lane. Good luck or skill had taken us into a first-rate position for defense; and the lull gave time to dress our line back to the road-side. Somehow, too, the run had cheered us up: in spite of the look of utter defeat the whole field had worn, we all now seemed to feel the contagion of confidence. Our fear had all gone; we examined our musket-locks; shoved cartridge-boxes round to the front of our belts, and picked out such slim shelter as the shallow little roadside ditch could afford. The lull didn't fool us a bit, though: we knew it was coming harder than ever, in a minute. Half a dozen brass Napoleon guns came up behind us and took position on the slight rise of ground there—I am afraid to say how slight or how near; positively, we could look right into their open mouths!

There was only a minute or two of silence, in which we stood expectant, and looked across the road into the pinewoods in front. A rattling crash of musketry—a screaming yell of men—the tramp of advancing lines coming through the woods! Then the Napoleons opened; and we opened too—the first shot we had fired that day. And we must have opened to some purpose—made it lively for the John-nies, I guess—for they never reached the fence in front. At any rate, I saw but one all the rest of the day—a big fellow, in full gray to the blanket—who climbed to the top of the fence and sat there, straddle, swaying back and forth, till he fell heavily inside.

But, oh! the brass guns behind us! How the gunners did dance with excitement and delight, as they poured in their fire! Bully guns, for short-range fighting! And every time they fired we had to duck down; and, even so, we got covered with grains of powder, and burning bits of flannel, and great puffs of hot smoke. I saw the gunners putting in the powder-bags when you could not bear your hand on the hot press.

We kept up our confidence and our courage, and seasoned the woods with the liveliest kind of firing, whenever the Rebs came marching up again; for they came back and tried it over again two or three times before they gave it up. But they made their mark upon our lines—you can bet on that! The wounded fell down just where they stood. One fellow wanted me to turn him over, that I might get at his cartridge-box, when my own should be empty, as he wouldn't want it himself. The poor fellow was dead before we left.

PRIVATE MILUS O. YOUNG

9th Georgia Infantry, G. T. Anderson's Brigade
As Anderson's brigade prepared to charge the summit of Henry Hill, one of the regimental commanders, Colonel William T. Wilson of the 7th Georgia, a planter from Houston County, gave an impromptu speech to encourage his men.

Anderson hollered "attention"—the boys shouldered arms. . . . Col. Billy Wilson [of the] 7th Georgia . . . rode out in front and said "Boys we have come back to our old stomping ground. If any of you . . . kill a Yankee . . . put on his shoes quick and if you get into a sutler store, eat all the cheese and crackers that you possibly can hold and if you get any good cigars give old Billy two. Forward." The boys raised a yell as usual.

By the time our Brigade marched through the old fields and struck the woods, Col. Billy Wilson was killed. . . . if he got his cigars I did not see him smoke them.

SERGEANT WILLIAM H. ANDREWS

1st Georgia Infantry, G. T. Anderson's Brigade
Although he had suffered two minor wounds during the Peninsula campaign, William Andrews, a 24-year-old soldier from Fort Gaines, Georgia, recovered to fight at Second Manassas. In the gathering dusk of August 30, heavy losses and exhaustion, combined with stiffening Federal resistance on Henry Hill, ended the Confederate advance.

Our line was lying down, every man shooting for all he was worth, looking like a solid sheet of flame from their guns. The double line of yankees were certainly giving us the best they had to offer in the way of hot lead. Besides the batteries in rear of their line on the hills near the Henry House was giving us what Paddy give the drum. The screech of their bursting shells as they crashed through the trees would have caused the heart of the bravest to quake with fear. To be actively engaged in battle is bad enough, but to be a passive spectator is simply awful. My first thought was to run to a tree, but there was none, only in our rear, about 30 feet distant. To run back was something I would not do, so there was nothing for one to do but stand and take what come.

Captain Angus M. McRae of the Douglas Rifles—Company G of the 23d South Carolina Infantry— was fatally wounded as his regiment, part of Evans' brigade, advanced on Chinn Ridge. McRae, a former merchant from Clio, South Carolina, left a wife and four young children.

SERGEANT JOHN V. HADLEY

7th Indiana Infantry, Thoburn's Brigade
As Pope's army retreated, Colonel Joseph Thoburn's brigade, part of the rear guard, collided with the Confederates on the Federal right flank north of the Warrenton Turnpike. When volleys flashed in the darkness, Thoburn's men broke and ran. Sergeant Hadley was wounded during the exchange. Captured in the Wilderness in 1864, Hadley escaped and returned to his regiment.

I then turned to follow my Reg. but a ball passing through my hat near the temples knocking me "non compis mentis" and I fell to the ground. How long I lay there I can't tell. But I guess not long. I was again on my feet but in that confusion I knew not where I was or what I was, what I ought to do or what I could do. I felt the blood running from my wound & knew not how bad it was but concluded that I would as soon be killed as to suffer and starve to death in their hands. So I seized my faithful rifle by the musle and gave her an unearthly hurl into the ranks of an approaching column about five steps distant. I was answered by a volley of about a dozzen guns but fortunately none struck me. I now lunged forward in [the] direction of our retreating forces but had not made more than a half dozzen steps when a greasy grey back presented his bayonet at my breast and demanded a halt. I thought perhaps it was not a joke and stopped, when he stormed out "What Reg. do you belong to?" I told him in my confusion correctly, but he mistook for 7th La. I am sure for he took down his gun and told me to get in rank. I obeyed him. Got into their ranks and joined them in their shouts of victory. They were going on a double quick after our forces and I continued with them about 1/4 of a mile when we struck a cornfield. I don't think there were many of them crossed onto the field but I did and took a separate row. And now you would have laughed to see the trammels come off of me. Haversack, canteen, cartridge box and everything that was loose went flying into the air and then to say I ran says nothing. You have read of antelopes taking 30 ft. at a bound. Well— I anteloped it. I might have exclaimed with great propriety,

"I am the rider of the wind,
  the stirrer of the storm,
  the hurricane I left behind,
  to be with lightning warmed."

"I suppose you appreciate the condition of affairs? It's another Bull Run, sir, it's another Bull Run!"

BRIGADIER GENERAL JOHN GIBBON

Brigade Commander, Army of Virginia

As the beaten Army of Virginia retreated across the Bull Run bridge toward Centreville, John Gibbon's Black Hat Brigade was ordered to form a battle line along the Warrenton Turnpike east of Henry Hill. There Gibbon encountered an embittered General Phil Kearny.

Whilst waiting in position I heard some one inquire in a short quick tone: "Whose command is this?" and turning to look, I recognized General Phil Kearny. I walked up to him and told him I was directed to act as rear guard. He was a soldierly looking figure as he sat, straight as an arrow, on his horse, his empty sleeve pinned to his breast.

Turning towards me, he said in his curt way: "You must wait for my command, sir." "Yes," I replied, "I will wait for all our troops to pass to the rear. Where is your command, General?" "Off on the right, don't you hear my guns? You must wait for Reno, too." "Where is he?" "On the left—you hear his guns? He is keeping up the fight and I am doing all I can to help."

Then in a short bitter tone he broke out with: "I suppose you appreciate the condition of affairs here, sir?"

I did not understand the remark and only looked inquiringly at him. He repeated:

"I suppose you appreciate the condition of affairs? It's another Bull Run, sir, it's another Bull Run!"

"Oh!" I said, "I hope not quite as bad as that, General."

"Perhaps not. Reno is keeping up the fight. He is not stampeded. I am not stampeded, you are not stampeded. That is about all, sir, my God that's about all!"

It is impossible to describe the extreme bitterness and vehemence with which he uttered these words as he rode away towards his command.

Lieutenant George W. Whitman, youngest brother of poet Walt Whitman, served with the 51st New York of Ferrero's brigade. At Second Manassas, the 51st was the last Federal force to leave Henry Hill. The men withdrew in orderly formation or "marching company front," as Whitman proudly wrote his mother.

Lieutenant Frederick A. Morton of the 6th Maine Battery carried this 1851 London Colt Navy Revolver at Second Manassas. The battery lost two guns and two caissons fighting a rearguard action on Matthews Hill, but Morton came through unharmed. He resigned a few weeks later.

SERGEANT WILLIAM E. DOUGHERTY

1st U.S. Infantry, Chapman's Brigade
Irish-born Dougherty enlisted in the U.S. Regulars in 1860. He ended the war with a rank of lieutenant and a brevet for gallantry at Vicksburg, and he retired in 1901 as a colonel after 41 years of service. Dougherty recalled the chaos along the Warrenton pike during the Federal retreat.

We encountered the most awful confusion here. The narrow space was packed with the broken brigades of Butterfield and Barnes, among whom were many wounded. In the midst of this throng were several ammunition wagons and Smead's battery. This battery had just descended the hill and was blocking the lane and unable to move. The battery commander had been killed and several of his men disabled. One of the latter, hit in the shoulder by a shell fragment, had been placed hastily on the footboard of a limber. In the struggle and commotion he was thrown heavily to the ground. A sergeant and two cannoneers lifted him to a caisson, where the sergeant secured him with a strap. As they raised him from the ground I saw his right arm fall backwards like the broken wing of a wounded bird. His clothing was drenched with blood, and it dripped in a steady stream from the sleeve. Not a word or a groan escaped him and his fine boyish face bore an expression of amazement rather than pain.

LIEUTENANT HENRY KYD DOUGLAS

Staff, Major General Thomas J. Jackson
In his memoirs, "I Rode with Stonewall," Lieutenant Douglas recorded an encounter between his chief, Stonewall Jackson, and a severely wounded soldier from the 4th Virginia Infantry.

On our return we came where the dead and wounded were lying thick. The General noticed a disabled soldier trying to climb up the railway embankment, where the fight had been so hot. He rode up to the soldier and asked if he was wounded. "Yes, General, but have we whipped 'em?" Answering him in the affirmative and dismounting as he did so, he approached the soldier and asked him to what regiment he belonged. "I belong to the Fourth Virginia, your old brigade, General. I have been wounded four times but never before as bad as this. I hope I will soon be able to follow you again."

An examination showed that the wound was a deep one in the flesh of the thigh, from which the pale soldier was suffering greatly. The General went to his side, placed a hand upon his burning head and in a low and husky voice said, "You are worthy of the old brigade and I hope with God's blessing, you will soon be well enough to return to it." He then directed several of the staff to carry the man to a more comfortable place and Dr. McGuire to give him what relief he could. He sent a courier for an ambulance to take him to a hospital. The grateful soldier tried to speak but could not; sobs choked him and tears ran from his eyes over his ashen cheeks: words would not come and he submitted to everything in silence. But the General understood.

A Signal Victory

On the overcast and drizzly morning of August 31, Pope pondered his next move as he tried to sort out the shambles of his beaten force at Centreville. As many as 13,000 Union soldiers had been killed, wounded, or captured in the three days of battle at Manassas, and many regiments were desperately rounding up stragglers. Still, Pope had something in excess of 60,000 men on hand. Both Franklin's Sixth Corps and Major General Edwin V. Sumner's Second Corps had been belatedly sent on from Alexandria, where McClellan had established his headquarters, and these fresh troops from the Army of the Potomac more than made up for those lost in action.

Lee, whose army had suffered some 8,700 casualties, was determined to maintain the initiative. Unwilling to risk an assault on the formidable defenses at Centreville, Lee ordered Longstreet to hold Pope's attention as Jackson's wing swung around the Federal right, moving behind the enemy force on the Little River Turnpike toward Fairfax. The road intersected the Warrenton Turnpike atop a ridge at Germantown, seven miles beyond Centreville. If Jackson got there before Pope did, the Union forces would be cut off from their line of retreat to Washington. Longstreet

would follow Jackson, as he had done successfully earlier in the campaign, and perhaps the South could achieve a decisive victory.

With Hill's division in the lead, Jackson's hungry and tired soldiers slogged through the intermittent rain. But they were simply too worn out to live up to their reputation for hard marching. Jackson bivouacked for the night near the estate known as Chantilly, aware that Federal scouts were shadowing his route and that surprise was thus out of the question.

In light of Lee's effort to strike at his line of retreat, Pope decided on September 1 to withdraw to the defenses of Washington and there reorganize his dispirited forces. Pope himself remained with a sizable rear guard at Centreville as his troops began retreating eastward on the Warrenton Turnpike toward Fairfax. General Isaac Stevens led two divisions of the Ninth Corps to block Jackson's Rebels on the Little River Turnpike before they reached the crossroad at Germantown.

Late on the afternoon of September 1, Stevens moved toward Ox Hill, southeast of Chantilly, where Jackson's troops had halted to allow Longstreet's column to close up. The rattle of skirmish fire and the salvos of Federal batteries alerted Jackson to the threat,

and he deployed his troops south of the turnpike, where a confused battle erupted as the skies opened in a torrential downpour.

With General Stevens leading the vanguard of the assault, the regiments on the Federal left charged across an open field and broke through Jackson's line near the junction of Lawton's and Hill's divisions. But Stevens was shot dead, the flag of the 79th New York in his hands, and the Yankees were sent reeling back. General Kearny began rushing his division of the Third Corps north to Stevens' support, and Brigadier General David B. Birney's brigade was soon locked in furious combat with Hill's troops along the edge of a large cornfield.

With characteristic recklessness, Kearny galloped forward to rally Stevens' retreating soldiers. As the thunder boomed and lightning flashed, Kearny spurred his horse into the cornfield, where in the driving rain and premature darkness he mistook a group of Georgians for Federal troops. As he turned to make his escape the Rebels let loose a ragged volley, and the one-armed division commander fell dead from the saddle. The firing soon sputtered out, and the contending forces disengaged, each side having lost some 500 men.

The indecisive clash at Ox Hill—known in the North as the Battle of Chantilly—proved to be the concluding action of the Second Manassas campaign. The outcome of this skirmish meant nothing, however, to the thousands of wounded left behind in the wake of the fighting on the Bull Run battlefield. The luckiest among them had been evacuated to dressing stations or hospitals; others had found their own shelter, cramming themselves into any structure with a roof between Gainesville and Centreville. But hundreds more, especially Northern wounded, were alone with their agony, scattered all across the battlefield, beyond the reach of their medical services for days. With the Federals in retreat and Lee determined to keep moving, too few remained to deal adequately with all the casualties.

The Confederates did manage to bury most of their dead, and some of the Union dead, in shallow mass graves before they moved on. As usual, the numbers of Rebel wounded overwhelmed the Army of Northern Virginia's medical corps, and only a portion were evacuated to hospitals farther south. Many of the rest were tended by civilian doctors and parceled out to homes all across the area, where in the next weeks they would be forced to play hide-and-seek with Federal cavalry patrols.

On September 2, under a flag of truce, the first small Union rescue parties reached the field, but not until the fourth was a real effort mobilized. By this time, those still alive were in wretched shape—near starvation, soaked by rains, and with wounds already festering. Over the next few days, hundreds of vehicles—many of them taxis and buses from Washington—hauled their miserable passengers back to the overflowing hospitals in the capital.

When John Pope completed his retreat to the defenses of Washington, he met with humiliation. Hailed by thunderous cheers from the Federal soldiers, George B. McClellan rode out to assume command of the army. President Lincoln, faced with the gravest crisis of the war, saw no alternative but to place the hopes of the Union in the hands of the contentious but undeniably charismatic McClellan. Pope was sent west to fight Indians, his reputation forever tainted by his defeat on the plains of Manassas.

In an unsurpassed display of strategic brilliance, Robert E. Lee had vanquished Pope. "General Lee has shown great Generalship and the greatest boldness," General William Dorsey Pender wrote. "There never was such a campaign, not even by Napoleon." Fired with confidence and buoyed with hope, Lee turned the Army of Northern Virginia toward the Potomac River, determined to win a crowning victory on Northern soil.

SECOND MANASSAS CAMPAIGN CASUALTIES

FEDERAL

Killed	1,724
Wounded	8,372
Missing	5,958
Total	16,054

CONFEDERATE

Killed	1,481
Wounded	7,627
Missing	89
Total	9,197

GENERAL ROBERT E. LEE

Commander, Army of Northern Virginia
Lee and his Army of Northern Virginia had decisively turned back the Federal
invasion and for the first time held the strategic initiative in the eastern theater.
At 10:00 p.m. on the evening of August 30, Lee sent President Jefferson Davis
a telegram informing him of the latest triumph.

This Army achieved today on the plains of Manassas a signal victory over the combined forces of Genls McClellan and Pope. On the 28th and 29th each wing under Genls Longstreet and Jackson repulsed with valour attacks made on them separately. We mourn the loss of our gallant dead, in every conflict yet our gratitude to almighty God for His mercies rises higher and higher each day, to Him and the valour of our troops a nation's gratitude is due.

Columns of Pope's defeated army trudge back through the fortifications at
Centreville on the day after the Second Manassas battle. In the foreground
the wounded pile up around a wayside cabin being used as a field hospital.

PRIVATE CHARLES H. VEIL

9th Pennsylvania Reserve Infantry, Hardin's Brigade
Veil's regiment was the hardest hit in Reynolds' division, suffering 99 casualties
in its brief but costly stand against Hood's Texans. But this defeat and the terri-
ble sights he witnessed afterward did not deter Veil, who went on to fight with
the 1st U.S. Cavalry until the end of the war.

As we passed through Centerville on our retreat I saw a sight I often think of. The surgeons were operating on the badly wounded, as they were brought in from the field. Long rows of wounded men were lying around; some had been operated on, while others were waiting to be. The surgeons were cutting off arms, feet, hands and limbs of all kinds in what looked like a little country school house. And as an arm or leg was cut off it was thrown out an open window. The cut-off limbs had accumulated so that they blocked the window, and a detail of a few men were hauling away the limbs with a wheelbarrow. It was an awful sight and one I have never forgotten. It had the appearance of a human slaughter house.

LIEUTENANT JOHN M. BLUE

17th Virginia Cavalry Battalion, Robertson's Brigade
Disaster though it was for the Federals, the outcome of Second Manassas did at least accelerate the establishment of a sorely needed ambulance corps. Scenes such as the one described here by Lieutenant Blue finally persuaded army officials to provide vehicles and men to speedily evacuate wounded.

The Yankees had asked, under flag of truce, permission to bury their dead and care for their wounded, which had been granted them. Capt. McDonald had been left behind to keep an eye on them while they performed this sad but necessary duty, and to await further orders. Capt. McDonald selected a place to camp, then for several days we rode over the battle field and talked with the northern people. Old men and their wives and daughters who had come out from Washington and from many of the northern States in search of fathers, husbands, sons and brothers, who were reported missing and supposed to be either dead, wounded or prisoners.

It was a sad, a sickening sight to see those old fathers and mothers turning the dead, who had fallen on their faces, to see if it was the loved ones for whom they were in search. The object of their search was often found cold in death. Then the scene was sometimes one calculated to melt a heart of stone, to see an old gray haired mother and father kneeling and kissing the lips of their idol, it may have been their only child. Then again a young girl, yet in her teens could have been sitting by the side of, it may have been an only brother, sobbing as though her heart would break.

I saw hundreds, I might say thousands of wounded men who had lain on that field of carnage for three days in a scorching August sun, or drenching rains, many with swollen discolored tongues protruding between their parched lips showed how terrible was their thirst. Many of them could move a hand or make a sign, yet their tongue and throat was so dry and swollen that they could not speak, though it was easy to understand that they were begging for water to quench their intolerable thirst. Many of their wounds were filled after three days with vermine. There were numbers of wounded still lying on the gory field, although an ambulance train which at a distance, might have been taken for a great serpent, had been slowly winding its way up on one side and down the other of the narrow valley.

"Let me implore that . . . it may be stated that General Pope has been outwitted, and that McDowell is a traitor."

COLONEL THORNTON F. BRODHEAD

1st Michigan Cavalry, Buford's Brigade
Brodhead was mortally wounded late on August 30 while leading a spirited charge near Lewis Ford. Captured by the Confederates, he lingered just long enough to write letters to his family, offering his farewells and strong words about his senior commanders.

My dear Wife:—
I write to you mortally wounded, from the battle-field. We have again been defeated, and ere this reaches you your children will be fatherless. Before I die let me implore that in some way it may be stated that General Pope has been outwitted, and that McDowell is a traitor. Had they done their duty as I did mine, and had led as I did, the dear old flag had waved in triumph. I wrote to you yesterday morning. To-day is Sunday, and to-day I sink to the green couch of our final rest. I have fought well, my darling; and I was shot in the endeavor to rally our broken battalions. I could have escaped, but

would not until all our hope was gone, and was shot,—about the only one of our forces left on the field. Our cause is just, and our generals,—not the enemy's,—have defeated us. In God's good time he will give us the victory.

And now, good by, wife and children. Bring them up—I know you will—in the fear of God and love for the Saviour. But for you and the dear ones dependent, I should die happy. I know the blow will fall with crushing weight on you. Trust in Him who gave manna in the wilderness.

Dr. North is with me. It is now after midnight, and I have spent most of the night in sending messages to you. Two bullets have gone through my chest, and directly through my lungs. I suffer little now, but at first the pain was acute. I have won the soldier's name, and am ready to meet now, as I must, the soldier's fate. I hope that from heaven I may see the glorious old flag wave again over the undivided country I have loved so well.

Farewell, wife and friends, we shall meet again.

COL. THORNTON F. BRODHEAD

WAS born in New Hampshire, in 1805. His father was a clergyman of distinguished reputation, learning and piety. In his early years Col. Brodhead went to Detroit, where he remained for nearly 20 years, honored by all with whom he came in contact. He served with great distinction in the Mexican war. At the commencement of the present rebellion he offered his sword to the Federal Government, and was placed in command of the 1st Michigan cavalry. He was mortally wounded at Centreville, on the 30th of August. On his person was found a letter severely censuring Gens. Pope and McDowell, which we copy:

"DEAR BROTHER AND SISTER—I am passing now from earth, but send you love from my dying couch. For all your love and kindness may you be rewarded. I have fought manfully, and now die fearlessly. I am one of the victims of Pope's imbecility and McDowell's treason. Tell the President, would he save the country, he must not give our hallowed flag into such hands.

"But the old flag will triumph yet—the soldiers will rebuild its poles, now polluted by imbecility and treason.

"John, you owe a duty to your country; write—show up Pope's incompetency, and McDowell's infamy, and force them from places where they can send brave men to assured destruction. I had hoped to live longer, but I die amidst the danger of battle as I could wish. Farewell! In you and the noble officers of my regiment, I confide my wife and children.   T. F. B.''

One of Colonel Brodhead's stinging last letters—addressed to "Dear Brother and Sister"—found its way into the newspapers (above). General McDowell responded by demanding an official inquiry regarding Brodhead's charges. Sixty-seven days of testimony uncovered no evidence for "treason," but it did reveal proof of incompetence sufficient to ruin McDowell's career.

Brigadier General Isaac I. Stevens, who died on the field at Chantilly, sits surrounded by his staff at Beaufort, South Carolina, in spring 1862. The general's son, Captain Hazard Stevens, stands third from the left.

CAPTAIN HAZARD STEVENS

Staff, Brigadier General Isaac I. Stevens

Hazard Stevens, son of General Isaac Stevens, was commissioned a lieutenant in the 79th New York Highlanders in 1861 and resigned that September to serve on his father's staff. He won the Medal of Honor for the capture of Battery Huger near Suffolk, Virginia, in 1863 and was breveted three times. At Chantilly he witnessed his father's death.

The troops, under the withering hail of bullets, were now wavering and almost at a standstill. Five color-bearers of the Highlanders had fallen in succession, and the colors again fell to the ground. At this crisis General Stevens pushed to the front, seized the falling colors from the hands of the wounded bearer, unheeding his cry, "For God's sake, don't take the colors, general; they'll shoot you if you do!" and calling aloud upon his old regiment, "Highlanders, my Highlanders, follow your general!" rushed forward with the uplifted flag. The regiment responded nobly. They rushed forward, reached the edge of the woods, hurled themselves with fury upon the fence and the rebel line behind it, and the enemy broke and fled in disorder.

The 28th Massachusetts joined gallantly in the charge, and the other brigades as gallantly supported the first. At this moment a sudden and severe thunderstorm, with a furious gale, burst over the field and the rain fell in torrents, while the flash of lightning and peals of thunder seemed to rebuke man's bloody, fratricidal strife.

General Stevens fell dead in the moment of victory. A bullet entered at the temple and pierced his brain. He still firmly grasped the flagstaff, and the colors lay fallen upon his head and shoulders. His noble, brave, and ardent spirit, freed at last from the petty jealousies of earth, had flown to its Creator.

CAPTAIN CHARLES F. WALCOTT

21st Massachusetts Infantry, Ferrero's Brigade

As the action drew to a close at Chantilly, Major General Philip Kearny accidentally rode into the Confederate lines. Captain Walcott tried in vain to warn Kearny, and he witnessed the fate of one of the Union's best fighting men. Later, as colonel of the 61st Massachusetts, Walcott was cited for his role in the capture of Richmond in the final days of the war.

General Kearny was following us up closely, and as we came to a halt fiercely tried to force us forward, saying that we were firing on our own men, and that there were no rebels near us. We had the proof in two prisoners—an officer and private of a Georgia regiment—brought in by our skirmishers, besides the warning cries of "Surrender," coming both from our right and front; but, unfortunately, Kearny's judgment seemed unable to appreciate the existence of the peril which his military instinct had caused him to guard against. Lieutenant Walcott, of the brigade staff, took our prisoners to him, saying, "General, if you don't believe there are rebels in the corn, here are two prisoners from the 49th Georgia, just taken in our front." Crying out fiercely, "God damn you and your prisoners!" the general, entirely alone, apparently in ungovernable rage at our disregard of his peremptory orders to advance, forced his horse through the deep, sticky mud of the cornfield past the left of the regiment, passing within a few feet of where I was standing. I watched him moving in the murky twilight through the corn, and, when less than twenty yards away, saw his horse suddenly rear and turn, and half a dozen muskets flash around him: so died the intrepid soldier, General Philip Kearny!

Brigadier General Isaac Stevens falls, shot through the temple while leading the 79th New York, in this engraving from the New York Illustrated News. "It was a heavy loss to us," the paper eulogized, "and the rebels will doubtless be especially jubilant when they learn that they have killed another of our best officers."

General Philip Kearny (left) was much admired by Yankees and Rebels alike. After he was killed at Chantilly, Robert E. Lee ordered that his body be escorted through the lines under a flag of truce. Edwin M. Stanton, Union secretary of war, called Kearny's death "a national calamity."

Kearny's brigadier general shoulder strap, worn at the time of his death, and the Confederate Minié ball that killed him on September 1, 1862, were preserved by his family. The gold Kearny Medal (right) was worn by officers of his old division to honor their late commander.

MAJOR WASHINGTON L. GRICE

45th Georgia Infantry, Thomas' Brigade
Major Grice, from Carroll County, Georgia, was in the Confederate battle line on the night of September 1 when a lone horseman approached the Georgia soldiers. Several Rebel units sought credit for the shot that felled Kearny, but Grice's claim for the 49th Georgia remains the most convincing.

Darkness had put an end to the conflict; the battle was over and the firing had ceased when General Kearney left his line and rode alone to the front of the 49th Georgia. Evidently he was trying to ascertain whether these men were friends or enemies, as there was some confusion on both sides caused by the growing darkness.

When close to our line, he asked: "What troops are those?" His question was answered by a similar one concerning his own belonging. Some of the men understood his reply to be "We are Confederates," while others thought he said "Federals." Discovering his mistake, he wheeled his horse and started to retreat. Capt. John H. Pate, of the 49th, gave the order to "Fire on him." General Kearney bent low down on the neck of his horse; and as he did so, [the] bullet entered his body directly from the rear, making no external wound. He fell from his horse, and died in a few minutes. . . .

. . . It had rained that evening while the battle was in progress, and the night air was chilly to men in wet clothes. At the regimental headquarters we built a fire, and to this fire the dead body was brought. We knew by the uniform that it was a Federal officer, but we did not know his name or rank. A Federal captain who had been wounded and captured had been brought to the same fire, as soon as he saw General Kearney with his one arm (the other having been lost in the Mexican War), told us who the dead man was. His body lay by that fire all night, a few hundred yards from where he fell.

. . . The next day General Lee sent the body, under flag of truce, to his own men, and he sent with it the red smoking cap which was found with the body.

CAPTAIN EVANS R. BRADY

11th Pennsylvania Reserve Infantry, Hardin's Brigade
In the aftermath of the Federal disaster, Captain Brady, a veteran of the Peninsula battles and Second Manassas, wrote a candid letter to his local newspaper, the Clearfield Republican. Despite his intention to resign, Brady continued in the service and was killed in action at South Mountain in September.

I have given up all hope of a restoration, and now look forward to a cessation of hostilities and a compromise, by an acknowledgement of the Southern Confederacy. I am sorry to admit this, yet I cannot see how it can be otherwise, so long as the people are determined to keep up the negro agitation. We have been led to believe that there was a strong Union feeling in the South; but my experience . . . has been otherwise. You may rely that the Southern men are united and determined—they act in concert and have every equipment necessary for an army. Our army is sadly demoralized—discipline has been overlooked, and our generals seem to be jealous of each other, lest some one may gain more honor than the rest.

The army is down on Pope and McDowell, and the restoration of McClellan to the command has inspired our men more than anything I have witnessed for a long time; the people of the North seem to be opposed to him; but I assure you the army has every confidence in his abilities. During the retreat on the Peninsula, the soldiers cheered and waved their caps for him while they lay in the mud and swamps—while McDowell might ride along his whole line and fail to elicit a single sign of approbation. I could write myself about the conduct of the war, if known would open the eyes of the people in the North; but I refrain, because I know I would not be believed, and my motives would be attributed to other than the real cause. I have made up my mind to resign and come home; if my resignation will be accepted.

SOPHRONIA E. BUCKLIN

Volunteer Nurse
Armed with numerous letters testifying to her abilities and character, New Yorker Sophronia Bucklin applied to Dorothea Dix, the government's superintendent of women nurses, for a post in an army hospital. In early September 1862, she was assigned to the Judiciary Square Hospital in Washington, D.C., which was overflowing with the wounded from Second Manassas and Chantilly.

The morning of the nineteenth of September dawned over the long low hospital, and my duties began. With silent prayers for courage, and struggling with the beating at my heart, armed with wash bowl, soap and towels, I went into the ward, and entered upon my first work as a hospital nurse, amongst those who had been wounded in fighting the second battle of Bull Run.

It was no small matter for me to apply the wet towel to the faces of bronzed and bearded men; it was no slight task to comb out the tangled hair and part it over foreheads which seemed hot with the flash of cannon. I had been nurtured in quietude, and had little conception of the actual state of things when the timid heart preferred to remain in that state, though the brain and hand were in rebellion to it, and held it down to the servitude. . . .

For several successive mornings one poor fellow, whose eyes were both shot out, with his head badly shattered, lay silent while his ablutions were being performed. I thought he had perhaps lost his speech in the untold terror of his sightless condition, but by-and-by he said, "Thank you," when the process of washing was completed.

I could not comb his hair, for the bandages were bound tightly over it, and, as he turned away after the simple recognition of thanks, I passed on without questioning him. A few days went by, then he said, "Did you ever notice that I never talked to you, as other patients did, when you first came to take care of us?" I replied, "I did."

"Then I will tell you why," he continued; "I was so thankful, that I had no words for speech—to think the women of the North should come down here, and do so much for us, being exposed to all kinds of disease, and to so much work and hard fare, all to take care of us poor soldiers, when we lie as I do."

SURGEON OLIVER S. BELDEN

5th New Jersey Infantry, Carr's Brigade
Recovering the remains of Civil War soldiers was largely a private affair.
For days, months, even years after a battle, relatives and friends would scour
the field looking for the right grave. One such attempt was made at Manassas
on January 1, 1863, by a party that included Belden and the father of Captain
Edward Acton, a soldier who was buried during the battle.

Mounting the first high hill beyond the first branch of the Bull Run stream, we soon came to the road along another branch of the stream which led directly to the place of burial at the foot of a high hill which overlooked the whole field of the battle. There, under a small tree, the body of the Captain, along with Lieutenant Abbott of the Seventh New Jersey and another of the Eighth New Jersey, was buried with an inscription on a small wooden head board, designating his name and rank. At this spot we arrived about eleven o'clock at night. After a faithful use of pick and shovel for an hour, under the light of the moon which had just begun to rise, we succeeded in removing the body from its resting-place, finding it buried in the Captain's military clothes surrounded by three or four

Captain Edward A. Acton (left) of the 5th New Jersey Infantry left behind a wife and three small boys when he enlisted in 1861. His Quaker family was greatly distressed by his decision, but Acton went off to war, fighting through the entire Peninsula campaign. On the afternoon of August 29, he was shot through the body and died shortly after. The next morning, his men buried him and placed a crude headboard over his grave.

thicknesses of canvas tent as a winding sheet, and, after a four months' burial, in such a remarkable state of preservation that the features of the countenance could very readily be recognized.

Such an occasion as the removal of a body from its temporary resting-place on the field of battle at midnight, under the light of the moon which seemed to have risen at that particular hour for the special benefit of this mission party of love and patriotism, beyond all protection from Union bayonets and in the heart of the enemy's country, could not fail to awaken, not merely in the heart of the bereaved father, but also in the minds of all the party, some very saddening thoughts and reflections. All of the party were ready to shed the tear of sympathy on that sad occasion, hallowed by so many sacred surroundings and associations.

BRIGADIER GENERAL LYSANDER CUTLER

Army of the Potomac
For months after Second Manassas, troops marching past the Groveton
crossroad on the heavily traveled Warrenton Turnpike often reported seeing
the remains of soldiers still lying out in the fields around Brawner's Farm.
Cutler, who had fought in the battle, oversaw their belated burial.

Headquarters First Division, First Army Corps. Bristol, Va., November 1st, 1863.
Editor State Journal:—Rumors have reached me, from time to time, that the remains of those men of the "Iron Brigade," and of the Fifty-sixth Pennsylvania and Seventy-sixth New York volunteers, who fell at Gainesville in the bloody fight of August 28th, 1862, were carelessly buried. Upon examination, a few days since, while passing the battlefield on our way to Thoroughfare Gap, it was found to be true. I have today had details from all the regiments who fought there sent to the ground, under the charge of Captain Richardson, of the Seventh Wisconsin. We have carefully interred the remains. Many of them could be recognized by the positions where they lay, or by articles found about them. As the friends of those who fell will doubtless hear of the loose manner of the first burial, I write to assure them that all has been done that could be to give them decent burial.

Very Respectfully,

L. Cutler

More than a year after the battle, members of the Iron Brigade and other units inter their long-dead comrades on the Manassas battlefield. Visible in the right background is a portion of the gap in the rail bed called the Dump, scene of some of the battle's fiercest fighting.

GLOSSARY

battery—The basic unit of artillery, consisting of four to six guns.

breastwork—A temporary fortification, usually of earth and about chest high, over which a soldier can fire.

brevet—An honorary title given for exceptional bravery or merit in time of war. It carries none of the authority or pay of the real rank.

Bucktails—Nickname for the 13th Pennsylvania Reserves. Recruits were required to bring in a deer's tail as proof of their prowess with a rifle. These bucktails were then worn in hats as regimental identification.

caisson—A cart with large chests for carrying artillery ammunition; it is connected to a horse-drawn limber when moved.

canister—A tin can containing lead or iron balls that scatter when fired from a cannon.

cap—Technically a percussion cap. A small, metal cover, infused with chemicals and placed on the hollow nipple of a rifle or revolver. When struck by the hammer the chemicals explode, igniting the powder charge in the breech.

carbine—A lightweight, short-barreled shoulder arm used especially by cavalry.

case shot—*Case shot* properly refers to shrapnel or spherical case. The term is often used mistakenly to refer to any artillery projectile in which numerous metal balls or pieces are bound or encased together. See also *shrapnel*.

change front—To alter the direction troops face to deliver or defend against an attack.

draw out guns—To move artillery pieces from cover or a staging area into a position from which they can fire on the enemy.

dress by the colors—To arrange troops into lines according to placement of the unit's flag.

Enfield rifle—The Enfield rifle musket was adopted by the British in 1853, and the North and South imported nearly a million to augment their own production. It fires a .577-caliber projectile similar to the Minié bullet.

enfilade—Gunfire raking an enemy line lengthwise, or the position allowing such firing.

15-20–second shell—An artillery projectile containing an explosive charge. Its fuse detonates the charge in the air near the enemy 15 to 20 seconds after the round is fired.

flank—The right or left end of a military formation. To flank is to attack or go around the enemy's position on one end or the other.

grapeshot—Iron balls (usually nine) bound together and fired from a cannon. Resembling a cluster of grapes, the balls break apart and scatter on impact. Although references to grape or grapeshot are numerous in the literature, some experts claim that it was not used on Civil War battlefields.

haversack—A shoulder bag, usually strapped over the right shoulder to rest on the left hip, for carrying personal items and rations.

idolized tea—A slang term for whiskey.

light marching order—To travel "light," leaving behind knapsacks and other nonessential items and carrying only a musket, powder, shot, and perhaps some rations and a blanket roll, in order to be less encumbered for rapid travel or battle.

limber—A two-wheeled, horse-drawn vehicle to which a gun carriage or a caisson is attached.

Minié ball—The standard bullet-shaped projectile fired from the rifled muskets of the time. Designed by French Army officers Henri-Gustave Delvigne and Claude-Etienne Minié, the bullet's hollow base expands, forcing its sides into the grooves, or rifling, of the barrel. This causes the bullet to spiral in flight, giving it greater range and accuracy. Appears as minie ball, minnie ball, Minnie ball, and minnie bullet.

Napoleon—A smoothbore, muzzleloading artillery piece developed under the direction of Napoleon III. It fires a 12-pound projectile (and therefore is sometimes called a 12-pounder). Napoleons were originally cast in bronze; when that material became scarce in the South, iron was used.

nigh-wheel mule—The mule closest to the left, front wheel of a wagon or limber.

oblique—At an angle.

parole—The pledge of a soldier released after capture by the enemy that he will not fight again until he has been properly exchanged.

Parrott guns—Muzzleloading, rifled artillery pieces. They are made of cast iron, with a unique wrought-iron reinforcing band around the breech. Patented in 1861 by Union officer Robert Parker Parrott, the guns are more accurate at longer range than their smooth-bore predecessors.

pas de charge—The official name for the drumbeat ordering a charge.

posse comitatus—The legal term for a group of individuals officially charged with carrying out a task. Here it means simply a unit of men.

rammer—An artillerist's tool used to force the powder charge and projectile down the barrel of a gun and seat them firmly in the breech.

redoubt—An enclosed, defensive stronghold.

rifle—Any weapon with spiral grooves cut into the bore, which give spin to the projectile, adding range and accuracy. Applied to cannon or shoulder-fired weapons.

rifle pits—Holes or shallow trenches dug in the ground from which soldiers can fire weapons and avoid enemy fire. Foxholes.

round shot—A solid, spherical artillery projectile.

secesh—A slang term for secessionist.

section of artillery—Part of a battery consisting of two guns, the soldiers that operate them, and their supporting horses and equipment.

shrapnel—An artillery projectile in the form of a hollow sphere filled with metal balls packed around an explosive charge. Developed by British general Henry Shrapnel during the Napoleonic Wars, it is used as an antipersonnel weapon. Also called spherical case.

skirmisher—A soldier sent out in advance of the main body of troops to scout out and probe the enemy's position. Also, one who fights in a skirmish, a small fight usually incidental to the main action.

solid shot—A solid artillery projectile, oblong for rifled pieces and spherical for smoothbores.

spherical case—See *shrapnel*.

sponge—An artillerist's tool used to clear a cannon barrel of grime, smoldering cloth, and other detritus between rounds.

sutler—A peddler with a permit to remain with troops in camp or in the field and sell food, drink, and other supplies.

vent—A small hole in the breech of a weapon through which a spark travels to ignite the powder charge and fire the piece.

Zouaves—Regiments, Union or Confederate, that model themselves after the Zouaves of French Colonial Algeria. Known for spectacular uniforms featuring bright colors—usually reds and blues—baggy trousers, gaiters, short and open jackets, and a turban or fez, they specialize in precision drill and loading and firing muskets from the prone position.

ACKNOWLEDGMENTS

The editors wish to thank the following individuals and institutions for their valuable assistance in the preparation of this volume:
Nancy C. Baird, Delaplane, Va.; Arthur Bergeron, The Louisiana Office of State Parks, Baton Rouge; John Mills Bigham, Confederate Relic Room and Museum, Columbia, S.C.; Beth Bilderback, South Caroliniana Library, University of South Carolina, Columbia; Mrs. John R. Blue, Romney, W.Va.; William F. N. Brewster, State of Wisconsin, Department of Veterans Affairs, Madison; Ray Brown, Manassas National Battlefield Park, Manassas, Va.; Jim Burgess, Manassas National Battlefield Park, Manassas, Va.; Gerry Caughman, State Capital, Hartford; Peggy Fox, Confederate Research Center, Hillsboro, Tex.; Mrs. Francis T. Greene, Warrenton, Va.; John K. Gott, Arlington, Va.; Randy W. Hackenburg, U.S. Army Military History Institute, Carlisle Barracks, Pa.; Scott Harris, The Manassas Museum, Manassas, Va.; Steve Hill, State House, Boston; John House, Mansfield State Commemorative Area, Louisiana Office of State Parks, Mansfield; Corinne Hudgins, The Museum of the Confederacy, Richmond; Larry Jones, Austin, Tex.; Howard Madaus, Cody Firearms Museum, Cody, Wyo.; Jackson Marshall, North Carolina State Archives, Raleigh; Steve Massengill, North Carolina State Archives, Raleigh; Lisa McCown, Special Collections, Leyburn Library, Washington & Lee University, Lexington, Va.; Bonnie Moffat, Confederate Relic Room and Museum, Columbia, S.C.; Janie Morris, Special Collections Library, Perkins Library, Duke University, Durham, N.C.; Dan Oates, Romney, W.Va.; David K. Parks, Macomb, Mich.; Marsha Rader, Baltimore; Ed Raus, Manassas National Battlefield Park, Manassas, Va.; Bobby Roberts, Little Rock, Ark.; William A. Turner, La Plata, Md.; David Wynn Vaughan, Atlanta; Michael J. Winey, U.S. Army Military History Institute, Carlisle Barracks, Pa.

PICTURE CREDITS

The sources for the illustrations are listed below. Credits from left to right are separated by semicolons, from top to bottom by dashes. Dust jacket: Front, U.S. Army Military History Institute (USAMHI), Carlisle Barracks, Pa., copied by A. Pierce Bounds; rear, courtesy William A. Turner. 6, 7: Map by Paul Salmon. 8: Library of Congress No. B8171-313. 9: Calligraphy by Mary Lou O'Brian/Inkwell, Inc. 12: Map by Peter McGinn. 14, 15: National Archives Record Group 111, courtesy Time Inc. Picture Collection. 17: USAMHI, Carlisle Barracks, Pa., copied by A. Pierce Bounds (2)— Library of Congress No. B815-544. 19: Frank & Marie-Thérèse Wood Print Collections, Alexandria, Va. 20: Courtesy D. Mark Katz; courtesy Special Collections, James Graham Leyburn Library, Washington & Lee University, Lexington, Va. 21: Courtesy Lewis Leigh, Centerville, Va., photographed by Larry Sherer; Tracey W. McGregor Library (*A 1863.C67), Special Collections Department, University of Virginia Library. 22: Mrs. Nancy C. Baird. 23: USAMHI, Carlisle Barracks, Pa., copied by A. Pierce Bounds. 24: U.S. War Dept. General Staff Photo No. 165-5B-4 in the National Archives— Library of Congress No. 418079. 25: Library of Congress No. 3217 B8184 7084-A. 26: Library of Congress No. 5253 B8171. 27: Calligraphy by Mary Lou O'Brian/Inkwell, Inc. 29: Map by Walter W. Roberts. 31: Courtesy Michael J. McAfee. 32: From *The Story of a Cannoneer under Stonewall Jackson,* by Edward A. Moore, published by J. P. Bell, Lynchburg, Va., 1910, copied by Larry Sherer—courtesy Homer Babcock, photographed by Larry Sherer. 33: Courtesy William A. Turner; from *Richard Snowden Andrews,* ed. by Tunstall Smith, Press of the Sun Job Printing Office, Baltimore, 1910; Maryland Historical Society, Baltimore. 34: Library of Congress. 35: From *With the Old Confeds: Actual Experiences of a Captain in the Line,* by Samuel D. Buck, H. E. Houck & Co., Baltimore, 1925, copied by Philip Brandt George. 36, 37: From *History of the Doles-Cook Brigade, Army of Northern Virginia, C.S.A.,* by Henry W. Thomas, The Franklin Printing & Publishing Co., Atlanta, 1903, copied by Philip Brandt George—Library of Congress. 39: National Archives Neg. No. CN-11190, copied by Evan H. Sheppard. 40: The Eleanor S. Brockenbrough Library, The Museum of the Confederacy, Richmond, photographed by Larry Sherer. 41: Courtesy William A. Turner, copied by Larry Sherer. 42: From *One of Jackson's Foot Cavalry,* by John H. Worsham, ed. by James I. Robertson Jr., McCowat-Mercer, Jackson, Tenn., 1964, copied by Larry Sherer. 43: Courtesy State of Connecticut General Assembly, Joint Committee on Legislative Management, photographed by Gus Johnson—The Museum of the Confederacy,

Richmond, photographed by Katherine Wetzel (2). 44: Courtesy Mrs. John R. Blue; courtesy Homer Babcock, photographed by Larry Sherer. 45: Courtesy of Stonewall Jackson Foundation, Lexington, Virginia. 46: Library of Congress No. 7662-B8151 10122. 47: Library of Congress. 48, 49: USAMHI, Carlisle Barracks, Pa., copied by A. Pierce Bounds; Library of Congress. 50, 51: USAMHI, Carlisle Barracks, Pa., copied by A. Pierce Bounds; Library of Congress No. 5253-B8171. 53: David Wynn Vaughan—Library of Congress No. B815-510. 54, 55: Library of Congress. 56: M. and M. Karolik Collection, courtesy Museum of Fine Arts, Boston. 57: Hargett Rare Book and Manuscript Library, University of Georgia, Athens. 58, 59: Library of Congress No. 5253-B8171-513. 60, 61: USAMHI, Carlisle Barracks, Pa., copied by A. Pierce Bounds. 62: Library of Congress No. 3217 B8171. 63: Calligraphy by Mary Lou O'Brian/Inkwell, Inc. 65: Map by R. R. Donnelley & Sons Co., Cartographic Services. 67: Library of Congress No. B8171-518. 68: USAMHI, Carlisle Barracks, Pa., copied by Robert Walch. 69: Library of Congress No. 418078; Library of Congress No. 3521. 70: Courtesy Adele Mitchell, copied by A. Pierce Bounds; Valentine Museum, Richmond. 71: From *War Years with Jeb Stuart,* by W. W. Blackford, Charles Scribner's Sons, New York, 1945, copied by Philip Brandt George. 72: Frank & Marie-Thérèse Wood Print Collections, Alexandria, Va. 74, 75: Drawing by Alfred R. Waud, Library of Congress No. 13468-42. 76, 77: Courtesy Lee A. Wallace Jr.—Library of Congress. 78: New York State Department of Military and Naval Affairs, photographed by Larry Sherer. 79: Frank & Marie-Thérèse Wood Print Collections, Alexandria, Va. 80: Mrs. Nancy C. Baird. 81: USAMHI, Carlisle Barracks, Pa., copied by A. Pierce Bounds—Library of Congress No. USZ62-12801. 82, 83: USAMHI, Carlisle Barracks, Pa., copied by A. Pierce Bounds. 85: From *Ham Chamberlayne—Virginian: Letters and Papers of an Artillery Officer in the War for Southern Independence,* by John H. Chamberlayne, ed. by C. G. Chamberlayne, Press of the Dietz Printing Co., Richmond, 1932, copied by Larry Sherer. 86: Library of Congress; Massachusetts Commandery of the Military Order of the Loyal Legion of the United States and the U.S. Army Military History Institute (MASS-MOLLUS/USAMHI), copied by A. Pierce Bounds. 87: Frank & Marie-Thérèse Wood Print Collections, Alexandria, Va. 88: Library of Congress, Neg. No. B8171-547. 89: Calligraphy by Mary Lou O'Brian/Inkwell, Inc. 91: Map by Walter W. Roberts, overlay by Time-Life Books. 92, 93: North Carolina Division of Archives and History; from *The American Heritage Century Collection of Civil War Art,*

ed. by Stephen W. Sears, American Heritage Publishing Co., New York, 1974, copied by Larry Sherer. 94: From *The Papers of Randolph Abbott Shotwell,* Vol. 1, ed. by J. G. de Roulhac Hamilton, The North Carolina Historical Commission, Raleigh, 1929, copied by Philip Brandt George. 95: Valentine Museum, Richmond. 97: Library of Congress No. USZ62-19201. 98: USAMHI, Carlisle Barracks, Pa., copied by A. Pierce Bounds. 99: USAMHI, Carlisle Barracks, Pa., copied by A. Pierce Bounds; Wisconsin Veterans Museum (2). 100: Wisconsin Veterans Museum; State Historical Society of Wisconsin. 101: Courtesy William A. Turner, photographed by Larry Sherer. 102: Painting by J. P. Walker, courtesy Virginia Historical Society, photographed by Larry Sherer. 103: From *Two Views of Gettysburg,* by Sir Arthur J. L. Fremantle and Frank A. Haskell, ed. by Richard Harwell, R. R. Donnelley & Sons Co., Chicago, 1964, copied by Philip Brandt George. 105: Map by Walter W. Roberts. 106: From *A Narrative of the Work of the Commission Appointed by an Act of the Legislature, of the State. . . .,* by Peter Wilson Ostrander, Eagle Press, Brooklyn, 1907, copied by Larry Sherer. 108, 109: From *The Story of a Cannoneer under Stonewall Jackson,* by Edward A. Moore, The Neale Publishing Co., New York and Washington, 1907, copied by Philip Brandt George; Frank & Marie-Thérèse Wood Print Collections, Alexandria, Va. 110, 111: USAMHI, Carlisle Barracks, Pa., copied by A. Pierce Bounds. 112: Photograph by Douglas Christian, courtesy Bureau of State Office Buildings, Commonwealth of Massachusetts. 113: Manassas National Battlefield Park, photographed by Larry Sherer (2); courtesy David Keith Parks, Macomb, Mich., photographed by Eric Smith. 115: USAMHI, Carlisle Barracks, Pa., copied by A. Pierce Bounds; courtesy Confederate Memorial Hall, New Orleans, photographed by Larry Sherer. 116: Library of Congress No. B8171-315. 117: Courtesy William B. Styple, photographed by Henry Groskinsky. 118: Virginia Historical Society. 119: Courtesy David Keith Parks, Macomb, Mich., photographed by Eric Smith. 120, 121: From *Still More Confederate Faces,* by D. A. Serrano, Metropolitan Co., Bayside, N.Y., 1992; South Caroliniana Library, University of South Carolina, Columbia (4). 122: From *A Confederate Surgeon's Letters to His Wife,* by Spencer Glasgow Welch, Continental Book Co., Marietta, Ga., 1954, copied by Philip Brandt George (2)—USAMHI, Carlisle Barracks, Pa., copied by A. Pierce Bounds. 123: South Carolina Confederate Relic Room and Museum, courtesy Annie McCullough Edwards Dargan—USAMHI, Carlisle Barracks, Pa., copied by A. Pierce Bounds. 125: Map by Walter W. Roberts, overlay by Time-Life Books. 126: Library of Congress; George Newton Wise Collection, Special Collections Library, Duke University—courtesy David Keith Parks, Macomb, Mich., photographed by Eric Smith. 128: Manassas National Battlefield Park. 129: Courtesy David Keith Parks, Macomb, Mich., photographed by Eric Smith (2); courtesy Louisiana Office of State Parks, photographed by Neil Johnson. 130: From *War Diary and Letters of Stephen Minot Weld*, privately printed by The Riverside Press, Cambridge, Mass., 1912; except bottom left, USAMHI, Carlisle Barracks, Pa., copied by A. Pierce Bounds. 131, 132: Library of Congress. 133: Brian C. Pohanka. 134: Beverly M. Dubose Collection, photographed by Larry Sherer; Confederate Research Center, Hillsboro, Tex. 135: Courtesy Don Troiani Collection, photographed by Larry Sherer; Smithsonian Institution, National Museum of American History, Washington D.C., photographed by Larry Sherer; New York State Museum, Albany, N.Y., photographed by Larry Sherer; Brian C. Pohanka. 137: Map by Walter W. Roberts, overlay by Time-Life Books. 138, 139: U.S. Army Military Institute, Fitzhugh McMaster Collection, copied by Robert Walch; Library of Congress. 140: The Western Reserve Historical Society, Cleveland. 142: Courtesy Private Collection, copied by Larry Sherer. 143: USAMHI, Carlisle Barracks, Pa., Bonnie Yuhas Collection, copied by Robert Walch. 144: Photograph by Douglas Christian, courtesy Bureau of State Office Buildings, Commonwealth of Massachusetts; Frank & Marie-Thérèse Wood Print Collections, Alexandria, Va. 145: Library of Congress. 146: USAMHI, Carlisle Barracks, Pa., copied by A. Pierce Bounds. 147: South Carolina Confederate Relic Room and Museum, courtesy Elizabeth McRae Hamrick. 148: Trent Collection, Special Collections Library, Duke University. 149: Courtesy David Keith Parks, Macomb, Mich., photographed by Eric Smith. 150: Calligraphy by Mary Lou O'Brian/Inkwell, Inc. 152: Library of Congress No. USZ621-15831. 153: Courtesy David Keith Parks, Macomb, Mich., photographed by Eric Smith. 154: Courtesy David Keith Parks, Macomb, Mich., photographed by Eric Smith; USAMHI, Carlisle Barracks, Pa., copied by A. Pierce Bounds. 155: Frank & Marie-Thérèse Wood Print Collections, Alexandria, Va. 156: Courtesy William B. Styple, photographed by Henry Groskinsky—courtesy William B. Styple Collection (2); New York State Museum, Albany, N.Y. 157, 158: USAMHI, Carlisle Barracks, Pa., copied by A. Pierce Bounds. 159: Library of Congress No. USZ62-19339.

BIBLIOGRAPHY

BOOKS

Andrews, W. H. *Footprints of a Regiment.* Atlanta: Longstreet Press, 1992.

Baird, Nancy Chappelear, ed. *Journals of Amanda Virginia Edmonds, Lass of the Mosby Confederacy: 1859-1867.* Stephens City, Va.: Commercial Press, 1984.

Blackford, Charles M. *Letters from Lee's Army.* New York: Charles Scribner's Sons, 1947.

Blackford, William W. *War Years with Jeb Stuart.* New York: Charles Scribner's Sons, 1945.

Blake, Henry N. *Three Years in the Army of the Potomac.* Boston: Lee and Shepard, 1865.

Blue, John M. *Hanging Rock Rebel.* Ed. by Dan Oates. Shippensburg, Pa.: White Mane, 1994.

Borcke, Heros von. *Colonel Heros von Borcke's Journal.* Winston-Salem, N.C.: Palaemon Press, 1981.

Bosbyshell, Oliver C. *The Forty-Eighth in the War.* Philadelphia: Avil Printing, 1895.

Buck, Samuel D. *With the Old Confeds: Actual Experiences of a Captain of the Line.* Baltimore: H. E. Houck, 1925.

Bucklin, Sophronia E. *In Hospital and Camp.* Philadelphia: John E. Potter, 1869.

Byrne, Frank L., and Andrew T. Weaver, eds. *Haskell of Gettysburg: His Life and Civil War Papers.* Madison: State Historical Society of Wisconsin, 1970.

Casler, John O. *Four Years in the Stonewall Brigade.* Guthrie, Okla.: State Capital Printing, 1893.

Chamberlayne, John Hampden. *Ham Chamberlayne—Virginian.* Richmond: Press of Dietz Printing Co., 1932.

Cheek, Philip, and Mair Pointon. *History of the Sauk County Riflemen.* Madison, Wis.: Democrat Printing, 1909.

Dawes, Rufus. *Service with the Sixth Wisconsin Volunteers.* Ed. by Alan T. Nolan. Madison: State Historical Society of Wisconsin, 1962.

Dedicatory Ceremonies Held on the Battlefield of Manassas, or Second Bull Run, Virginia, October 20, 1906 and May 30 (Memorial Day), 1907. . . . Brooklyn: Eagle Press, 1907.

Denison, Frederic. *Sabres and Spurs.* Central Falls: First Rhode Island Cavalry Veteran Association, 1876.

Douglas, Henry Kyd. *I Rode with Stonewall.* Chapel Hill: University of North Carolina Press, 1968.

Duncan, Russell, ed. *Blue-Eyed Child of Fortune: The Civil War Letters of Col. Robert Gould Shaw.* New York: Avon Books, 1992.

Early, Jubal A. *Autobiographical Sketch and Narrative of the War between the States.* Philadelphia: J. B. Lippincott, 1912.

Forbes, Edwin. *Thirty Years After*, 2 vols. New York: Fords, Howard & Hulbert, 1890.

French, Samuel Bassett. *Centennial Tales.* Comp. by Glenn C. Oldaker. New York: Carlton Press, 1962.

Fulton, William Frierson. *Family Record and War Reminiscences.* Alabama: n.p., n.d.

Gaché, Louis-Hippolyte. *A Frenchman, a Chaplain, a Rebel.* Chicago: Loyola University Press, 1981.

Gibbon, John. *Personal Recollections of the Civil War.* New York: G. P. Putnam's Sons, 1928.

Gilmor, Harry. *Four Years in the Saddle.* New York: Harper & Brothers, 1866.

Gould, John M. *History of the First-Tenth-Twenty-Ninth Maine Regiments.* Portland, Maine: S. Berry, 1871.

The Guns of '62. Vol. 2 of *The Image of War: 1861-1865.* Garden City, N.Y.: Doubleday, 1982.

Haight, Theron W. "Gainesville, Groveton, and Bull Run." In *War Papers Read Before the Commandery of the State of Wisconsin. . . .* Vol. 2. Milwaukee: Burdick, Armitage & Allen, 1896.

Haynes, Martin A. *A History of the Second Regiment.* Lakeport, N.H.: n.p., 1896.

Hennessy, John J. *Return to Bull Run.* New York: Simon & Schuster, 1993.

Hickerson, Thomas F., ed. *Echoes of Happy Valley.* Chapel Hill, N.C.: Bull's Head Bookshop, 1962.

Houghton, W. R., and M. B. Houghton. *Two Boys in the Civil War and After.* Montgomery: Paragon Press, 1912.

Krick, Robert K. *Stonewall Jackson at Cedar Mountain.* Chapel Hill: University of North Carolina Press, 1990.

Lang, Theodore F. "Personal Reminiscences." In *Loyal West Virginia.* Baltimore: Deutsch Publishing, 1895.

Lee, Robert E. *The Wartime Papers of R. E. Lee.* Ed. by Clifford Dowdey. Boston: Little, Brown, 1961.

Long, Armistead L. *Memoirs of Robert E. Lee: His Military and Personal History.* New York: J. M. Stoddart, 1886.

Loving, Jerome B., ed. *Civil War Papers of George Washington Whitman.* Durham, N.C.: Duke University Press, 1975.

Lusk, William Thompson. *War Letters of William Thompson Lusk.* New York: private printing, 1911.

[Lyon, James S.] *War Sketches.* Buffalo: Young, Lockwood & Company's Steam Press, 1882.

Marvin, Edwin E. *The Fifth Regiment, Connecticut Volunteers.* Hartford: Press of Wiley, Waterman & Eaton, 1889.

McClendon, William A. *Recollections of War Times.* Montgomery, Ala.: Paragon Press, 1909.

Moore, Edward A. *The Story of a Cannoneer under Stonewall Jackson.* Lynchburg, Va.: J. P. Bell, 1910.

Neese, George M. *Three Years in the Confederate Horse Artillery.* New York: Neale Publishing, 1911.

Polley, J. B. *A Soldier's Letters to Charming Nellie.* New York: Neale Publishing, 1908.

Sheeran, James B. *Confederate Chaplain: A War Journal.* Ed. by Joseph T. Durkin. Milwaukee: Bruce, 1960.

Stearns, Austin C. *Three Years with Company K.* Ed. by Arthur A. Kent. Rutherford, N.J.: Fairleigh Dickinson University Press, 1976.

Stevens, Hazard. *The Life of Isaac Ingalls Stevens.* Vol. 2. Boston: Houghton, Mifflin, 1900.

Thomas, Henry W. *History of the Doles-Cook Brigade, Army of Northern Virginia, C.S.A.* Atlanta: Franklin Printing and Publishing, 1903.

Townsend, George A. *Rustics in Rebellion.* Chapel Hill: University of North Carolina Press, 1950.

United States War Department. *The War of the Rebellion,* 128 vols. Washington, D.C.: U.S. Government Printing Office, 1902.

War Diaries and Letters of Stephen Minot Weld: 1861-1865. Boston: Massachusetts Historical Society, 1979.

Welch, Spencer Glasgow. *A Confederate Surgeon's Letters to His Wife.* Marietta, Ga.: Continental Book Co., 1954.

White, William S. *Sketches of the Life of Captain Hugh A. White of the Stonewall Brigade.* Columbia: South Carolinian Steam Press, 1864.

Worsham, John H. *One of Jackson's Foot Cavalry.* New York: Neale Publishing, 1912.

Yeary, Mamie. *Reminiscences of the Boys in Gray.* Dayton: Morningside, 1986.

Zettler, Berrien M. *War Stories and School-Day Incidents for the Children.* New York: Neale Publishing, 1912.

PERIODICALS

Ames, John Worthington. "The Second Bull Run." *Overland Monthly,* 1872, Vol. 8.

Barnes, Edward L. "The 95th New York: Sketch of Its Services in the Campaigns of 1862." *National Tribune,* January 7/14, 1886.

Chandler, Stephen E. "In the Thick of It: What the Iron Brigade Experienced in the Old Dominion." *National Tribune,* October 17/24, 1895.

Cooper, T. A. "A Confederate's Reminiscences." *National Tribune,* January 9, 1908.

Dougherty, William E. "An Eyewitness Account of Second Bull Run." *American History Illustrated,* December 1966.

Goldsmith, W. L. "Who Killed Gen. Phil Kearney?" *Confederate Veteran,* June 1907.

Hammond, Mary Acton. "'Dear Mollie': Letters of Captain Edward A. Acton to His Wife, 1862." *The Pennsylvania Magazine of History and Biography,* January 1965.

Hendricks, James M. "The March to the Rear of Pope's Army." *Confederate Veteran,* 1909, Vol. 17.

Lamont, Eneas N. "Second Battle of Bull Run." *Philadelphia Weekly Times,* March 1, 1884.

Law, Evander M. "The Virginia Campaign of 1862." Philadelphia Weekly Press, October 26/November 2, 1887.

"Letters of Evans R. Brady." *Clearfield Republican* (Pa.), October 1, 1862.

McCrady, Edward. "Gregg's Brigade of South Carolinians in the Second Battle of Manassas." *Southern Historical Society Papers,* 1885.

Patteson, William H. "A Boy in the Camp of Lee." Ed. by A. J. Emerson. *Confederate Veteran,* September 1916.

Strother, David H. "Personal Recollections of the War." *Harper's New Monthly Magazine,* August 1867.

"Webster's Only Son." *The Baker Library Bulletin* (Dartmouth College, N.H.), December 1949.

OTHER SOURCES

Albergotti, Thomas C. Memoir. Charleston: South Carolina Historical Society, 1903.

Barbour, Lucian. Letter, October 6, 1862. Washington, D.C.: Library of Congress, Manuscript Division.

Beardsley, Samuel. Collection. Carlisle Barracks, Pa.: U.S. Army Military History Institute, n.d.

Blue, John M. Memoirs. *Civil War Times Illustrated* collection. Carlisle Barracks, Pa.: U.S. Army Military History Institute, n.d.

Brown, Campbell. "Military Reminiscences of Major Campbell Brown." Brown-Ewell Papers. Nashville: Tennessee State Library and Archives, n.d.

Catton, Bruce. Research notes for Bruce Catton's *Centennial History of the Civil War,* made available by Doubleday. Washington, D.C.: Library of Congress, n.d.

Davenport, Alfred. Letter, March 1862. New York: New York Historical Society.

Drewry, Albert Sidney. Memoir. Carlisle Barracks, Pa.: U.S. Army Military History Institute, n.d.

Fitzpatrick, Marion H. Papers. Southern Historical Collection. Chapel Hill: University of North Carolina, n.d.

Giddings, Allan. Collection. Kalamazoo: Western Michigan University Archives and Regional History Collections, n.d.

Hunter, Alexander. "Four Years in the Ranks." Unpublished manuscript. Richmond: Virginia Historical Society, n.d.

Hutton, John W. F. Memoirs. Washington, D.C.: Library of Congress, Manuscript Division, n.d.

Kauffman, Joseph F. Diary. Southern Historical Collection. Chapel Hill: University of North Carolina, n.d.

Lowry, Samuel Catawba. Diary. Columbia: University of South Carolina, South Caroliniana Library, n.d.

McLean, Joseph. Papers. Mohnton, Pa.: Bonnie McLean Yuhas, n.d.

McLeod, William. Letter, September 28-30, 1865. William Oland Bourne Papers. Washington, D.C.: Library of Congress, Manuscript Division.

Norton, Joseph Jeptha. Diary. Columbia: University of South Carolina, South Caroliniana Library, n.d.

Parker, George C. Letters. *Civil War Times Illustrated* collection. Carlisle Barracks, Pa.: U.S. Army Military History Institute, n.d.

Pearson, Henry H. Letter, September 5, 1862. Leigh Collection. Carlisle Barracks, Pa.: U.S. Army Military History Institute.

Pryor, Shephard Green. "Letters 1861-1863 of Captain Shephard Green Pryor of The Muckalee Guards. . . ." Unpublished manuscript. Atlanta: Georgia Department of Archives and History, 1940.

Quincy, Samuel M. "History of the Second Massachusetts Regiment of Infantry." Paper read at the Officers' Reunion, Boston, May 11, 1877. Washington, D.C.: Library of Congress.

Todd, Westwood A. "Reminiscences of the War between the States: April 1861-July 1865." Southern Historical Collection. Chapel Hill: University of North Carolina.

Veil, Charles Henry. "An Old Boy's Personal Recollections and Reminiscences of the Civil War." Civil War Miscellaneous Collection. Carlisle Barracks, Pa.: U.S. Army Military History Institute, n.d.

Warren, William P. Unpublished personal account. James Garver Collection. Carlisle Barracks, Pa.: U.S. Army Military History Institute, n.d.

Wise, George N. Diary entries, August 1862. Durham, N.C.: Duke University, William R. Perkins Library.

Woods, Micajah. Papers. Charlottesville: University of Virginia, Alderman Library, n.d.

Young, Milus O. "History of the First Brigade." Atlanta: Georgia Department of Archives and History, n.d.

INDEX